threads
FITTING
FOR EVERY
FIGURE

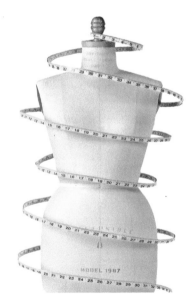

editors of
THREADS

The Taunton Press

The Taunton Press
Inspiration for hands-on living®

The Taunton Press, Inc., 63 South Main Street, Newtown, CT 06470-2344
e-mail: tp@taunton.com

Editor: Renee I. Neiger
Technical Editors: Carol Fresia and Pam Hoenig
Copy Editor: Betty Christiansen
Indexer: Cathy Goddard
Jacket/Cover design: Laura Palese
Interior design: Carol Singer
Layout: Cathy Cassidy

Library of Congress Cataloging-in-Publication Data

Threads' fitting for every figure / editors of Threads.
     pages cm
  Includes bibliographical references and index.
  ISBN 978-1-60085-396-8
1. Clothing and dress measurements. 2. Dressmaking--Pattern design. 3. Tailoring. I. Threads (Newtown, Conn.) II. Title: Fitting for every figure.
  TT520.T56 2012
  646.4'072--dc23

                         2012022120

Printed in the United States of America
10 9 8 7 6 5

ACKNOWLEDGMENTS

The secret to great-looking clothes is a flattering fit; a flattering fit comes from understanding your figure, your pattern, and your garment. There are many ways to approach fitting—from tweaking the seams and darts on a commercial pattern, to drafting or draping a garment to your personal measurements—and different projects call for different methods. Happily, the authors who have contributed to this book know that and have shared a wide range of techniques for making garments that look custom-made, rather than home-sewn.

This volume would not have been possible without the expertise of the many teachers, designers, custom clothiers, alterations specialists, and patternmakers whose work is represented here. Their knowledge of garment fitting is matched only by their enthusiasm for the subject. *Threads* magazine and The Taunton Press are grateful to all our authors who, for more than a quarter of a century, have demonstrated both their mastery of the art of sewing in all its forms and their devotion to an audience of avid sewers who care about producing garments they're proud to wear. Their commitment teaches us more than technique: It shows us, too, that this timeless craft is worth studying, preserving, and updating.

Thank you to our editors, Carol Fresia, Pam Hoenig, Renee Neiger, and Shawna Mullen. Many thanks to Judith Neukam for her expert advice and fine-tuning of the information in this book.

CONTENTS

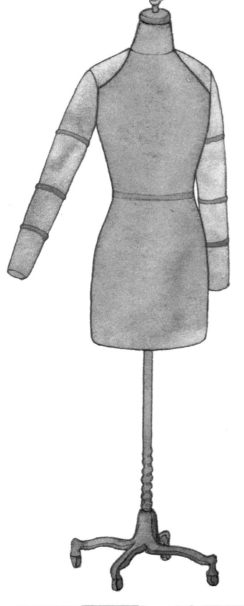

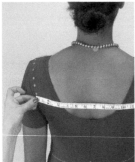

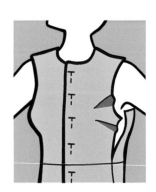

INTRODUCTION

At *Threads* magazine, we understand how home sewers strive to create garments that fit. For the past 25 years, we have been engaging our readers in the fitting debate and enlisting the help of top sewing experts and designers. Our staff, too, brings their own point of view, so we test and test and test again the steps for projects, tips, and techniques. After all, we want our readers be the best home sewers they can be.

We understand that not all sewers have the same approach to achieving good fit. Some want to do just what's needed while others want, and are skilled enough, to tackle more involved techniques. And then there are those with advanced skills who will settle for nothing less than a couture fit. No matter what your personal approach might be, there is something for you in our new guide, *Threads Fitting for Every Figure*.

Our answer to your many fitting queries is the special book you now hold in your hands. You will find a handy reference to the basics of fitting, working with patterns and muslin, fitting the bodice, fitting pants and skirts, and a section on special fitting techniques. Two contributors in particular warrant special mention: Carol Fresia, who took on the task of pulling the book together, and her editor, Judith Neukam, *Threads* senior technical editor, who made sure that it all made good sense.

We wish you the best of luck in your fitting endeavors and hope you continue the conversation with us at www.threadsmagazine.com, where we always look forward to your comments and feedback.

—Deana Tierney May, Editor

I

FITTING BASICS

The first step in sewing clothes that are comfortable and flattering is collecting all the data you need about the figure you're trying to fit. Accurate body measurements are your starting point, and it's essential to take the time to measure and record methodically.

Once you know what size you are, it's helpful to know what size your most flattering clothes are. You'll learn to measure your best-fitting garments, giving you a target size to work toward when altering patterns to suit your figure. Quantifying your ease and length preferences eliminates much of the guesswork involved in working with commercial patterns.

For a home sewer who is serious about excellent fit (and you don't have to be an advanced sewer to care about fit), a personalized dress form can make all the difference. You can purchase a standard-size form and pad it to your size, or you can make your own form, molded to replicate your silhouette exactly. The time or money you invest in developing a custom form will be paid back many times over in well-fitting garments that make you look like a million dollars.

Measuring

By following the steps shown on pp. 6–10, you will acquire a set of measurements to use for fine-tuning the fit of commercial patterns or creating hand-drafted designs. If you are working with pattern-drafting software, you'll be able to adapt these methods as you follow brand-specific instructions. (Each company has its own marking and measuring protocols that you should follow exactly.)

Preparing to Measure

Body shape, and subsequently fit, can be greatly affected by the undergarments worn when measurements are taken—bras in particular. To ensure an accurate fit, wear the undergarments you normally do. Be prepared to mark on them if necessary for recording reference points. Our model was photographed in a leotard, but you'll get more accurate measurements if the person being measured wears only her best-fitting undergarments.

The most important aid in the measurement process is a measuring buddy. (There's just no way to accurately measure your own body.)

Tips on Measuring

- Measurements should be taken with the subject standing with natural posture.

- Arm measurements should be taken with the arm relaxed and slightly bent at the elbow.

- Keep the tape smooth and level when measuring around the body.

- Don't measure loosely or with a finger under the tape to build in ease.

- It is very common for there to be significant asymmetries in a body. For this reason, it is important to measure both sides of the body; if you find discrepancies greater than ½ in., adjust or draft the pattern with distinct right- and left-side pattern pieces.

Measuring Reference Points

Mark the body so you'll have consistent reference points while you measure.

WHAT YOU'LL NEED

- A short, fine chain necklace—to establish a natural neckline
- Washable markers—to draw lines on skin and/or undergarments
- ¼-in. adhesive dots
- Pins
- Narrow elastic—to locate and mark the waistline
- Flexible but stable measuring tape
- 12-in. ruler

Optional:

- A form-fitting T-shirt with set-in sleeves—to help identify an armhole
- Twill tape/cotton cording for marking crotch length

Ⓐ NECKLINE

Identify the natural neckline with a short chain necklace that settles comfortably just below the slight hollow at the base of the neck.

- Mark the exact center front of this neckline with a small adhesive or pen dot.
- Mark the prominent vertebra at the top of the spine with an adhesive or pen dot. (Bend the head forward to make the vertebra easier to find.)
- Mark a point on each side of the neck, in line with the hollow just behind the earlobe.

Ⓑ SHOULDER POINT

Feel for the end of the flat bone at the end of the shoulder, or raise your arm until a dimple appears at the end of your shoulder and feel for the shoulder bone in this depression. It is important to identify an exact shoulder point.

- Mark it with an adhesive or pen dot.

Ⓒ BUST POINT

Mark the nipple location with a cross of two pins on the bra fabric or with an adhesive dot.

Ⓓ WAISTLINE

Depending upon body proportions, there are two possible waistlines: a natural waist or, for people who do not have a naturally indented waist, a de facto (chosen) waist, where the top of skirts or trousers sits. Find the natural waist by tying a piece of elastic around the person's waist and having her bend from side to side until the elastic settles comfortably in the hollow around the middle of her body; take the waist measurement here. If the person does not have an indented waist, adjust the elastic on her body to sit at the de facto waist. This often entails moving the elastic above or below the natural waist, sometimes to be higher at the back and lower at the front.

- Once established, mark the waistline on the body with a pen; the elastic can shift while measuring.

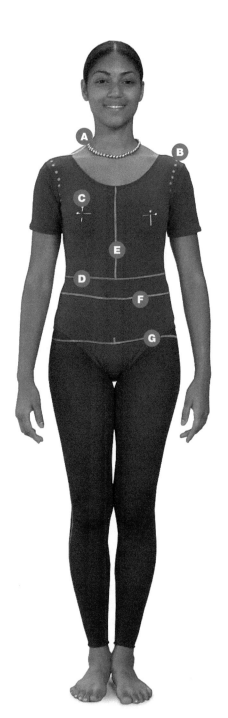

E CENTER FRONT AND CENTER BACK

Draw a series of dots perpendicular to the floor from the hollow of the neck to the waist. Repeat from the nape of the neck.

F ABDOMEN

Mark a line parallel to the floor across the fullest part of the abdomen.

G HIPS

Find the widest part of the lower body by wrapping a measuring tape around the hip area and sliding it down the body; note that the widest part may be anywhere from a few inches to more than 12 in. below the waist.

• Where the measurement is largest, mark a line parallel to the floor all around the body.

H SHOULDER SEAMLINE

Draw a line on the body, from the side-neck point marked on the neckline, along the top of the shoulder, to the shoulder point.

I ARMHOLE

Mark with a dotted line. Starting from the shoulder point, mark down into the crease formed by the body joining the arm, on both the front and back. (If locating the armhole is difficult, duplicate one from a form-fitting T-shirt, slipping one hand under the sleeve to trace the seamline onto the body.)

J SIDE SEAMS

Draw a line perpendicular to the floor from the underarm to the ankle on both sides of the body.

POINTS OF INTERSECTION

Be sure all horizontal markings clearly intersect all vertical markings so you'll be able to identify the exact center front, center back, and side seam locations. (Note the center front of your waistline may not be in line with your navel.)

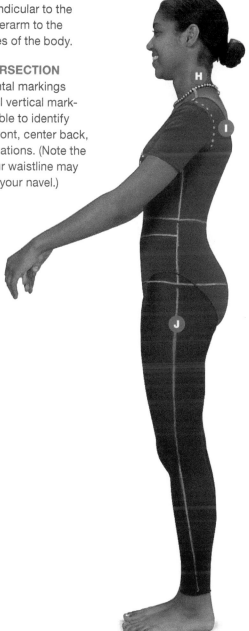

Measuring the Body

SHOULDERS

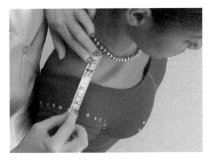

SHOULDER LENGTH: Measure from the side-neck point to the shoulder point.

SHOULDER-TO-SHOULDER/FRONT: Measure between the shoulder points in a straight line across the front.

SHOULDER-TO-SHOULDER/BACK: Measure between the shoulder points in a straight line across the back.

BACK WIDTH: Measure between the arm-holes (make sure the tape doesn't get caught up in the shoulder blades).

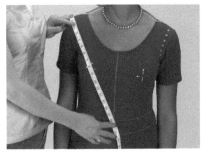

FRONT SHOULDER SLOPE: Measure from the shoulder point to the waistline center front in a straight diagonal line, through the bust point.

BACK SHOULDER SLOPE: Measure from the shoulder point to the waistline center back.

ARMS

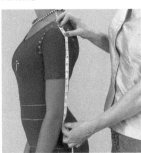

ARM LENGTH (sometimes called over arm): Keep the arm relaxed with a slight natural bend at the elbow. Take this measurement in two steps, from the shoulder point to the elbow, and then from the elbow to just below the wrist bone.

BICEPS/UPPER ARM: Measure around the biceps with the arm slightly bent and the biceps relaxed.

ARMHOLE DEPTH: Slide a ruler, horizontally, high up under the arm; with the tape, measure from the shoulder point to the ruler.

BUST

 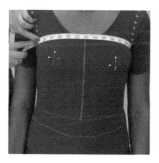  

BUST CIRCUMFERENCE: Measure the fullest part of the bust with the tape parallel to the floor.

UPPER BUST: Measure the circumference above the bust, with the tape up against the armpit.

UNDER BUST: Measure the circumference under the bust, holding the tape in line with the bottom edge of the bra.

CHEST WIDTH: Measure above the bust from armhole to armhole, holding the tape parallel to the floor.

NECK

NATURAL NECKLINE: Holding the tape so it stands on edge, measure around the base of the neckline as defined by the necklace.

NECK EDGE TO BUST POINT (also called bust depth): Measure from the side-neck point to the bust point.

NECK EDGE TO WAIST: Measure from the side-neck point to the waistline in a straight line, through the bust point.

WAIST AND HIPS

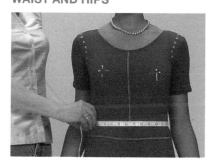 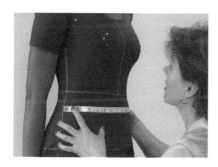 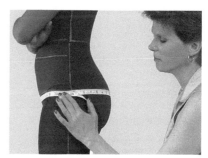

WAIST: Measure the circumference of the marked waistline.

ABDOMEN: Measure from side to side across the fullest part of the abdomen.

HIP CIRCUMFERENCE: Measure around the fullest part of the hips with the tape parallel to the floor. (When the hip is not the fullest lower body measurement, take another measurement at the fullest part.)

continued

Measuring the Body continued

LEGS

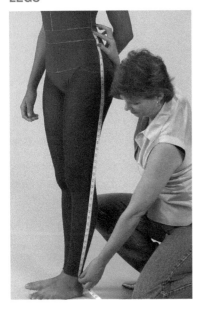

OUTER SEAM: Measure from the side waist to the preferred pants hem.

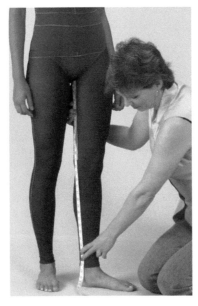

INSEAM: Measure from the lowest part of the crotch to the preferred pants hem. Tape the measuring tape to a 12-in. ruler to comfortably take this measurement. Don't spread legs any wider than necessary.

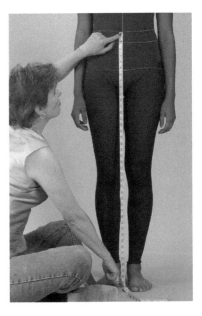

WAIST TO FLOOR/FRONT AND BACK: Measure the perpendicular distance from the waistline to the floor at the center front and center back.

CROTCH

CROTCH LENGTH/FRONT AND BACK: Measure from the waistline center front to the waistline center back through the legs, holding the tape comfortably close to the body. Note the distance from the center front to the inseam (crotch front length) and subtract it from the total to derive the crotch back length. (Or mark and then measure a length of twill tape to determine these dimensions.)

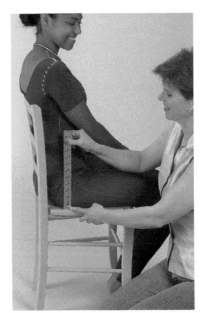

CROTCH DEPTH: Have the person sit on a flat chair, and use a ruler to measure from the marked waistline to the chair seat. Keep the ruler perpendicular to the seat.

Measuring Garments for Fit

Measuring your body is a crucial step in garment fitting, but it's also essential to identify the fit you're looking for. To do so, simply measure the clothes you own that have the most flattering fit. Areas that benefit from this approach are armhole depths, neck widths, and sleeve-cap heights, as well as overall ease throughout a garment. Follow the instructions below for taking measurements from articles of clothing, and compare these to prospective patterns. If you know the dimensions you like, you can easily and quickly alter patterns to suit your shape and style.

Select a few garments that you feel comfortable wearing, in styles that are similar to the kinds of patterns you like to make. Make notes about the weight and drape of the fabrics in each measured garment. In addition, it can be enlightening to measure a few poorly fitting garments, so your measurement ranges include definite danger zones, too.

Lay each garment flat to measure vertically and horizontally, as shown below. If you have a gridded cutting surface, align the garment center with a gridline, and do the same thing when measuring patterns. This will make the comparisons between your clothes and your patterns faster and more intuitive, especially as you measure more of them. If desired, draw a quick outline of each garment you've measured, and indicate on these sketches where you measured the garment, to simplify making comparisons.

Comparing New Patterns

Lay out each new pattern and measure it horizontally and vertically in the areas in the same way; don't forget to leave out the seam allowances when you measure. This helps you quickly determine whether the pattern's fit, ease, and style are going to suit you or if you need to make some changes—or whether you should choose another pattern. Be sure to compare the fabric you're using with the fabric of the garments you measured. Fabrics with lots of drape can handle much more ease than stiffer fabrics, so, just as with garment styles, you'll get the best results if you're comparing similar fabrics.

To ensure that your new garment has the fit and comfort characteristics of your favorite clothes, you can make basic pattern alterations using your measurement chart (see p. 12) as a reference guide: Identify the same points on the pattern and the garment chart, mark them on the pattern to match the chart, and then redraw the pattern lines to reflect the new positions.

Patterns with unusual pieces and silhouettes, and with complex seams and details, will not be as easy to compare, but once assembled, they will often present the same issues of fit. Measure carefully across multiple pattern pieces to make the comparisons.

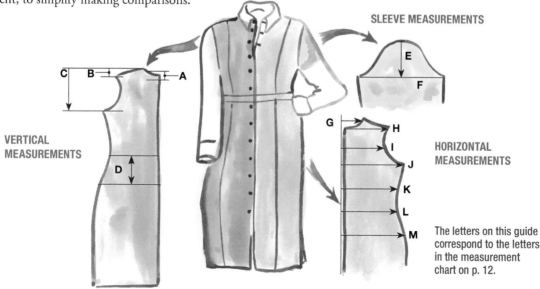

SLEEVE MEASUREMENTS

VERTICAL MEASUREMENTS

HORIZONTAL MEASUREMENTS

The letters on this guide correspond to the letters in the measurement chart on p. 12.

Detail Measurements from Your Favorite Clothes

Use this chart to record the garment measurements you take following the instructions on p. 11.
Letters A–M correspond to a letter on p. 11.

GARMENT DETAILS—VERTICAL	
Measure vertically from neckline/ shoulder-point level or waist level; measure sleeve heights vertically from top of cap to underarm level.	A. Neckline depth, round neck
	A. Neckline depth, V neck
	A. Neckline depth, other
	B. Shoulder-point drop
	C. Armhole depth, fitted tops
	C. Armhole depth, nonfitted tops
	C. Armhole depth, overgarment
	D. Length from waist to full hip
	E. Sleeve cap height, fitted set-in sleeve
	E. Sleeve cap height, nonfitted set-in sleeve

GARMENT DETAILS—HORIZONTAL	
You need only half-widths to compare to patterns. Measure horizontally from center front; measure chest width at narrowest level.	F. Sleeve width, fitted
	F. Sleeve width, nonfitted
	G. Neckline width
	H. Shoulder-point width
	I. Chest width, fitted set-in armhole
	I. Chest width, nonfitted set-in armhole
	J. Underarm width, fitted top
	J. Underarm width, nonfitted top
	K. Bust width, fitted top
	K. Bust width, nonfitted top
	L. Waist width, fitted top
	L. Waist width, fitted skirt/pants
	M. Hip width, fitted top
	M. Hip width, nonfitted top
	M. Hip width, fitted skirt/pants
	M. Hip width, nonfitted skirt/pants

OVERALL GARMENT LENGTHS (NOT PICTURED ON P. 12)	
Measure vertically from neckline/ shoulder-point level or waist level.	N. Bodice/cropped top
	N. Hip-length top
	N. Tunic-style top
	N. Dress
	N. Short skirt
	N. Long skirt
	N. Pants
	N. Other

The Importance of Ease

The amount of ease in a pattern (the difference between your actual measurements and those of the tissue) can make or break fit, regardless of size. Ease allows for movement; the amount of ease varies with the garment style.

Typically, a pattern company builds around 2 in. of ease into its basic sloper (a base pattern that represents the dimensions of a specific figure, without additional design features) and adds additional ease based on the style of the garment. A fitted dress, for example, may have 3 in. to 4 in. of ease at the bust, and a loose-fitting dress may have up to 8 in. of ease.

Some pattern companies provide all the finished measurements (bust, waist, hip, hem width) on the envelope and let you figure out the ease for yourself. Other companies note ease information on the envelope. In addition, on their Web sites, both Vogue and Butterick® include an in-depth ease chart that lists the ease allowed in a variety of silhouettes.

It is important to figure out how much ease you want in the bust, hip, and finished width of a garment. To do so, see "Determining a Garment's Ease," at right.

Determining a Garment's Ease

To measure the ease on any garment, put it on, then pinch out the loose fabric on each side at the bust, hip, or biceps. Try to distribute the ease equally between your hands, then measure the pinch depth in one hand and multiply the result by 4 to get the total ease. Multiply the biceps pinch depth by 2 to get the total sleeve ease.

Record these measurements in the chart on p. 191, "Ease Measurements from Your Favorite Clothes," and do the math to determine the total garment circumference needed to reproduce the fit.

The Dress Form

A dress form shows exactly what's happening with a garment's fit, proportions, and construction, and it helps you fix the problems it reveals. If you don't have a trusted sewing buddy to lend a hand with fitting, a dress form can do the job and is available to you anytime at all, without an appointment.

Even though a dress form is not essential, beginning sewers who follow patterns to the letter and line will find them useful. No matter how simple the garment, you'll understand its structure and fit better when you can see it on a three-dimensional human shape. If you're venturing into design and want to make changes to a commercial pattern or draft your own patterns, a dress form enables you to verify that your flat patterns will translate correctly into the garment you've envisioned. And if you're interested in draping garments from scratch (designing directly on the form, usually using muslin, and without a pattern), a dress form is essential equipment.

Sewers who routinely make clothing for others can use a dress form for interim fittings and to support garments between fittings. Even those who sew for children and men can find forms to suit their needs.

Fitting Form to Figure

A dress form is most helpful when it's an exact duplicate of your figure, but few of us resemble the standardized shapes of commercial dress forms. Any form can be customized with the addition of padding; some are sold with pads and batting for this purpose. Others have dials that increase or decrease the height and girth of the form.

Because most garments hang from the shoulders, this area is the most important to fit accurately. If, for example, your shoulders are narrow but your bust is full, you're better off purchasing a form that matches your shoulder width and then padding the bust to size. In fact, many sewers dress their forms in one of their best-fitting bras, to shape and position the bust area properly for a good fit.

For body types that are outside the range of standard dress sizes, plus-size and petite forms exist, although not in as many varieties. Very tall or very lean, columnar individuals—or those with extremely asymmetrical figures—may have trouble finding a form that can be made to resemble them closely enough. In this case, it's worth considering a custom form or making your own (see pp. 16–23).

If you sew for a number of people who are somewhat close in size but not identical in measurements, look for a form that can be adjusted in both vertical and circumferential dimensions.

Using a Dress Form

From the earliest stages of selecting a pattern to putting the finishing touches on a garment, you'll find your dress form an invaluable aid. Here are some ways yours can help you:

- Assemble a tissue test garment by pinning the pattern pieces to the form.
- Fit a muslin to check dart placement, shoulder width, neckline depth, and overall girth and length.
- Construct and shape a garment; if your form can tolerate steam-pressing, you can shape clothing directly on the form.
- Fine-tune a garment's fit.
- Mark hems and button placement and spacing.
- Experiment with design adaptations.
- Drape an original design.

Dress Form Features

Your sewing habits and needs dictate the type of form that's best for you. When buying a dress form, consider the features shown here.

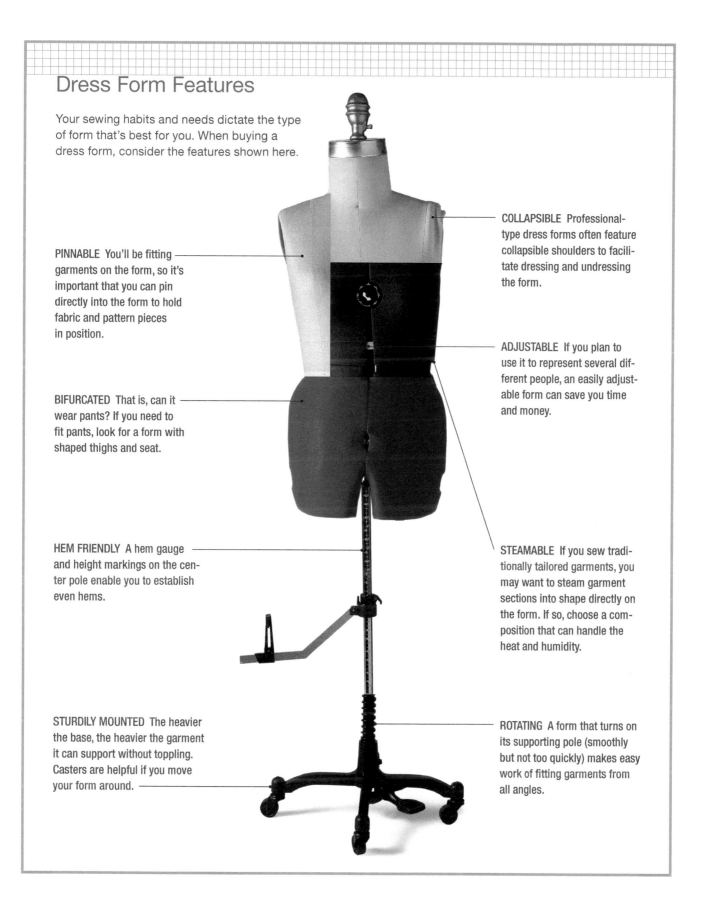

COLLAPSIBLE Professional-type dress forms often feature collapsible shoulders to facilitate dressing and undressing the form.

PINNABLE You'll be fitting garments on the form, so it's important that you can pin directly into the form to hold fabric and pattern pieces in position.

ADJUSTABLE If you plan to use it to represent several different people, an easily adjustable form can save you time and money.

BIFURCATED That is, can it wear pants? If you need to fit pants, look for a form with shaped thighs and seat.

HEM FRIENDLY A hem gauge and height markings on the center pole enable you to establish even hems.

STEAMABLE If you sew traditionally tailored garments, you may want to steam garment sections into shape directly on the form. If so, choose a composition that can handle the heat and humidity.

STURDILY MOUNTED The heavier the base, the heavier the garment it can support without toppling. Casters are helpful if you move your form around.

ROTATING A form that turns on its supporting pole (smoothly but not too quickly) makes easy work of fitting garments from all angles.

Making Your Own Dress Form

If you have $15 (the approximate cost of the supplies needed), a willing helper, and about two hours, you can make your own customized duct-tape dress form.

You will need two to three 60-yd. rolls of 2-in.-wide duct tape. The brand makes a difference, because some tape shrinks over time, which changes the size of your dress form. The house brand from Ace Hardware® holds up well, as does Duck Tape®. Using an old pair of scissors (the tape adhesive will gum them up, so you do not want to use your good pair), cut the tape into 4-in. to 6-in. strips, plus longer strips for the waist and crossing the chest.

1. Dress to Fit
Wear well-fitting undergarments. Tape a 2-in.-wide strip cut from a file folder or heavy paper to your skin and over your underwear, down your center back from your hairline to below your hips. This protects you and your underwear when you cut off the dress form. Then put on a long T-shirt. This remains inside the form, so choose one you don't mind sacrificing to the project. The T-shirt needn't be too tight, because the tape pulls it in. A turtleneck T-shirt is ideal, or you can fill in around the neckline with plastic wrap before taping. Start wrapping under the bust. Wrap snugly, but not so tight as to rearrange or compress the body. At the waist, wrap a little more loosely on the first layer, allowing folds to form in the tape as you follow the contour, if necessary. Proceed to a "cross-your-heart" taping that goes from one shoulder under the opposite breast, then around to the back, to define the bust area.

2. Apply the Tape
Wrap the tape horizontally at the bottom, down to mid-thigh (**2a**).

At the bust and underarm, cut the T-shirt sleeves, if needed, to allow the tape to follow the figure, and use shorter pieces fanned out over the bust. Tape the edges at the neckline (over the turtleneck or plastic wrap) and armholes similar to those you'd want on a fitted bodice, giving your form a neck. When the first layer is complete, wrap twice more, first vertically, then again horizontally, further compressing the waistline to fit each layer more closely, and smoothing over any wrinkles this causes with more tape. If you'd like, for the final layer, use patterned duct tape to give your dress form some style (**2b**).

3. Mark and Remove the Form
When finished, but before removing the form, have the "wrappee" bend slightly sideways to reveal her waistline, and mark it (and any other points you want identified) with permanent marker. Mark the final layer carefully with plumb lines at the center front and center back, and around the waist, and carefully establish the proper height and posture by marking a line parallel to the floor below the hip level around the form. Then cut through the tape from lower center back up to the neckline, and remove the form.

4. Create a Base
Cut along the horizontal line at hip level to establish a baseline. Trace around the base of the dress form, cut a cardboard or ½-in.-thick foam-core base to match, and cut a hole in it if you plan to fit it on a stand pole. A strong wooden hanger placed inside the shell supports the shoulders. Tape the hanger to a PVC pipe or a wooden pole if you plan to make a stand, and tape it inside the form before stuffing it. Otherwise, you can use the hanger on a ceiling-hung chain or hook to hang your dress form.

5. Stuff the Form
If the bust contour needs additional support (larger bust shapes tend to cave in over time without support), tape or glue a foam raglan shoulder pad inside the form in each breast. Stuff and tape over the armholes and neck, and solidly stuff the entire form to support it. Use a fiberfill designed for toys or pillows. Push the foam core base into the bottom of the dress form, and tape it in place. Compare the wrappee's measurements to the form. If necessary, you can adjust the form by cutting slits to create darts, or by squeezing or padding the form to the new dimension and retaping.

Cover areas that the T-shirt doesn't with plastic wrap before taping.

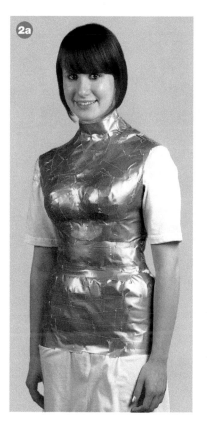

Wrap snugly but not so snugly as to compress or rearrange the body. Apply three layers of tape.

For decorative effect, you can use patterned duct tape for the outermost layer of tape.

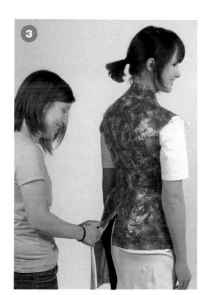

Cut through the tape and T-shirt layers up the center back, with your scissors sliding along the paper strip you taped on the body. Carefully step out of the form.

Cut and fit the base to the form, and tape it in place.

After stuffing the dress form, it can hang on a chain from the ceiling when you're using it and hang in your closet when you're storing it.

USE COMMERCIAL SET-IN SLEEVE PATTERN

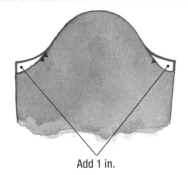

Add 1 in.

MARK PLACEMENT LINES

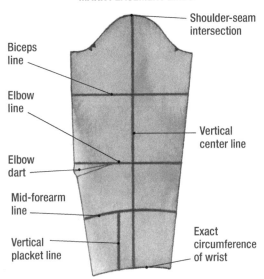

Shoulder-seam intersection

Biceps line

Elbow line

Elbow dart

Mid-forearm line

Vertical placket line

Vertical center line

Exact circumference of wrist

Mark placement lines on sleeve muslin.

USE MUSLIN TO MAKE PATTERN

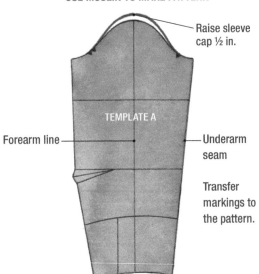

Raise sleeve cap ½ in.

TEMPLATE A

Forearm line

Underarm seam

Transfer markings to the pattern.

Add an Arm to a Dress Form

Add an arm to a commercial dress form, and you'll increase your fitting power. The shape of a sleeve cap, placement of elbow darts, and sleeve length and drape become instantly visible. Drag lines formed by a cap that's too high or low can be adjusted without a lot of trial and error. Additionally, you can fine-tune the fit of raglan, dolman, and various dropped-shoulder sleeve styles; refine special details such as placket placement or an unusual cuff; or use the form to drape an interesting sleeve of your own design.

Copy Your Arm

Use a tight-fitting commercial set-in sleeve pattern with an elbow dart and a close-fitting cap (not puffed or darted) for the foundation of your own sleeve-form pattern. The sleeve that comes with a pattern sloper, available from major pattern companies, is a good choice. Add 1 in. to the underarm seams at the top of this pattern, so the sleeve extends high into the armpit area.

Cut and sew the pattern in muslin, then put it on. With the help of a friend, pin-fit the muslin sleeve snugly to your arm (see pp. 29–31). The idea is to copy your arm as is, without adding ease for movement. Next, with arm bent, have your friend mark the placement lines on the muslin, corresponding to those shown at center left. Now take off the muslin.

Use the Muslin to Make a Pattern

Trace your fitted muslin onto pattern paper, transfer and true markings, and raise the sleeve cap ½ in. Draw a forearm line to correspond to the wrist shape; all lines should match at the underarm seam. This is the sleeve-form body (template A, bottom left).

CUT TEMPLATES TO COMPLETE THE SLEEVE

Enlarge templates B, C, and D below to fit your measurements (approximately 400 percent equals a size 10). Add a ½-in. seam allowance to all pattern pieces.

PIN SHOULDER SUPPORT

Pin template B's center line to the shoulder line on the dress form so it extends 1 in. beyond the form. Pin the front and back of B to the dress form; trace the form's armhole seamline onto the shoulder support. Mark front and back on pattern piece.

ADJUST LENGTH OF ARMHOLE

Measure the length of the armhole on template A at the seamline. Subtract 1 in. Enlarge/adjust template C so it has a circumference equal to the measurement.

ADJUST WRIST MEASUREMENT

Enlarge/adjust template D so it has a circumference equal to your wrist measurement.

PIN SHOULDER SUPPORT

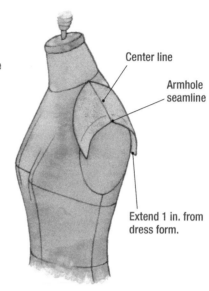

Pin template B so it extends 1 in. beyond the form; transfer markings.

Center line

Armhole seamline

Extend 1 in. from dress form.

ADJUST LENGTH OF ARMHOLE

Measure length of armhole on template A.

ENLARGE AND CUT OUT TEMPLATES

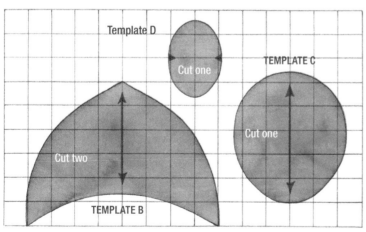

Template D

Cut one

TEMPLATE C

Cut one

Cut two

TEMPLATE B

☐ = 1 in.

Enlarge and use these templates to complete the sleeve form.

Construct the Sleeve Form

Cut the adjusted template pieces out in fabric and transfer all placement lines. Use canvas, poplin, or duck instead of muslin; the form will hold up to lots of use, and garment sleeves will slide on and off the form smoothly. Use soutache braid to indicate placement lines. Because soutache is narrower (⅛ in.) than the ¼-in.-wide style tape normally used to define style lines on a dress form, it is more precise. And soutache can be felt through layers of muslin or fabric, unlike flat style tape.

SEW PATTERN PIECE A

Stitch the elbow dart. On the right side, topstitch soutache braid over the horizontal style lines, and placket and forearm lines. Trim; seal with Fray Check™. Next, sew the underarm seam, leaving 6 in. unsewn for stuffing. Sew gathering stitches in the cap seam allowance. Gather slightly.

SEW PATTERN PIECE B

With right sides together, stitch the two shoulder support sections together, leaving the curved armhole edge open. Turn, press, and topstitch ⅛ in. from edge. Baste the armhole edges of the shoulder support, then baste it to the sleeve cap's right side. Staystitch the armhole and the wrist seamline, and clip.

Finish the Sleeve Form

With right sides together, baste, then stitch the armhole insert (piece C) to the sleeve, securing the shoulder support (piece B) at the same time. Stitch the wrist insert (piece D) to the wrist end.

Match the centers of the oval's long edges to the underarm and center line to make sure that the oval represents the wrist in its natural position. Stitch; turn right side out through the opening.

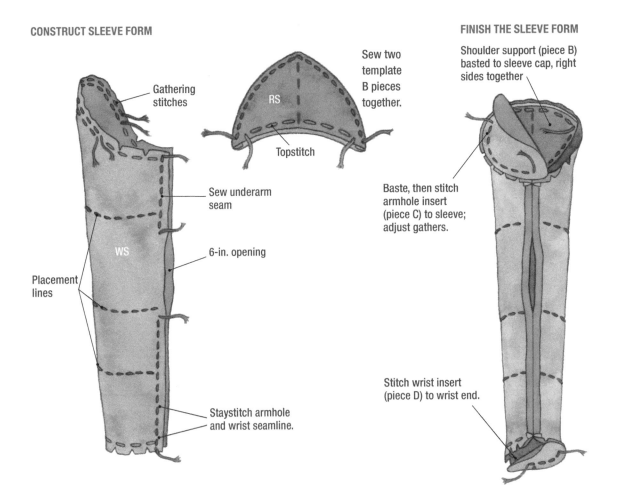

CONSTRUCT SLEEVE FORM

Gathering stitches

RS

Sew two template B pieces together.

Topstitch

Sew underarm seam

WS

6-in. opening

Placement lines

Staystitch armhole and wrist seamline.

FINISH THE SLEEVE FORM

Shoulder support (piece B) basted to sleeve cap, right sides together

Baste, then stitch armhole insert (piece C) to sleeve; adjust gathers.

Stitch wrist insert (piece D) to wrist end.

STUFF AND ATTACH SLEEVE FORM

After sewing the sleeve form, it's time to stuff it (polyester batting, such as Fairfield's Soft Touch® Poly-fil Supreme, is a suitable choice for stuffing). Stuff the arm as firmly as possible, but don't overstuff the shoulder area. If the arm is too tightly packed, it will stand away from the dress form instead of hanging naturally. Pin the sleeve form to the dress form at the shoulder support to check the fit before stitching the sleeve's opening closed.

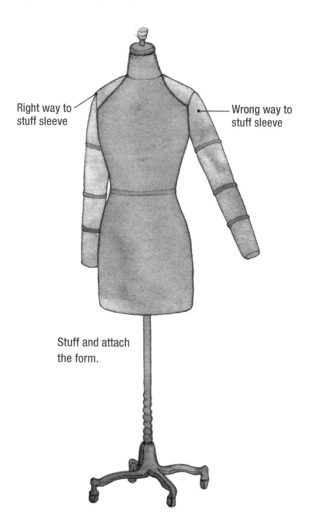

Right way to stuff sleeve

Wrong way to stuff sleeve

Stuff and attach the form.

 TIP To give the shoulder of a homemade dress form a smoother look, place batting in a bag made from panty hose.

Sleeve for a Homemade Dress Form

Making a sleeve form to fit a homemade dress form is a little more challenging than making one for a commercial form. Using a pattern based on a raglan sleeve works for any of these variations in the shoulder/armhole area.

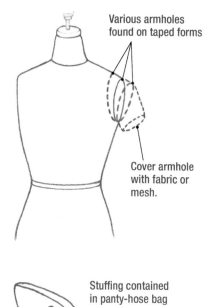

Various armholes found on taped forms

Cover armhole with fabric or mesh.

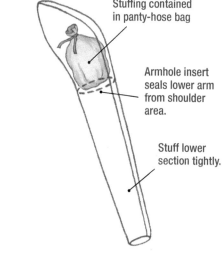

Stuffing contained in panty-hose bag

Armhole insert seals lower arm from shoulder area.

Stuff lower section tightly.

The Pants Form

Making a soft-filled custom pants form isn't difficult, and it will make fitting pants significantly more accurate.

Start with a simple pants pattern that fits reasonably well (one with no pleats, yokes, or other style details). With it, you can make a soft, stuffed pants form that will work for draping, fitting, and altering projects, even if it doesn't exactly mimic all body contours. Because you can easily reposition the legs during fitting, this type of pants form may be easier to work with than a stiff form, especially for those who have little or no space between the thighs when standing normally.

Make the Pants Form

DIVIDE THE PATTERN PIECES

Divide the front and back pattern pieces in half lengthwise down the center of the leg. Add ½-in.-wide seam allowances to the center lines to make four new pattern pieces: one center and side piece for both the front and back. Adjust the hemline to the exact anklebone point, and raise the crotchline 1 in. True all the seamlines (see the top left photo on the facing page).

CUT THE PATTERN OUT

Cut the pants pattern out in muslin. Ask a helper to pin-fit the muslin skintight by reshaping each seam and dart (see the top right photo on the facing page). Mark the fitting lines, unpin, and transfer the altered outline to the paper pattern.

MEASURE THE ANKLE

Measure the circumference of the ankle and make a corresponding oval pattern to use as an ankle cap. Cut all pieces from canvas, poplin, or duck.

MARK THE PLACEMENT LINES

Stitch all vertical seams except the inseam, then apply the soutache to the fitting lines. Mark a standard zipper length 7 in. down from the waist. Measure and mark placement lines for capri, knee-length, Bermuda, and shorts hem lengths as desired. Sew soutache at these pants lengths perpendicular to vertical soutache lines (see the bottom left photo on the facing page). Stitch the inseam, matching soutache ends.

ASSEMBLE THE FORM

Interface the ankle-cap pieces, then assemble the fronts and backs into a complete lower torso, stitching the oval ankle caps with the longer dimension oriented front to back. Turn right side out.

MAKE A PLYWOOD WAIST PLATE

Hold two L-squares around your waist so they intersect at right angles to establish a rectangle that represents your waist shape. Have a helper mark the intersections with masking tape. Place them flat on pattern paper, and transfer and true the rectangle shape that represents your waist cross section. Some waists will be more rectangular and others more square. Measure your waist circumference, then shape a tape measure so that it stands upright within the rectangle at that measurement into an oval that follows your waist-rectangle shape (see the bottom right photo on the facing page). True the oval and use as a pattern to cut a plywood end cap. Paint or varnish the cap if desired.

FINISH THE PANTS FORM

Insert screw eyes into the waist plate, spaced about 6 in. apart in line with the side seams. Alter the canvas torso to fit the waist plate snugly. Cut and sew a 1-in.-wide waistband around the top edge. Press under the band seam allowance, and edgestitch closed. Stuff the entire form through the waistline opening (a heavy, foot-long dowel can be a useful aid) with polyfiber stuffing (you'll need four or five 24-oz. bags), then insert the plate. Using about 36 upholstery tacks or wooden staples, secure the fabric to the plate at center front, center back, and side seams, then evenly space tacks in between, about 1½ in. apart. Use a chain and hook to hang the finished form.

DIVIDE PATTERN PIECES

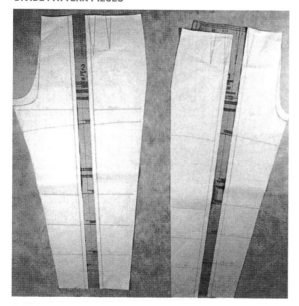

Divide the front and back pattern pieces in half lengthwise down the center of the leg.

MARK PLACEMENT LINES

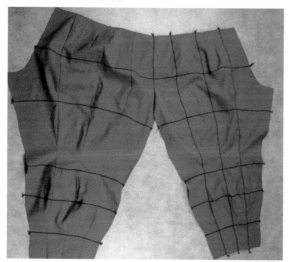

Cut the pieces from the form fabric and stitch the seams except the inseam. Apply soutache to horizontal placement lines for capri, knee-length, Bermuda, and shorts hem lengths.

CUT PATTERN OUT IN MUSLIN

Pin-fit the muslin skintight by reshaping the seams and darts.

MAKE PLYWOOD WAIST PLATE

You'll need two L-squares, pattern paper, and a measuring tape to make a finishing plywood waist plate for your pants form.

II

WORKING WITH PATTERNS AND MUSLIN

Most sewers use commercial patterns when they make clothing. These patterns are drafted for standardized figures and usually need a few adjustments to fit properly. You can alter pattern circumference by simply changing pattern size, but you'll also likely need to change the length.

It's least complicated to make any length adjustments first. Most patterns are drafted for a person between 5 ft. 4 in. and 5 ft. 6 in., depending on the pattern manufacturer. Measure between your shoulder and waist and compare the length to the pattern. If the pattern is too long, fold a horizontal pleat below the bust and above the waist to subtract the extra length. If the pattern is too short, cut a horizontal line in the same location, spread it the additional length needed, and tape paper in the opened space. Add or subtract the same amount to the front and back pattern pieces. You can check waist, sleeve, pant, and skirt lengths as well and make corrections in the same manner. After adjusting all lengths, change the circumference measurements, if necessary.

Once you've made the initial alterations to a tissue pattern, try it on. Do this by pinning the tissue together and fitting it on your body; this is called tissue-fitting. Alternatively, sew a test garment called a muslin. For many garments, tissue-fitting, which involves only a half garment, is sufficient for confirming that lengths and widths are satisfactory. If you're working on a complex project, such as a fitted gown or tailored jacket, make a muslin, so you can pin-fit and restitch without stressing the fashion fabric through multiple alterations.

By checking the pattern and then testing your adjustments before committing them to final fabric, you'll spare yourself hassle and heartache. You can resolve your fitting issues in practice fabric and can be sure that the garment fits and flatters perfectly.

Fitting

To get a great fit in clothes you sew, there are two techniques to try: *Tissue-fit* the pattern before cutting into the fabric, which gives you a good idea of how the pattern will fit and how the resulting garment will hang, or *pin-fit* the garment as you sew to refine its fit. The time you spend on fitting will pay off in great sewing results.

The Tissue-Fit

Tissue-fitting involves pinning or taping the pressed pattern pieces together, trying on the paper half-garment, noting areas that need correcting, making fitting adjustments to the pattern, and then repeating the process until you're happy with it. If your body is fairly symmetrical, you can work with the half pattern and adjust only one side (making the other side the same), but if you're noticeably different on each side, copy the pattern pieces so you have a full paper garment, and tissue-fit the sides individually.

CHECK THE AMOUNT OF EASE
First, decide how much ease you want in your garment. It helps to compare the pattern with an old, trusted pattern or garment. Check the shoulder width, neckline, armhole depth, bustline, waist, hip, and length. If you know your figure irregularities, you can begin to adjust for them before you tissue-fit.

PREPARE THE PATTERN
Join pattern pieces with Scotch® Removable Tape (blue label), which can be positioned over and over, or simply pin the pattern together. Patterns without seam allowances, like Neue Mode and older Burda patterns, are easy to tape together and tissue-fit, and will give very accurate results.

Patternwork Principles

There are several key points in the anatomy of a pattern. And because they are universal to all garments, they exist on almost every pattern you use. Use the principles listed here as a guide or checklist to proofread your patterns, and you'll eliminate many initial pattern glitches. As you apply these principles, your mastery of pattern alterations will develop, and you'll enjoy sewing better-fitting garments.

KEY REFERENCE POINTS

- The upper shoulder point—where a jewel neckline crosses the shoulder seam—is the key pattern reference point on a garment. The garment hangs from this point, and it marks where you should begin most length and depth measurements.

- Lengthwise grainlines usually run parallel with the center front and center back lines, and perpendicular to the hipline and biceps line.

- At the point where two pattern-piece corners join front to back—for example, at a pants waist side seam, the underarm side seam, or each end of a shoulder seam—the combined corner angles equal 180 degrees, usually from the right angles at each corner. This prevents seams from having undesirable bumps at the edge.

- On contoured body styles, when the side seam angles in or out, or the garment is A-line or flared, use a curved hem. This is true for bodices, coats, skirts, and any garment that flares or angles.

- A standard jewel neckline width is approximately one third of the total shoulder width. The front neckline depth is approximately half of the neck width. The back neckline is generally ¾ in. deep on most sizes.

- Darts must always point toward the apex on the body (i.e., the bust point), but they don't reach it. Keep the dart point ½ in. to 1¼ in. from the apex so it ends gracefully and doesn't accentuate the bust point.

- Use seam allowances on large darts and fold and sew smaller darts as a wedge. Removing the extra fabric provides a smoother fit.

- The shoulder slope is essentially a dart, hidden in the seam, allowing the garment to hang on the straight of grain. The slope on your pattern must match your own shoulder slope for a bodice to fit properly.

- When adding more than 1½ in. of flare to a pattern piece (to each garment quadrant), make the addition internally, not on the side seam. The allowable amount of flare you can successfully add at the side seam increases as the pattern piece becomes longer. Adding excessive flare at the side seams can leave you with a garment that looks like it has fins.

- The front waistline is generally longer than the back by approximately 1 in. Conversely, the back hipline is longer on the back by the same amount.

ARMHOLES

Alter the armhole first and then adjust the sleeve cap. The proper armhole fit makes the whole bodice hang better. And of course, the right armhole is essential for a properly fitted sleeve.

- The upper chest width is generally narrower than its corresponding shoulder point. On a size 10, the armhole curves in approximately ¼ in. to ⅜ in. on each side.

- The front armhole angles toward the center front from the shoulder point down about two-thirds of the armhole depth before starting its curve around to the side seam.

- The back armhole curves toward the side seam halfway down the armhole depth. You need the greater scoop in the front to accommodate forward arm movement.

- The lower armhole flattens for approximately a quarter of the armhole inset. As garments become less fitted, the lower armhole points drop and widen.

SLEEVES AND SLEEVE CAPS

When you alter an armhole, it's likely that both the sleeve cap and the biceps length of the sleeve need to change, too.

- The sleeve cap height on a fitted garment measures approximately two-thirds to three-quarters of the length of the armhole depth, which is measured vertically from the shoulder point to the underarm.

- When you deepen an armhole, you need to increase the biceps circumference and shorten the cap, creating a looser-fitting sleeve.

- When you increase the width of a garment at the side seam (resulting in a greater armhole inset on the pattern), the cap height of the sleeve needs to increase.

PANTS AND SKIRTS

Pants and skirt patterns offer opportunities to hide darts in seams, which can be helpful once you know where they're located.

- The side seam curve on pants and skirts should curve to the depth of the fullest part of the hip, and then fall straight. The fullest part on some people may be the abdomen or thighs.

- Commercial pants and skirts generally have, on each side, one dart in the front and two darts in the back. The front hip curve is a sharper curve than the back, and is essentially a hidden dart. Front darts generally drop 3½ in., and back darts drop 5 in.

- To allow for longer crotch lengths that accommodate a full abdomen or buttocks, raise the center front or back seam above the normal waistline.

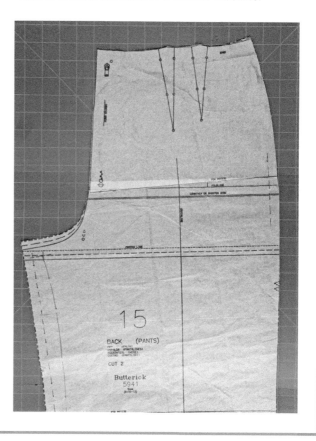

For patterns with seam allowances, it's easiest to fold back one seam allowance (clipping the edge, if needed) and lap it over the second one, matching the seamlines. Reinforce the clipped area with tape or fusible interfacing when you're ready to cut out the garment.

To prepare the pattern, attach the bodice front and back at the sides and shoulders. If your pattern has a skirt, attach it to the bodice, matching seamlines. Pin the sleeve together, and attach the cuff, if any. Pin up the hemlines, then pin a length of seam tape or ribbon around the waistline of the pattern. On a close-fitting garment, put the ribbon on the outside; on a loose-fitting garment, pin the ribbon loosely to the inside to hold it at the waistline. If you plan to use a shoulder pad, pin it in place now.

TRY ON THE TISSUE

Wearing the underwear and any clothing you'll wear beneath the finished garment, slip the tissue on your body and tie the ribbon around your waist. Pin or tape the pattern to your clothing at the neckline, bust, waist, and hip, in front and back. Slip the sleeve on and pin it to the bodice at match points in the front armhole and shoulder. You can ask for help or work alone.

Now, evaluate your pattern in front of a full-length mirror, using a hand mirror to see the back. Since a pattern hangs from the shoulders, begin at the top and check the following points:

- The shoulder seam should lie on the top of the shoulder and end at the shoulder point, so adjust as needed.
- Bust darts should point to the bust and end before its fullest point.
- Check to make sure the pattern tissue reaches the center front and center back. If it doesn't, let out the side seams.
- Vertical seams should hang perpendicular to the floor. If they don't, adjust them at the shoulders or waist.
- The sleeve should fit comfortably around the arm; check to be sure that any elbow shaping actually occurs at the elbow.
- Bend your arm to check the length.
- In many instances, you'll need to raise the cap of the sleeve, as well as the sleeve/bodice underarm seam, to increase mobility. If you end up with too much cap, or if the underarm is too high, cut off the excess during assembly.
- The seam tape or ribbon around the waist makes it easy to check the bodice length. Lifting your shoulders without tearing the tissue ensures a comfortable amount of blousing.

ADJUST AND REFIT

Take the paper pattern off and make any necessary adjustments to it, then try the tissue on again and check the fit. When you're finally happy with the pattern, you're ready to cut the fabric, but be sure to leave generous seam allowances in the fitting seams (shoulder, side, waistline, and sleeve) for any additional adjustments you make as you sew. (If you're working with expensive fabric and you have any doubts, make a trial garment first.)

Try on the taped pattern tissue.

TIP If your body is fairly symmetrical, you can work with the half-pattern and adjust only one side, but if you're noticeably different on each side, copy the pattern pieces and tissue-fit each side.

The Pin-Fit

As you sew your garment, pin-fit to customize the fit. Your choice of fabric influences the fit, and one alteration may affect or correct another. As soon as you assemble the main pieces of the garment, try it on right side out and check the fit. Don't overfit—your garment should allow you to move comfortably.

Since pin-fitting is done on the right side of the garment, you'll need to transfer changes accurately to the wrong side in order to incorporate them into your construction and blend the new seamline with the original one. A fast method of stitching a pin-fitted seamline is to slip-baste the seam as shown in the bottom left drawing, then open and machine-stitch on the basted line. The drawback is that it's difficult to transfer changes to the other side of the garment or to the pattern.

For a marking method that's easy to transfer to the other side, use pins or thread tracing to mark both sides of the corrected seam, where the two fabric layers touch. You can refer to these points as the *touch*

(where the fold touches the underlayer) and the *turn* (where the upper layer folds), as shown in the bottom right drawing. After marking, remove the pins and make the adjustment on the other side of the garment and on the tissue. Stitch the pin-fitted seams on the new seamlines.

Pin-Fit Fixes

The following are some fine-tuning suggestions that are useful when pin-fitting a garment:

ESTABLISH BODY WIDTHS

Chest, waist, and hip fitting depends on vertical seams. Take them in, or let them out until the wrinkles or drag lines ease. Correct the fit in body width by letting out or taking in vertical seams.

FIT THE SHOULDER

Lift to smooth the front chest area. You may have to drop the armhole after this. A bad fit in the shoulder often reveals itself in a drag line across the chest.

FIX THE CHEST

Scoop the armhole section that joins the bodice as it crosses the chest. This most-common fit problem

TWO WAYS TO PIN-FIT

SLIP-BASTE THE SEAM

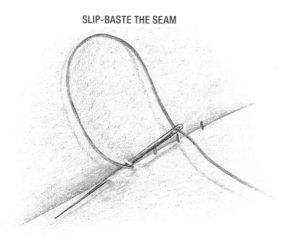

Mark the altered seamline to stitch it. Slip-baste to mark. Working from right to left, pick up thread on back layer, insert needle in fold of front layer, and pull through to complete stitch. Repeat to end. Remove the garment, then open and machine-stitch on the basted line.

TRANSFER CHANGES EASILY

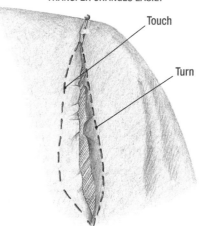

Touch

Turn

Pin or thread-trace along the "touch" and "turn." Remove the pins, mark seam changes on the other half of the garment, and stitch the new seams.

happens when there is too much width right above the chest. Reduce the width across the chest by shaving fabric from the front armhole.

ADJUST THE SLEEVE CAP AND ARMHOLE

Always pin your sleeves with the seam allowance turned inward as if it were sewn in. Give a little pinch for the ease in the front and back of your shoulder.

CHECK THE PANTS

Try lifting the center back to smooth out drag lines under the seat.

If there are "smile" lines in front, release the inseam at the back crotch to give enough saddle for the inner thigh. Not all back-rise length problems are at the waist. This problem is best resolved in the muslin-fitting stage, but if you have your final garment already cut and basted, you can add a wedge along the straight grain to the back leg at the top of the inseam.

CURVE DARTS

You may want to curve the shoulder seams and bust and hip darts so that they fit the contours of your

ESTABLISH BODY WIDTHS

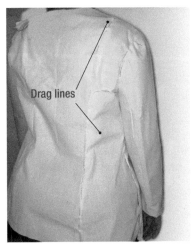

Drag lines

Drag lines across the chest or back can be an indication of a bad fit in the shoulders.

FIT THE SHOULDER

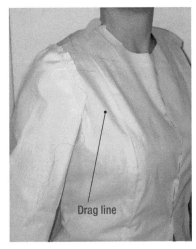

Drag line

You can correct wrinkles or drag lines across the chest, back, waist, and hip by letting out or taking in vertical seams.

ADJUST THE SLEEVE CAP

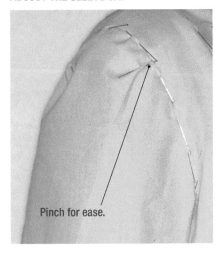

Pinch for ease.

Be sure to add a pinch for ease in the front and back of the sleeve cap seam.

CHECK THE PANTS

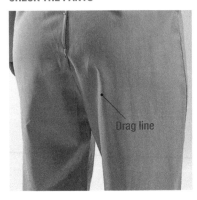

Drag line

A drag line under the seat can sometimes be eliminated by taking in the upper inseam on the back seam allowance.

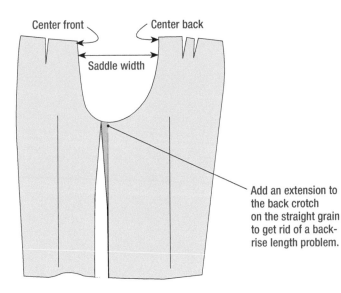

Center front   Center back

Saddle width

Add an extension to the back crotch on the straight grain to get rid of a back-rise length problem.

body. Check the ease in the bustline and the fit across the back and at the waistline.

Also, check the hang of the sleeve. Check to see that front and back sleeve seamlines appear vertical, and make sure that you can move your arms to the front and back comfortably.

Using a Camera to Fit

One of the most useful fitting aids available today is a digital camera. It enables you to keep a visual record of fittings to serve as a reference to the corrections needed.

Getting the Most Useful Photographs

- Photograph yourself as you stand comfortably without distorting your muslin test garment.
- Shoot the entire garment: front, back, and side. Fill the frame as much as possible. If you don't

have someone who can snap your pictures, you can take them yourself in the mirror. It's best if you have a full-length mirror for skirts, pants, and dresses. To minimize glare, be sure to override your camera's flash.

- Shoot at the highest resolution possible; this allows you to zoom in on areas of interest later when you study your photos for fitting clues.

Analyze the Photos

Your digital photos will reveal many more telltale wrinkles than you would see in the mirror. Note the areas that seem to need work, and zoom in to take a better look. Print the photos you want to examine closely, and save the photos so you can refer to them as you work on your pattern adjustments.

Look for drag lines, which occur when one area of a garment is pulling. They point your eye to the source of the problem.

Wrinkles form when a garment is too tight or too loose. If it's too loose, try lifting the area or pinching it in to see if the excess can be eliminated. If the garment is too tight, extra fabric is needed in the seams.

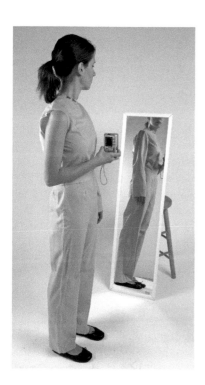  

When evaluating the muslin or the final cut, stand in front of a mirror and use a digital camera to take snapshots, then use the images to record and analyze your changes.

Make a Muslin

Sometimes, the fear of making a mistake can actually lead to procrastination. Whipping up a test garment in muslin is an excellent way to end your procrastination woes. But a muslin does not have to be made of muslin. Any inexpensive fabric works. Just pick a weight that's similar to the fashion fabric you're using. If you're sewing a knit, use a knit. Even old fabric you have on hand works. By creating a muslin, you can experiment with the pattern and happily make mistakes, without fear of ruining expensive fabric. It might sound like twice the work, but in fact, it halves the potential frustration of sewing blind with your fashion fabric.

Once you sew a muslin, you'll become a convert. Why? Because practice makes perfect and stress-free sewing. Think of a muslin test garment as the practice session of the sewing world—it allows you to explore techniques and fine-tune and streamline the garment-making process. It offers spot-on fit and style, down to the hems. With a muslin test garment, you can take in, let out, and otherwise tweak the fit allowing you to spare wear and tear on your

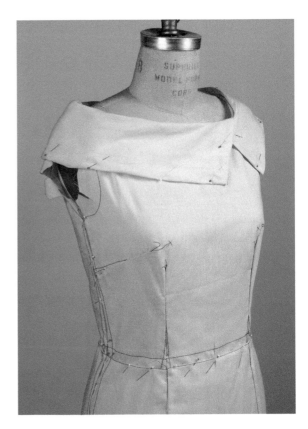

A muslin made from inexpensive fabric.

Preparing the Muslin Pattern and Yardage

A properly marked pattern and pressed muslin are essential to the creation of an accurate test garment.

DETERMINING THE SEAMLINES

Locate the seamlines on your commercial pattern. With the advent of multisize patterns, seamlines are no longer printed on commercial patterns; typically, they're 5/8 in. in from the cutting lines, but always check the pattern instructions. Measure in from the cutting line for your size using a ruler, and mark all the seamlines on your pattern.

Before you move on to the fabric, make any necessary adjustments, such as length or size alterations, to the paper pattern. You'll refine things later, of course, but if there are changes that you know you'll have to make, such as bodice and sleeve length adjustments, now is the time to make them.

PREPARING MUSLIN FABRIC

Unless you're working on a particularly wide skirt or bias garment, 45-in.-wide unbleached muslin fabric is sufficient and is easier to handle than wider fabrics. Don't get anything too thin or too thick; some muslin is so thick that it's difficult to pin through, and that's too inflexible for your purposes.

It isn't necessary to prewash the muslin fabric, but you must steam it thoroughly so it doesn't shrink. Press it carefully, and be sure to align the selvages perfectly. Pin the selvages together to ensure that the fold is on the vertical straight of grain.

fashion fabric. Because you adjust fit and figure out hem placement in a muslin, you don't need to leave extra fabric in the seam and hem allowances. By testing your seam placement first, you won't have to rip out stitches, which can leave behind tiny pinpricks or tears and can stretch seams.

In the long run, a test garment saves time. A muslin test run may add a little extra time at the beginning of the pattern-fabric relationship, but think of it as the ultimate icebreaker—it's a way to slowly get to know a pattern, learn its idiosyncrasies, and coax it into shape before committing to it in fashion fabric.

2. Press all seam allowances as you would in a final garment. You can cut many corners in a muslin, but never skip pressing steps. Press the seam allowances open, and then press again from the right side of the garment. Whenever possible, don't trim or clip seam allowances in the muslin, as you might need to let out seams in the fitting process.

Try it on to evaluate the fit, style, and length. If you're fitting the test garment on yourself, enlist the help of a buddy. If the fit looks strange across the shoulders, sew on the other sleeve for a clearer view of where the fit is going wrong.

Simple Steps to Make a Muslin

Crafting a test garment out of scrap fabric is really quite easy. Begin by choosing a size using the measurement chart on the pattern as your guide, and press all pattern pieces with a warm, dry iron—folds and wrinkles can affect the fit. Then cut out the main garment pieces. No need to spend time on cuffs, facings, or pockets, unless it is a section of the garment you particularly want to practice or check. Be sure to cut two sleeves. (You'll sew and attach one sleeve first, then check the fit. Only if things look too tight or too loose across the shoulders do you need to attach the other sleeve.)

Mark darts, grainlines, waist, and bust points with permanent marker. Mark the center front lines, zipper or buttonhole placement, and the seamlines too, if you like. Mark pocket outlines directly on the muslin to judge placement. Baste hemlines, because the line of thread is easier to feel and press; staystitch the neck edges by sewing a line of straight stitches on the seamline.

1. Baste the garment pieces together using long stitches; press. Following your pattern instructions, construct the garment, skipping steps for details you didn't include. Don't sew closures; simply pin those closed. Press up, and loosely pin the hems. To make stitch removal easy, back-tack only at stress points.

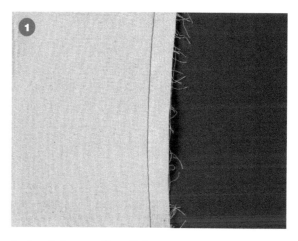

Baste with long machine stitches.

Don't include facings. Press seam allowances open.

3. Pin out any changes or release basting stitches. Write any notes directly on the muslin. Pin any changes. When satisfied with the fit and style, remove the garment, and lay it flat on a hard surface.

4. Mark the pinned sections with a permanent marker. Using a dotted line, mark both sides of pinned alterations.

5. Release the pins, press, and transfer changes. Measure the differences between the original markings and your adjustment marks. Transfer these changes to your pattern. If you make major adjustments, you might want to make another test garment to double-check the fit.

Label and save your muslins. There is no need to start from scratch every time: A muslin doesn't take up much room, and it will come in handy months or years down the road when you want to sew a favorite pattern in a different fabric. If you've lost or gained weight, or wish to make subtle style changes, you can just shake out the muslin, try it on, then make minor adjustments. Just be sure to write the date, pattern name, and size directly on the muslin in permanent marker before you store it away.

TIP Get a smooth start. Before you cut, press your muslin fabric, and make sure it is on-grain so you can cut your pattern accordingly.

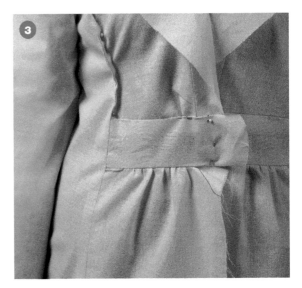

Pin to take in seams.

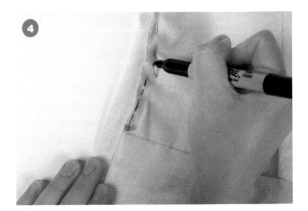

Mark pinned sections.

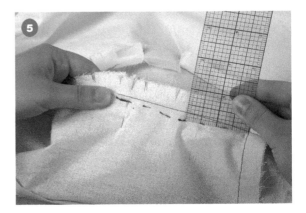

Measure the distance of the change, and transfer the alteration to your pattern.

Possible Fit Adjustments to a Muslin

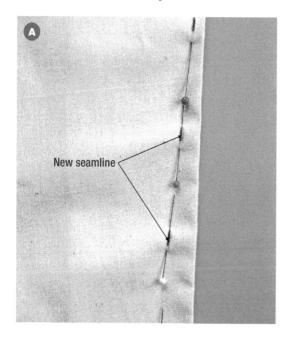

TAKE IN LOOSE SEAMS. If a section is too loose, pin it to fit, and mark the new seamline.

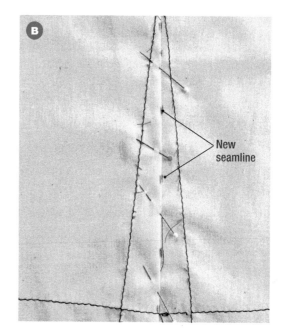

LOOSEN TIGHT SEAMS. If a section is too tight, open the seam, then pin and mark the new seamline.

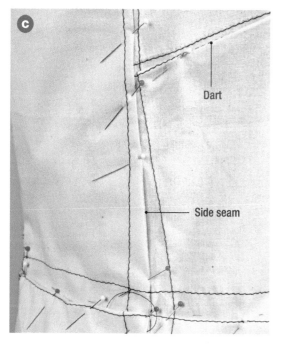

ADJUST DARTS. Pin them in place during the fitting, then mark any changes carefully.

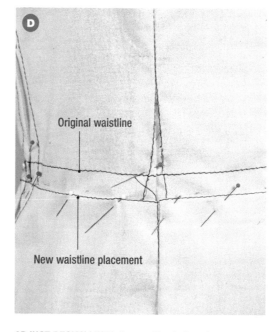

ADJUST DESIGN LINES. Assess the design elements and adjust them as necessary. Here, the waistline was lowered, which altered the dress proportions.

III

FITTING THE BODICE

For women, fitting the bodice of a garment can be a challenge. Simply understanding that a commercial pattern is, typically, drafted for a B-cup figure can get you started with pattern alterations. In this chapter, you'll learn how to increase, reduce, reposition, or add a bust dart that truly flatters your figure.

The shoulder slope, shape of the back, and armscye all influence how a garment lies on the body. Simple diagnoses and alterations help you eliminate gaps at the neckline and armhole, and ensure that a blouse, jacket, coat, or dress hangs smoothly from the shoulders down. Once you've resolved these trouble spots, you can perfect the sleeve. A sleeve that fits properly looks neat, reduces visual bulk from the torso, and increases your comfort.

In many cases, a careful, detailed fitting in fabric is the best way to solve multiple issues in the bodice. An in-depth discussion of fitting a bodice and sleeve muslin is offered in this chapter, along with a technique for fitting knits.

Fitting the Bust

Whether you're full busted or small busted, no top or jacket fits just right unless the garment's cup size matches yours. You may also need to adjust the position of a dart so it delivers fullness where you need it—not above or below.

Tips for Patternwork

- When enlarging a front pattern piece, divide the needed extra amount by two. That way, any enlargement you undertake on the pattern half will also take effect on the other side of the garment.

- When buying a new pattern, pick one that matches your high-bust body measurement as closely as possible—it's easier to let out the bust than to take in the rest of the garment. If you are between sizes, pick the larger size and decrease the pattern.

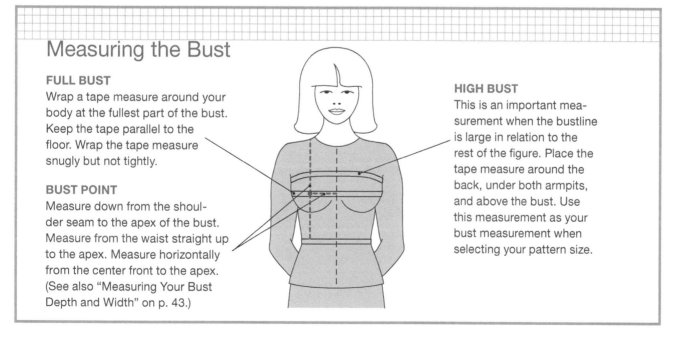

Measuring the Bust

FULL BUST
Wrap a tape measure around your body at the fullest part of the bust. Keep the tape parallel to the floor. Wrap the tape measure snugly but not tightly.

BUST POINT
Measure down from the shoulder seam to the apex of the bust. Measure from the waist straight up to the apex. Measure horizontally from the center front to the apex. (See also "Measuring Your Bust Depth and Width" on p. 43.)

HIGH BUST
This is an important measurement when the bustline is large in relation to the rest of the figure. Place the tape measure around the back, under both armpits, and above the bust. Use this measurement as your bust measurement when selecting your pattern size.

Adjusting a Pattern for a Fuller Bust

If your garments pull across the bust, your darts point in the wrong direction, or your side seams pull forward, it's time to fit the bust.

Here are three ways to alter a pattern for a fuller bust size. You will need your pattern, extra pattern paper, pencil, tape measure, ruler, and glue stick. Remember that a full bust alteration shouldn't change the original fit through the sleeves and back. Correct only the front pattern piece.

Follow the directions in "Measuring the Bust" on p. 37 and then transfer the information to your tissue pattern using one of the methods described below. Test your fit by making a sample garment from inexpensive fabric. You can be enjoying a custom-fit wardrobe in no time with these simple pattern adjustments.

Slash-and-Spread

Use this method when the side seams pull to the front or don't run straight down the side of the body. This technique keeps the side seams vertical after the alteration.

1. After copying and cutting out your pattern, cut the pattern parallel to the grainline from the shoulder point to the waist.

2. Separate the pattern pieces by half the extra amount needed based on your bust measurement. Lay over graph paper.

3. Ensure your pattern piece edges are parallel, then use a glue stick to adhere the pattern pieces to the paper.

4. Connect the original pattern lines on the top and bottom edges and trim the excess paper. Correct the front neckline to fit with the back pattern.

SLASH-AND-SPREAD METHOD

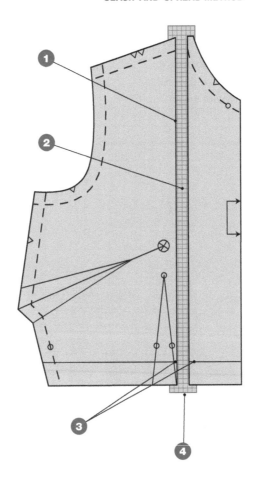

Alter for Extra Room

This method provides extra room for a full, low bust without changing the length of the shoulder seam.

1. After tracing the pattern onto paper and cutting it out, cut a line from the bottom edge to the shoulder seam as shown at top right. Don't cut the pattern into two pieces. (See "A Perfect Pivot Hinge" below.)

2. Pivot the pattern to add half the extra amount, and fill the opening with backing paper.

Note: Pin-fit your pattern tissue to see if you also need to adjust the dart points. You may also benefit from adding a second dart at the waistline.

Use Compound Alterations

If a bodice is tight around the bust and the side seam sits forward, alter the bodice from the waist and the side seam. Use this technique if you are adding more than 3 in.

1. After tracing your pattern onto paper and cutting it out, cut the pattern up from the waistline to the shoulder point, but do not cut the pattern into two pieces.

2. Pivot the pattern to add a quarter the needed amount and add backing paper.

3. Add a quarter the needed amount to the front side seam. Also, extend the side dart and adjust the front sleeve seam.

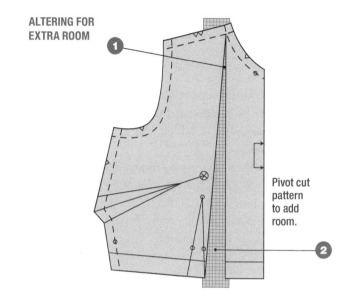

ALTERING FOR EXTRA ROOM

Pivot cut pattern to add room.

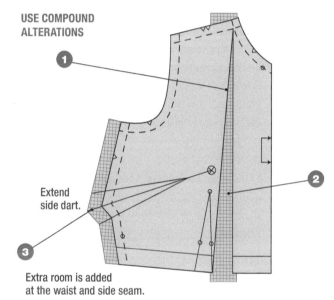

USE COMPOUND ALTERATIONS

Extend side dart.

Extra room is added at the waist and side seam.

A Perfect Pivot Hinge

To avoid getting a funny buckle at the pivot point on a pattern seam, create a hinge of tissue so the pattern can swing or pivot.

A. Before cutting the tissue, reinforce the pivot point with a small piece of transparent tape.

B. Cut the tissue up to the seamline but not through the seam allowance.

C. Then, from the seam allowance, clip a wedge inward, leaving a 1/16-in. hinge. Now the pattern opens smoothly with no buckling, pouching, or distorted seam.

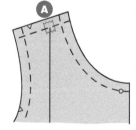
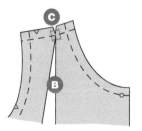

39

Adding or Altering Darts for the Fuller Bust

When placed properly, a couple of darts make your bustline look perfect and flatter your waistline, too. Fortunately, they aren't difficult to add to a pattern, or to alter.

After determining your correct bra size (see "Measuring for a Bra," p. 173), you can follow a simple formula to add darts of the right size to your patterns. You'll end up with a better fit than you'll ever find in ready-to-wear.

Adding Bust Darts

This alteration will add vertical and horizontal fabric to accommodate a fuller bust.

1. Measure your bust depth (see "Measuring Your Bust Depth and Width," p. 43). From the intersection of the neckline and shoulder seam down the front of the pattern (parallel to the grainline), measure your bust-depth distance and make a dot. This is not your bust point; it only indicates bust-point depth. The bust-point dot is placed in step 3.

2. Draw a horizontal line through the dot. Draw a line perpendicular to the grainline from the center-front line through the dot to the side seam.

3. Mark the bust point. Starting at the center-front line, measure the distance along the horizontal line, and draw a large dot. This dot is the correct bust point.

4. Add a diagonal line. Draw a second line from the bust point to the notch in the armscye. If there is no notch, divide the armhole curve into thirds, and draw the line to the lower third of the armhole.

5. Add a vertical line. Draw a third line parallel to the grainline from the bust point to the bottom of the garment.

6. Slash to the bust point. Cut the pattern along the horizontal line from the side seam to—but not through—the bust point. Slide a piece of tissue under the pattern.

7. Cut the vertical line. Cut from the bottom of the garment front to the bust-point dot. Continue to cut along the diagonal line to the armscye seamline, and leave a hinge. When the pattern is spread to accommodate the bust, the seamline at the armhole stays the same length. Cut the tissue at this same point from the edge of the armhole to the seamline; keep the hinge.

8. Carefully spread the vertical line. Slide the pattern tissue in the direction of the arrow, keeping the vertical slash lines parallel. Spread the pattern according to your cup size, using the "Increases for Bust Darts" chart on the facing page. Add this amount to the width of the vertical gap—not the width of the "dart" section. The bust-dart section will open as the pattern is spread. Although it looks as if the dart is forming, the wedge-shaped area is not quite right yet.

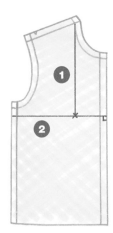

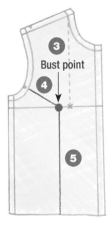

Bust point

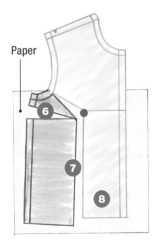

Paper

9. Cut along the horizontal bustline. Cut from the bust point to the center-front line. Slide the pattern section down until the two pattern hemlines align. Tape the vertical cut edges to the tissue underneath. Draw a center-front line to connect the upper and lower portion of the pattern.

10. The wedge shape that has formed is not the true dart. To find the true dart, draw a line from the bust point to the side seam in the center of the wedge opening. This is the center foldline of the dart.

11. Mark according to size. If you are making a size smaller than 16, mark a dot on the foldline 1 in. away from your original bust-point dot. If you are making a size 16 or larger, place the dot 2 in. to 2½ in. away from the bust-point dot. The dart point should never end exactly at the bust point.

12. Draw the dart legs. Mark a line from the top and bottom edges of the wedge shape to the new dart-point dot.

Last, fold the center dart line, and bring the two legs together. Then fold the dart up, as if pressing it into position. When you press the side darts up for a full bust, it makes the bustline look higher. Cut off the excess paper along the side seam. When the paper dart is released, a small divot of paper will form along the side seam. This will be needed when sewing your garment.

Increases for Bust Darts

Think of a dart as the space between spokes on a wheel, with your bust point at the hub. Sew two consecutive spokes together, and a cone will form. Sew a different pair of consecutive spokes together, and the cone will be the same shape even though the seam is on a different axis.

CUP SIZE	AMOUNT TO SPREAD PATTERN
C	½ in.
D	¾ in.
DD/E	1¼ in.
DDD/EE	1½ in.
F	1¾ in.

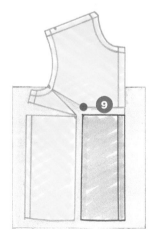
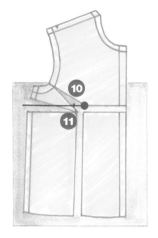
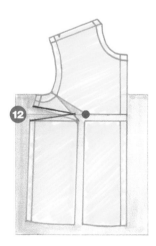

REDIRECT THE SIDE-SEAM BUST DART

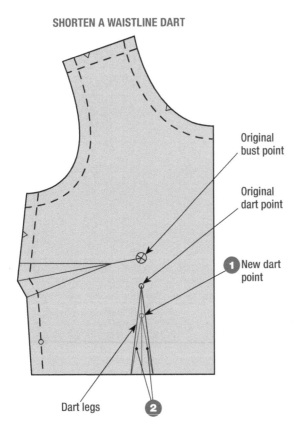

Original bust point

New bust point

1 2

SHORTEN A WAISTLINE DART

Original bust point

Original dart point

1 New dart point

Dart legs

2

Redirecting a Side-Seam Bust Dart

You can lower a dart point to correspond to the lower bust point that often accompanies a full bust.

1. Draw a line along the middle of the dart pointing toward the new bust point. Measure the length of the original dart and mark on the line just drawn.

2. Using the original dart-leg starting points, draw in the new dart, finishing at the new bust point.

Shortening a Waistline Dart

If the darts in a pattern don't point to the fullest part of the bust, you can shorten the waist dart to allow for fullness below the bust point.

1. Draw a line centered on the dart through the original dart point. Establish a new dart point along the line 1 in. lower than the fullest part of the bust.

2. Using the original dart-leg starting points, redraw the legs to end 1 in. from the new bust point.

Altering Princess Seams for a Full Bust

Altering a princess-seamed garment for a large bust requires several steps and careful truing. Buy a pattern according to your high-bust measurement (taken above the bust at the underarm), not your full-bust measurement, so you'll start out with a better fit through the shoulders and neckline.

1. Determine exactly where your bust point is in relation to the pattern's. Find your bust span by measuring between your bust points, and divide the measurement in half. Find your bust level by measuring from your neck point to your bust point, or from midshoulder to bust point if your pattern has a wide neckline. Lay out your front pattern piece on a large piece of paper, and make a vertical line on the paper parallel to the pattern's center front and half the bust span distance away from it, then mark the bust depth on the vertical line. This is your bust point.

   Compare your bust point to the pattern's, noting the difference vertically and horizontally. On the pattern, the bust point should be marked on the princess seamline with a symbol or line. This point is usually marked only on the front piece, so you'll need to transfer the bust point mark to the seamline of the side front piece as well.

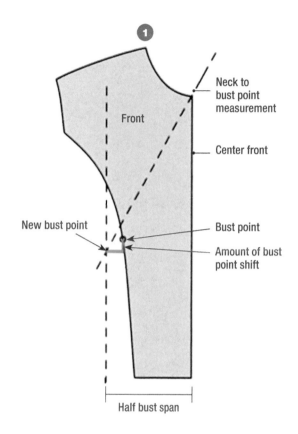

1

Front

Neck to bust point measurement

Center front

New bust point

Bust point

Amount of bust point shift

Half bust span

Measuring Your Bust Depth and Width

Knowing your bust depth and width will help you alter a pattern for better fit. Put on a good-fitting bra. The band should be horizontal around the circumference of your body, and the straps should be secure so they don't fall off your shoulders. Adjust your straps so the apex of your bust is above the halfway point of your upper arm. The higher your bust, the more youthful (and thinner) your figure appears.

To measure your bust depth, stand in front of a mirror, and measure from the shoulder seamline directly below your ear to your bust point.

To measure your bust width, measure the distance between your bust points. Then divide this measurement in half; this is the distance of your bust points from the pattern's center front.

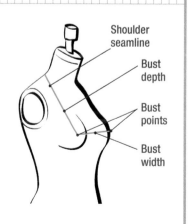

Shoulder seamline

Bust depth

Bust points

Bust width

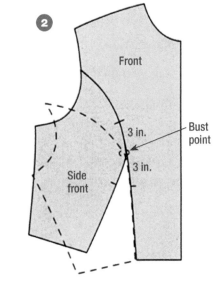

2. With the front and sidefront seamlines matched above the bust point, make a crossmark perpendicular to the seamlines, about 3 in. above the point. Realign the pieces at their bottom edges, match seamlines below the point, and make a second crossmark 3 in. below the point. These marks will help you align the repositioned seamlines after you move the bust point.

3. On each pattern piece, draw a rectangular box around the bust point, about 1 in. above and below the crossmarks and parallel vertically to the grainline. As long as both vertical sides are parallel to the grain, boxes on each don't have to be the same size

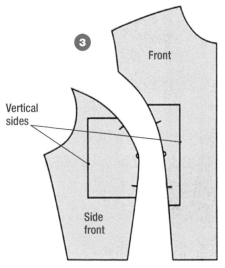

4. On the front pattern piece, cut out the box and move it vertically and horizontally by the amounts determined when you compared your bust point with the pattern's, placing your point directly on the seamline and making sure that you keep the box parallel to the grainline. On the side-front piece, move the box by the same amounts, also keeping the vertical side of the box parallel to the grainline.

5. To true the pattern, start at the original armscye or shoulder seam. Where the pattern jogs, split the difference between the jogs and blend to the point. Do the same thing from the bottom up to the bust point. Extend the crossmarks to the trued seamlines. Although it may look as though you've eliminated some shaping here, the actual

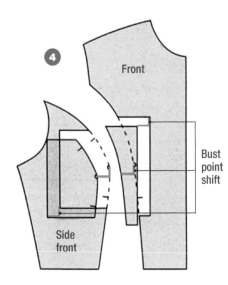

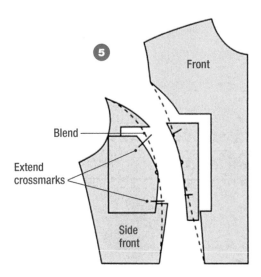

dart space between the princess seams remains the same, as does the armscye shape.

6. After you've repositioned the bust point, you'll need to add length and width to your pattern to accommodate a larger-than-B-cup bust. We'll add width on the side-front piece and length on the front piece. On the side front, add to the bust point ¼ in. for every cup size over B, as shown in the drawing at top right. Blend out to the seamline about 4½ in. above and below the bust point. On the front piece, draw an adjustment line at the bust point, perpendicular to the grainline. Cut and spread on this line the same amount that you shifted vertically on the side front. If your pattern is a shoulder- or classic-style princess, the basic steps are the same as just described.

7. If you've adjusted for a much wider bust span, it will probably be more flattering to change the location of the princess line at the shoulder. In this case, during the truing process, move the seamline above the bust point on the front piece toward the shoulder, and remove an equal amount from the side-front panel. If the garment has princess seams in back, these will have to be moved to match at the shoulder seam.

To check the fit, cut out the garment with 1-in.-wide seam allowances. Don't staystitch or clip the seam allowances yet; just match the crossmarks, ease the seams together, and baste. Fine-tune the seamlines if needed before you stitch them permanently.

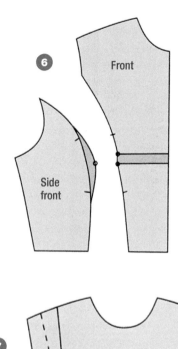

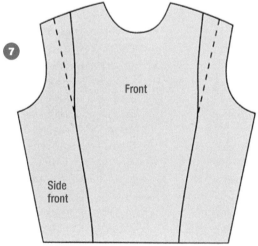

TIP

When altering a garment for a large bust, buy a pattern according to your high-bust measurement, not your full-bust measurement, so you'll start out with a better fit through the neckline and shoulders.

Fitting the Full-Busted Petite

If you're petite, and especially if you're a full-busted petite, you need to remove length through the torso of a garment, but you also need to add length to accommodate the bust fullness. The secret is to place extra length where you need it, and take it away from areas—like the armscye—where you don't. Don't expect your altered patterns to look like the pattern pieces outlined on the pattern's instruction sheet.

STANDARD VS. FULL-FIGURED PETITE SLOPERS

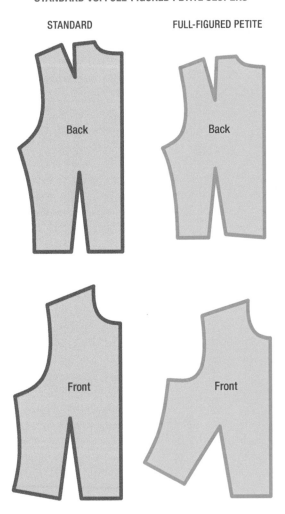

These slopers match only at the high bust level, indicating that both figures have the same circumference in the upper rib cage.

Full-figured petites change from small circumferences to large ones within a short distance, compared to the shape of the dress forms patterns are drafted to fit, so petite patterns will look quite different once they are adjusted to fit. In other words, you can't decrease the distance between shoulder and bustline without distorting the armhole, but once "distorted" correctly, the armhole fits.

At left, you'll see two slopers compared; one is made to fit a large-busted petite and the other to fit a misses size that has the same high-bust measurement as the petite figure (with a smaller bust), but it's about 5 in. taller. Notice that the two backs don't look very different except in length, while the fronts are noticeably dissimilar. The center-front lengths are more similar than the center-back lengths, because the petite's full bust requires more length, and the bust dart on the petite sloper is much bigger, which places its side seam on a greater angle. Also, notice the curve of the armhole, which is much more curved on the petite sloper than on the taller, less busty sloper.

This curve allows for the fullness of the bust and keeps the armhole close fitting with no gaps. The curve follows the same logic as a circular ruffle, cut with an extreme curve, which, when sewn to a straight seam, flares out at the opposite edge. By cutting a highly curved armhole, then straightening it out somewhat when it is put on the figure, you cause the fabric to flare out at the bustline, which is just what's needed for a full bust. In the drawings on the facing page, you'll see several typical top styles, first as drafted for a standard-size dress form and then as drafted for a full-figured petite, so you can see how various styles need to be "distorted" to work for this figure type. The best way for sewers to make changes of this sort is to start by making a sloper for themselves. It's the fastest way to get to know how to fit your own curves. By seeing the size of your darts and shape of your fitted armhole, you'll naturally develop a better understanding of what your patterns need to look like. You'll also have a fabulous tool, your fitted sloper, to use to compare and alter patterns.

Comparing Garment Styles for the Full-Figured Petite

These diagrams show how various garment styles evolve from fitted slopers, for both standard and full-figured petite figures. In each case, the petite version(s) provide less length; shorter, tighter armholes; and more dart control.

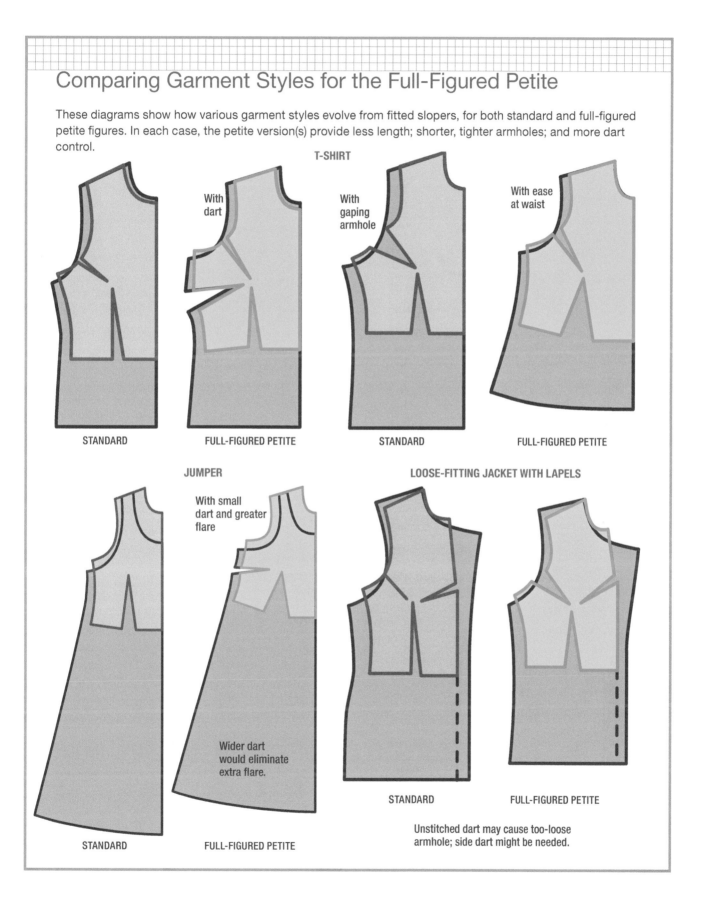

T-SHIRT

With dart

With gaping armhole

With ease at waist

STANDARD

FULL-FIGURED PETITE

STANDARD

FULL-FIGURED PETITE

JUMPER

LOOSE-FITTING JACKET WITH LAPELS

With small dart and greater flare

Wider dart would eliminate extra flare.

STANDARD

FULL-FIGURED PETITE

STANDARD

FULL-FIGURED PETITE

Unstitched dart may cause too-loose armhole; side dart might be needed.

Altering Patterns for a Smaller Bust

For a small bust, measure high bust as if you were taking a full-bust measurement, shifting the tape up from the front only.

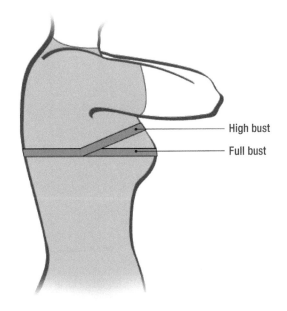

High bust

Full bust

Measurements you'll need to alter for a smaller bust.

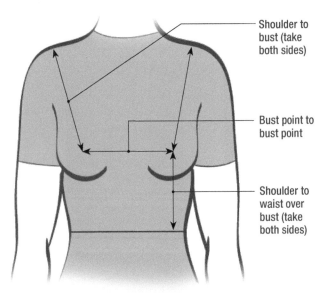

Shoulder to bust (take both sides)

Bust point to bust point

Shoulder to waist over bust (take both sides)

Commercial patterns are generally drafted for a B-cup bust. To alter them for an A-cup figure, it's important to reduce both the length and width of the pattern front, not just the dart size, when reshaping the pattern. Also, smaller busts may require a change in the bust-point position. But assuming that the pattern fits in all other respects, neither the back pattern nor the width of the front pattern between the armhole notches will be affected by the alteration for a smaller cup size.

A B-cup pattern is specifically sized for figures with a full-bust measurement 2 in. greater than their high-bust measurement, while an A cup represents a 1-in. difference. To check your own measurements, position the tape as if you were taking a full-bust measurement, then shift it up in front only, across the chest (about where the top edge of a strapless dress would fall), to find your high-bust measurement, as shown in the top left drawing. Add 2 in. to your high-bust measurement and use the resulting number as your bust measurement when purchasing a pattern. Additional measurements you'll need are from bust point to bust point, from shoulder to bust starting at the shoulder line midpoint, and from shoulder line midpoint to the waist over the bust, as shown in the bottom left drawing.

Using Darts and Seams to Fit an A Cup

On the facing page are instructions for reducing the fronts on three bodice styles, including correcting the front length and repositioning the side seam to reduce the front bust circumference. The examples all start with a bust-point shift, which might not be necessary on your figure. If your pattern has vertical darts, pin-fit them after making the adjustments shown here. Dartless styles can also be reduced, if necessary, simply by locating the likely positions of the unstitched darts in the pattern and following the same steps as those shown for the darted style with a similar shape.

ALTERING A SIDE-SEAM DART

1. Reposition the bust point if necessary, and move the dart so it points to the new bust point. Don't redraw the side seam until step 3.

2. Fold a horizontal tuck across the pattern, through the dart, making the shoulder-to-waist measurement match yours and reducing the side dart opening.

3. Fold the dart closed and redraw the side seam, removing ½ in. at the bust level and tapering to no change at the top and bottom.

ALTERING AN ARMHOLE DART

1. Reposition the bust point if necessary, and move the dart so it points to the new bust point.

2. Slash through the dart to the bust point and then down to the garment hipline or hem.

3. Fold a horizontal tuck across the center-front piece at bust level, making the shoulder-to-waist measurement match yours.

4. Pivot the side front from the hip-level slash line over the center-front piece at the bust by ½ in. Tape to secure. Redraw the dart legs from the compressed dart opening to the point.

ALTERING A PRINCESS SEAM

1. Reposition the bust point if necessary.

2. Fold a horizontal tuck across the center-front piece at bust level, making the shoulder-to-waist measurement match yours.

3. Keeping the waist and hip levels aligned, overlap the entire side front on the center-front piece by ½ in. at bust level. Tape to secure.

4. Draw new princess stitching lines that pass over and drop vertically from the bust point. Make the seamline on the side piece the same length as the seamline on the front piece by shortening the side-piece seamline at the underarm as needed.

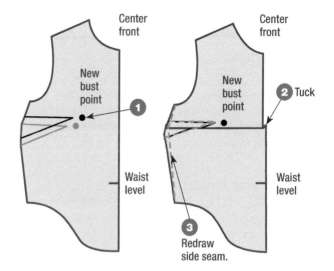

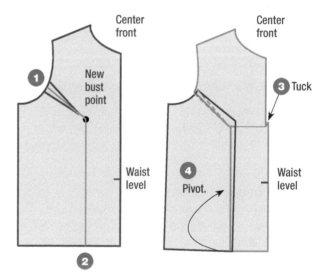

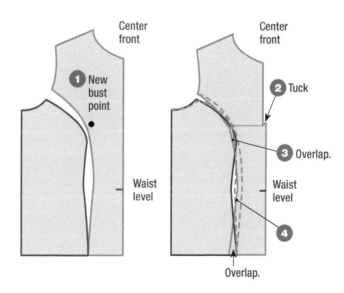

Shoulder-Slope Problems

Folds, wrinkles, and drag lines in the upper bodice hint strongly that the slope in the pattern is wrong for your shoulders. Put on an existing top that's your size, and assess the fit.

SQUARE SHOULDERS

A relatively high shoulder point scoots the armscye up, leaving the shoulder seam and neckline unsupported. Thus, the neckline stands away from the neck or horizontal wrinkles form across the upper torso in front or back.

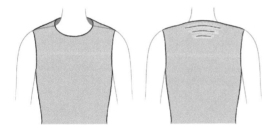

SLOPING SHOULDERS

When the shoulder point is low, the armscye might droop or gape on top and be tight under the arm. Tightness under the arm may cause diagonal wrinkles to form from the neckline to the armscye.

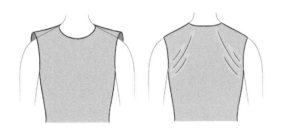

The Shoulder Slope

Your shoulders are like a clothes hanger: Every top, jacket, and dress you put on hangs from them. If you want your clothes to look better on you than on a hanger, you need to perfect the fit in the shoulders. Basically, you need to match the garment's shoulder slope to yours.

The slope of the shoulders is the angle starting below your ear at the base of the neck to the shoulder point—in other words, from where a short necklace would fall at the side of the neck to where you'd like the seam of a set-in sleeve to lie. If your shoulders are more square or more slanted than the garment's, you'll see evidence of that everywhere, from the neckline to the upper chest, the back, the sleeves, and even the hemline.

The instructions below explain how to pinpoint your shoulder-slope problems and to trace the silhouette of your body to make a master template of the shoulder area. You can then use the shoulder template to alter garment patterns.

SQUARE OR SLOPED SHOULDERS If your garments lie flat around the neck and hang smoothly over the top of the shoulder and the upper chest and back with no wrinkles or pulling, the slope of the pattern probably matches your shoulder shape well. For many of us, though, a standard pattern droops or pulls, creating wrinkles we'd rather not see. Fitting problems are usually caused by either square or sloped shoulders.

On *square-shouldered* figures, a garment's neckline may stand away from the base of the neck at the back and sides. The upper torso may display horizontal wrinkles across the collarbone region and just below the back neck. On *slope-shouldered* figures, you're likely to observe vertical wrinkles and drooping from the outer end of the shoulder down the sides of the torso, or diagonal wrinkles from the neckline to the armscye. Looseness at the shoulder seam, or an armscye that stands away from the shoulder point, is another telltale sign of sloping shoulders.

UNEVEN SHOULDERS Asymmetrical wrinkles suggest uneven shoulders. Many of us have one "normal" shoulder and one that's more sloped or square. If this is the case for you, you'll need to fit the right and left sides of your garments independently. In most cases, the best solution is to fit for the higher shoulder and pad the lower shoulder to match.

Shoulder wrinkles can be confusing; they sometimes mimic the symptoms of a fitting problem in the neck, sleeve, back, or bust. But by correcting the shoulder slope on your garments first, you'll solve other apparent fitting issues at the same time.

Finding Your Shoulder Slope

Determining your shoulder slope is as easy as tracing your silhouette onto a sheet of paper—and you'll have an instant custom-fitting tool. Enlist a friend to help.

Draw a line down the center of the paper, which will be perpendicular to the floor. Hang the paper on a wall so that the upper edge is a few inches above the top of your head.

1. Wear a tight-fitting top or underwear. Stand with your back against the paper, your feet slightly parted, and your arms hanging naturally at your sides. Align your body so that the line is centered at the top of your head and between your legs.

   Enlist a friend to trace your torso. To establish the outline of the figure, have her keep the pencil perpendicular to the wall (for clarity, the tracer is holding her pencil at an angle in our photo) and draw around the body. For a shoulder-slope tracing, trace from the waist up, including the sides of the neck. Don't worry if the pencil line looks a little wobbly. Step away from the paper and draw over the pencil line with a marker, smoothing out small bumps in the original tracing.

2. Remove the tracing from the wall, and lay it out on a table. Lay your garment pattern over the tracing, aligning the center front or center back along the vertical line and matching the neckline end of the shoulder seamline to the drawing. Compare the pattern's shoulder slope with yours. You'll see instantly whether you need to raise or lower the outer end of the shoulder seam.

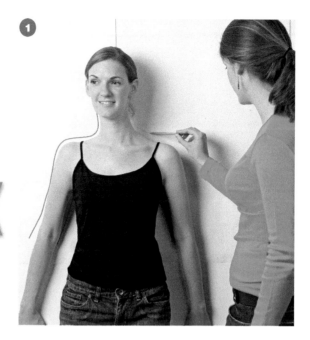

Find your shoulder slope by tracing the outline of your torso on a piece of paper taped to a wall.

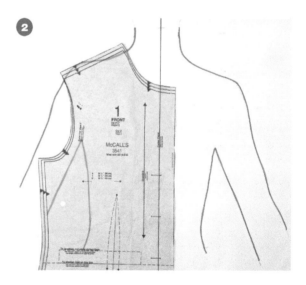

Compare the shoulder slope of your pattern with your actual slope. In this case, the pattern's seamline slopes at a noticeably steeper angle than the body's shoulder line.

ALTERING FOR SQUARE SHOULDERS

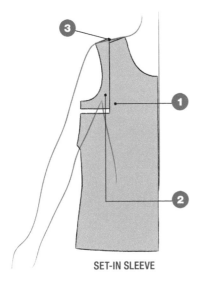

SET-IN SLEEVE

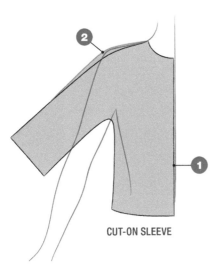

CUT-ON SLEEVE

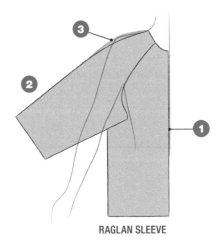

RAGLAN SLEEVE

Altering for Square Shoulders

Square shoulders need a seam that slants less steeply from the neck to the shoulder point than it does on the pattern piece. Make these alterations on both the front and the back pattern pieces.

Cuts for a Set-In Sleeve

1. Cut around the armscye, keeping the vertical cut parallel to the grainline and the horizontal cut perpendicular to it.

2. Slide the armscye section up as needed to meet the shoulder point on your shoulder template. Tape into position.

3. True the shoulder seamline by connecting the ends with a straight line.

Shoulder Shaping in a Cut-On Sleeve

Even if a cut-on, or kimono, sleeve has enough ease to accommodate a square shoulder, it can pull uncomfortably if the shoulder shaping is too shallow.

1. Lay the bodice section of the pattern over your shoulder template, aligning center fronts.

2. Redraw the shoulder seam to follow your shoulder line.

Adjusting a Raglan Sleeve

Work from the center front or center back to adjust raglan sleeves.

1. Lay the garment front pattern over your shoulder template, aligning center-front or center-back lines.

2. Lay out the raglan sleeve pattern, aligning the upper raglan notches.

3. Redraw the shoulder seam to add room for a square shoulder.

Altering for Sloped Shoulders

Sloped shoulders need a seam that slants more steeply from the neck to the shoulder point than it does on the pattern piece.

Cuts for a Set-In Sleeve

1. Cut around the armscye, keeping the vertical cut parallel to the grainline and the horizontal cut perpendicular to it.

2. Slide the armscye section down as needed to meet the shoulder point on your shoulder template. Tape into position.

3. True the shoulder seamline by connecting the ends with a straight line.

Shoulder Shaping in a Cut-On Sleeve

With sloped shoulders, too much of a curve in the upper sleeve seam of a cut-on sleeve can lead to unattractive folds of fabric.

1. Lay the bodice section over your shoulder template, aligning center fronts.

2. Redraw the shoulder seam to follow your shoulder line.

Adjusting a Raglan Sleeve

Work from the center front or center back to adjust raglan sleeves.

1. Lay the garment front pattern over your shoulder template, aligning center-front or center-back lines.

2. Lay out the raglan sleeve pattern, aligning the upper raglan notches.

3. Redraw the shoulder seam to reduce the shoulder ease.

ALTERING FOR SLOPED SHOULDERS

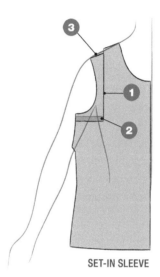

SET-IN SLEEVE

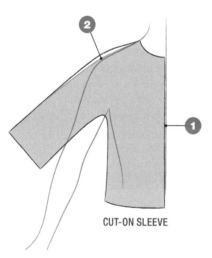

CUT-ON SLEEVE

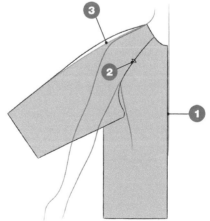

RAGLAN SLEEVE

Fitting the Armscye

The armscye, or armhole, should lie close to the body and encircle the shoulder smoothly. A full bust, a forward-thrust shoulder, prominent shoulder blades, or a curved upper back can all cause gaping at the front or back of an armscye. Instead of lying smoothly along the front and back shoulder, the armhole forms loose folds and ripples, usually above the bust or near the shoulder blade. To best illustrate why the gapes occur, take a stable woven fabric and drape it over your hand. Notice how the fabric falls into folds. Fabric can bend around the body, or it can bend over it, but when you ask it to bend both around and over it simultaneously, folds or ripples occur at its edge.

These folds are exaggerated versions of what happens when fabric tries to curve around the bust (or back) in all directions at once: A ripple of fabric—essentially an unstitched dart—escapes at the armhole, which is the closest open edge, and makes the armhole gape.

Fixing a Gaping Armhole with Darts

Imagine the shape of a wagon wheel, complete with spokes. If you sew consecutive spoke lines together to make a dart, two things happen: The circumference of the circle (wheel) is reduced, and the flat circle becomes a cone. As long as the spokes are the same distance apart at the circumference, the angle between any two consecutive spokes is the same, and it makes no difference which pair you sew together—you'll always get the same results. And even if the spokes were extended beyond the circumference, making the dart appear larger because of its length, the dart angle, which is often called the dart control, would remain the same. Herein lies the fix for your gaping armholes: Reduce the circumference of the armhole with a dart that makes the ripple disappear. And once you know the dart angle (the control), you can rotate the dart around the apex (or hub, using the wheel analogy), away from the armhole to exit on any edge of the pattern piece. For garments, some exit points just look better.

PIN OUT THE GAPE

Have a friend help you fit the pattern tissue or muslin by pinning the ripples into darts in the front and back armholes as needed to take up the excess fabric. You'll end up with a temporary dart in the armhole. This pinned-out dart establishes the amount of dart control you need to distribute elsewhere on the pattern piece.

How to Reposition a Dart

To move a dart from one position to another on a pattern, pin the dart closed and then slash the pattern from any point on the edge toward the dart point, along an imaginary spoke. Make the cut as long as is needed for the pattern to lie flat when the cut edges are spread apart. This spread opening is the new dart; its angle will be the same as the angle of the original dart.

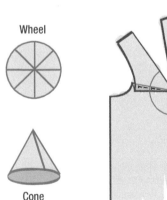

Wheel

Cone

ADD OR ENLARGE THE ARMHOLE DART

To add a dart, determine its position, and mark the place where it will cross the pattern edge. (For some ideas, see below.) Cut the pattern from this mark toward the bust (or shoulder blade) apex (not to the existing dart point).

Or, to enlarge an existing dart, cut along its center line. With the fitting dart still pinned at the armhole, flatten the pattern, allowing it to spread along the dart line you just cut. Tape the pattern to permanently close the pinned-out armhole dart. Patching the tissue, tape the new dart opening into place; then mark its seamlines, tapering them to meet 1 in. to 1½ in. before the bust (or shoulder blade) point/apex.

A Dartless Solution for a Gaping Armhole

If the armhole ripples are minimal, this fix will give the control of a dart without actually being one. Gather or ease the excess fabric into the armhole seam and secure it with stay tape, thus reducing the circumference of the armhole. You'll need to adjust the facing or the lining correspondingly, preferably by darting the excess out of the pattern.

Repositioning Dart Control

Once you understand the principle of dart control, you can explore myriad ways to relocate the excess fabric that makes a vest armhole gape.

A. MOVE THE EXCESS FABRIC TO A TRADITIONAL DART POSITION

Fitted vests are often shaped with darts placed horizontally and vertically at the bust; dropped vertically from the middle of the shoulder; or extended up diagonally from the side seam. Add the extra fabric from the vest armhole to an existing dart or move it to create a dart in one of these positions.

B. INCORPORATE DART CONTROL INTO SEAMS

If your vest has princess seams passing through the shoulders, move the excess fabric from the armhole to the top of the princess seam. If there are princess seams at the armholes, they offer a natural place for removing the excess, as does a yoke.

C. CREATE DESIGN INTEREST WITH NONTRADITIONAL DART POSITIONS

Relocating the dart control often enhances a design. You can break a single dart into two or more smaller darts as part of the repositioning. The positions don't need to be the same on each half of a garment.

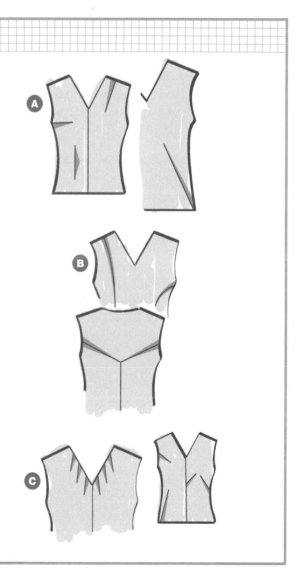

Perfecting the Armscye Fit

There's more to fitting an armscye than you may think—it requires fitting the bust dart, shoulders, and side seams. The best way to fit an armscye is to use a muslin—the test garment made from inexpensive fabric described on pp. 32–35. The muslin is pin-fit right on the body; the object is to make the fabric skim the body with no signs of wrinkles or strain lines. Following is a straightforward method for fitting an armhole and developing a well-fitting bodice muslin that accurately reflects the shape of the body.

Follow this order when fitting: bust, back, underarm, shoulder seam placement and slope, shoulder point to underarm, and side seams. Then adjust the pattern tissue using the fitted muslin as your guide. Such a completed pattern can be used as a reference to position darts and establish the armhole shape in future patterns. You'll end up with a perfect pattern for a closely fitting bodice with or without set-in fitted sleeves.

Make a Muslin

Select a fitted blouse pattern intended for woven fabrics that includes bust darts in the side seam or armscye. Make sure the finished bust measurement printed on the pattern is between 1½ in. and 2½ in. greater than your actual full bust measurement to allow enough wearing ease (see "The Importance of Ease," p. 13). Use a stable woven fabric without spandex, and follow the pattern to make your sleeveless, collarless muslin. Sew seams using a long machine stitch, and use a thread color that contrasts with the muslin fabric so that you can easily see to clip and release seams during fitting.

You'll need an assistant for the fitting process. Consider hiring a dressmaker to help you. Plan on making several muslins to get the right fit; the results are well worth the effort.

The first muslin serves as the rough draft for blocking out the major fitting changes. Plan on making at least one additional muslin to check your first fitting results. If you're a beginner, it's better to make more muslins with fewer changes to each than to try too many changes at once. Don't try fitting a muslin

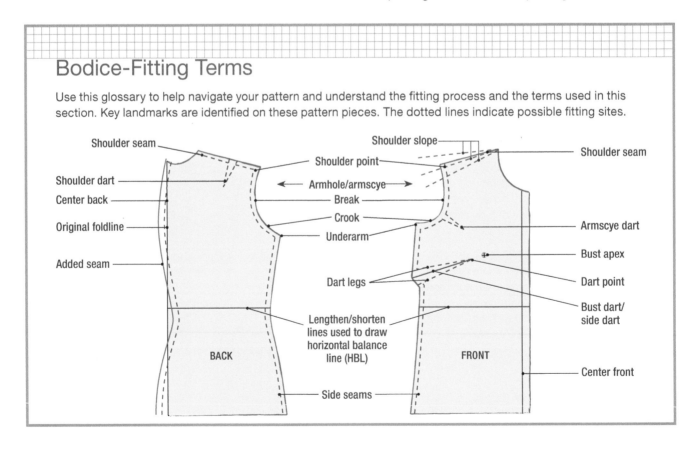

Bodice-Fitting Terms

Use this glossary to help navigate your pattern and understand the fitting process and the terms used in this section. Key landmarks are identified on these pattern pieces. The dotted lines indicate possible fitting sites.

Shoulder seam

Shoulder dart

Center back

Original foldline

Added seam

Shoulder slope

Shoulder point

Shoulder seam

Armhole/armscye

Break

Crook

Underarm

Armscye dart

Bust apex

Dart point

Bust dart/ side dart

Dart legs

Lengthen/shorten lines used to draw horizontal balance line (HBL)

BACK

FRONT

Center front

Side seams

that's a size too small because the tightness distorts the overall fit. For example, if you get a strain line between the bust points, start over using a larger size pattern (see the top right drawing).

It's important to make sure the bodice stays level around the body and doesn't dip in the front or back during the fitting. Draw a horizontal balance line (HBL), on the face of the muslin so you have a point of reference that you can easily see while fitting. You can use the lengthen/shorten line (between the waist and underarm rather than at the hem) as your HBL. While fitting, periodically check the level on the front and back HBL. If the back HBL dips, pin a wedge out of the upper back to level the line (see the center right drawing).

Reading the Muslin

To get started, study the general fit of the muslin and make any obvious adjustments. If the side seam strains over the hip, open both side seams from the hem upward until the muslin falls nicely (see the bottom drawing.) If the shoulder seam is too loose, pin out the excess fabric. The muslin should fit without strain but not loose and baggy. Remember, to get a pattern that reflects the shape of the body, you'll want to develop a fitting muslin that fits like a second skin—snug but not tight. Add design and additional wearing ease later.

In most cases, you need to fit only one side of the muslin after making the HBL level. If the person is particularly asymmetrical, overfitting can actually accentuate an uneven body. In general, if one side of the bust is larger, fit the larger side; if one shoulder is higher, fit the higher side, and adjust the low shoulder with a pad.

TIPS FOR FITTING A BODICE MUSLIN

Don't fit a muslin that's too small.

Use the horizontal balance line (HBL) to help you keep the pattern level.

If the side seams strain, open them over the problem area.

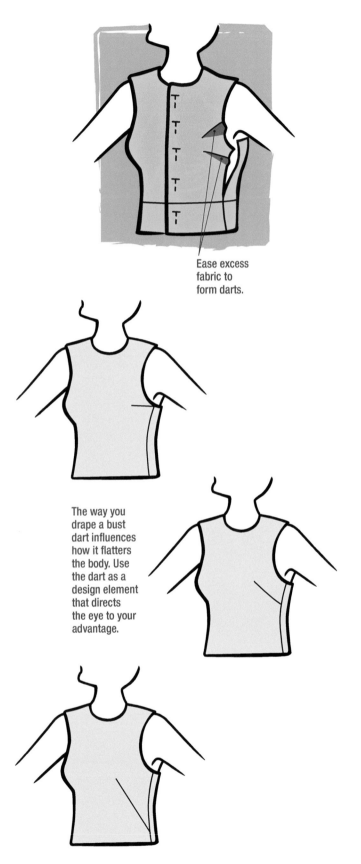

Ease excess
fabric to
form darts.

The way you
drape a bust
dart influences
how it flatters
the body. Use
the dart as a
design element
that directs
the eye to your
advantage.

Assess How the Muslin Fits at the Bust

Darts contour the fabric to accommodate the swell of the bust while keeping the garment looking trim. Anyone with a full A cup or larger benefits from properly placed bust darts, which make the center front of the garment fall straight to the waist and not swing away from the body. This results in a more flattering silhouette. The correct bust dart also keeps the armhole from gaping.

Some women carry bust tissue under their arms; other women carry it in front. Experiment with positioning the angle of the dart until it's most flattering. The dart placement alone can visually slenderize the figure. It's easiest to use side darts in a base pattern such as this, but pinching out a dart in the armscye to eliminate the gape and then moving the dart to a better location later is a good approach (see "Fixing a Gaping Armhole with Darts," p. 54). Use your fingers to ease up any drag line—in this case, a diagonal fold of fabric occurs between the bust apex and the side seam—into a side bust dart. Set the point of a dart closer to the apex for a smaller bust, farther away for a full bust. Don't be surprised if your dart seems larger than usual as long as you're getting a smooth fit. A very large dart may be needed to fit a very full bust. If this causes an unattractive bubble at the dart point, two parallel darts will solve the problem. Pin in the required dart or darts that best fit the bust (see the top left drawing).

Increasing the size of a side-seam dart lowers the front armhole. Fill the vacancy with a small piece of fabric to bring it up to the original height and redraw the armhole seamline. Stand back and evaluate whether the dart point hits in a pleasing place on the bust. If the dart's too low, it looks matronly, and if the dart's too high, it can look unflattering as well. The way you drape the dart influences how it flatters the body. Decide whether a slanting or straight dart fits you best (see the bottom left drawings on the facing page).

Correct the Fit of the Bodice Back

Now that you've adjusted the bodice front, check the back for excess fabric or undue strain at any point and assess the fit in the same way you did on the front. If the back armhole gapes, release the side seam and push the side back toward the front to diminish the gape and redraw the side seam, as shown in the top right drawing. If there is considerable roundness in the back, adding darts at the shoulder seams or even adding a center-back seam for extra curvature is a good solution, as shown in the bottom right drawing. If an armscye dart is needed to fit a muscular back, incorporate the dart amount in a princess line (back armscye darts are not traditionally used). The object is always to reduce any excess fabric in the circumference of the armscye.

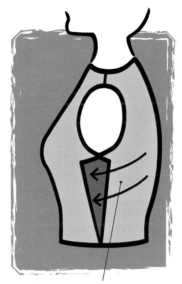

If the back armhole gapes, reposition the side seam.

Add princess seams and a center-back seam to accommodate extra back curvature.

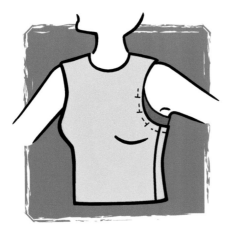

You can add a piece of fabric if the armhole is cut too low.

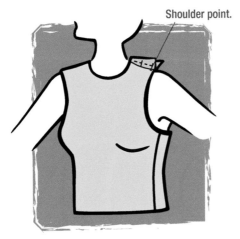

Shoulder point.

To change a shoulder seam, draw a line from the shoulder point to where the arm and shoulder come together.

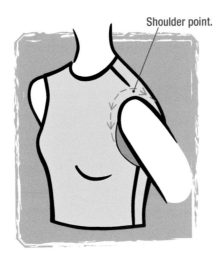

Shoulder point.

From the shoulder point, follow the body curvature and draw a new armhole.

Place the Armscye

Now that you've draped darts to match your curves and removed excess fabric from the back of your muslin, the shape of your armhole has probably changed. Deciding where the armhole hits under the arm is partially personal preference. Remember that an armhole cut high up under the arm is generally more comfortable because it allows a greater range of movement in a garment with sleeves; this is often counterintuitive to a beginning fitter. A sleeveless garment is only ½ in. higher under the arm than a fitted garment with a sleeve.

If the armhole is cut too low under the arm, add a piece of fabric and draw in a new depth (see the top left drawing), or make a note to raise the underarm a specified amount on your pattern tissue. If you hold a ruler under your arm as high as is comfortably possible, the underarm seamline should fall barely below where the ruler is touching the flesh.

Change Your Shoulder Seam

Whether you change your shoulder seam is a judgment call. The seam should lie along the top of the shoulder at a place that balances the body front to back and follows the natural slope of the shoulder. The shoulder point falls on the shoulder seam at the exact place the arm and shoulder come together—at the dent that forms when you lift your arm.

On the muslin, draw a line that falls from the shoulder point to the "crook" of the arm (where the arm attaches to the body) and then runs under the arm at the "break" of the arm (where the curve begins to go under the arm; see the center left drawing). Draw the curvature of the armhole on the muslin to follow the body curvature from the shoulder around the arm on both the front and the back (see the bottom left drawing).

Check that the side seam hangs straight. Make adjustments by releasing and repinning the seam so that it's perpendicular to the floor. Assess if it divides the side of the body attractively.

Transfer Muslin Alterations

Mark the seam and dart lines directly on the muslin, and follow any instructions noted on the muslin during the fitting. Use a permanent marker and always mark and concentrate on the actual seamlines. To reduce confusion, ignore seam allowances until later. The muslin is now a road map of the changes needed on the pattern.

Go back to your original pattern and transfer the muslin corrections to the tissue. It's best not to use the muslin as a pattern because fabric molds to the wearer's body and stretches with cuts across grainlines. Plus, it's easier and more reliable to "walk" and "true" seamlines (see "How to Walk and True a Seam" at right) in paper because paper doesn't stretch or distort.

Once the changes are made to your pattern, it may look substantially different from the original, especially in the front armhole. On a large bust, the armhole might now have an L shape. We're accustomed to seeing a long, gradual curve on commercial patterns, but that isn't the shape many of us need.

Concentrating on the stitching lines, add new tissue to your pattern where it's needed. Pin in the new darts and walk the corresponding seams as described in "How to Walk and True a Seam." After the seamlines have been corrected and trued, draw and cut the new seam allowance while the darts are folded so the correct dart legs automatically form.

Now make your second muslin. This time, staystitch the armhole seams. The armhole is much higher now, and you'll probably need to clip the curves to the staystitching for a comfortable fitting (see the drawing below). The new armhole curve should not be tight but should just skim the body. The second muslin will most likely require few dramatic changes. Follow the same steps as before, this time fine-tuning the fit and the position of the seamlines.

How to Walk and True a Seam

In the course of adding darts and making other fitting adjustments, you have also made multiple changes to the seams. Now you have to determine that both sides of a seam are the same length. To do this, you walk and true the seam.

To walk the seams on your paper pattern, first pin in the darts and then compare the stitch lines of adjacent seams (side front to side back, or shoulder front to shoulder back) in 1-in. increments from one end of the seam to the other. If the seams aren't the same length, use the HBL (horizontal balance lines), notches, and key landmarks to determine where length should be added or subtracted. It is essential to compare actual seamlines excluding the seam allowance; the seamlines must match in length to enable precise construction.

After walking the seam, true it by using a fashion ruler or designer's curve to blend any jagged seamlines that may have formed during the alteration process, drawing a new smooth line to bridge the gap. If you're unsure what the ideal blending line is, it's safe to split the difference between two lines—and remember, you're making another muslin and will have another opportunity to fine-tune the fit and seamlines again.

TIP If a garment is too snug in the underarm area, and you don't want to take out the sleeve and alter it in the conventional way, try this: Turn the garment inside out, and sew a new seam lower than the original underarm seam to increase the body space. This technique is fast and easy, and the results are perfect.

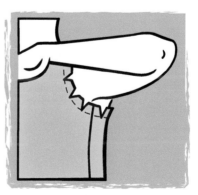

Clip to the staystitching around the armhole to enable armhole fit assessment.

Fitting the Sleeve

With a well-fitted bodice and armscye, you want a sleeve that not only fits into the armscye, but also fits comfortably around your arm. You can approach this goal by working with the measurements of your arm, or the measurements of a garment with sleeves that fit you well.

Perfecting the Fit

You've probably been told over and over never to change the sleeve cap, because if you do, it won't fit into the armhole properly. Let's venture into that sacrosanct sleeve cap and break tradition by fitting the sleeve cap to your arm instead of to your pattern's armscye. All you need to know is how much bigger a sleeve cap can be in proportion to the armscye opening, and how to draft an alternative sleeve to accommodate a fuller upper arm.

As for most custom-fitting projects, you'll need a pattern, a person to assist you with fitting, and muslin fabric to test the fit. When you're finished, you can combine the well-fitting armscye explained on pp. 58–61 with your custom sleeve for a beautifully fit bodice.

Alter the Sleeve

Measure your upper arm, or biceps circumference, at the high underarm, and your cap height from the shoulder point (the exact point at which the arm and shoulder join—identified as the dent that forms when the arm is lifted) to the biceps, and add the prescribed ease. Now use these two measurements to adjust your sleeve pattern following one of the methods shown here. These include a traditional method for enlarging a sleeve's upper arm, as well as two alternative methods.

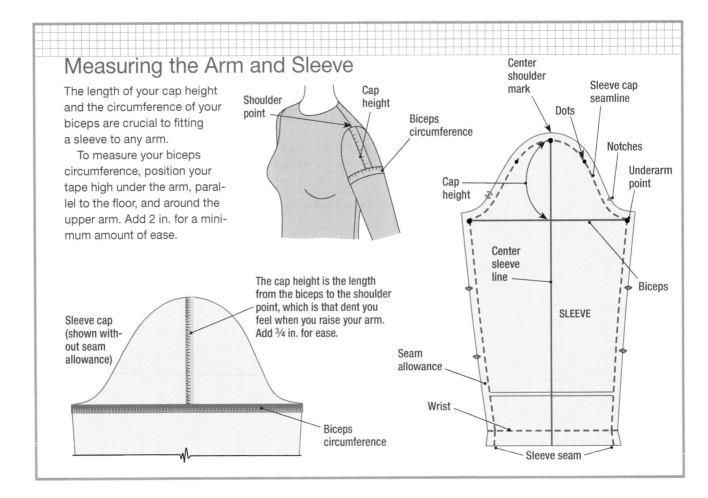

Measuring the Arm and Sleeve

The length of your cap height and the circumference of your biceps are crucial to fitting a sleeve to any arm.

To measure your biceps circumference, position your tape high under the arm, parallel to the floor, and around the upper arm. Add 2 in. for a minimum amount of ease.

Shoulder point

Cap height

Biceps circumference

Center shoulder mark

Sleeve cap seamline

Dots

Notches

Cap height

Underarm point

Center sleeve line

Biceps

SLEEVE

Sleeve cap (shown without seam allowance)

The cap height is the length from the biceps to the shoulder point, which is that dent you feel when you raise your arm. Add ¾ in. for ease.

Seam allowance

Biceps circumference

Wrist

Sleeve seam

CUT AND SPREAD THE PATTERN

Cut the pattern from the shoulder point to the wrist, and from the left underarm point to the right underarm point. Then spread the two underarm points in opposite directions until their distance apart matches your biceps circumference. Even though this method maintains the original sleeve cap length, it lowers the cap height.

INCREASE THE SEAM ALLOWANCES FOR ADDED EASE

Add up to ¾ in. to each sleeve seam, and increase the seam allowance on the sleeve cap to ensure ample fitting space.

MAKE VERTICAL CUTS TO EXPAND THE SLEEVE CAP

If more room is needed, cut from the shoulder point to the wrist and spread the pattern to add 1 in. If you need to add still more room, cut parallel lines 1½ in. from the first cut and distribute the remaining amount between those two cuts by spreading the pattern horizontally.

CUT AND SPREAD

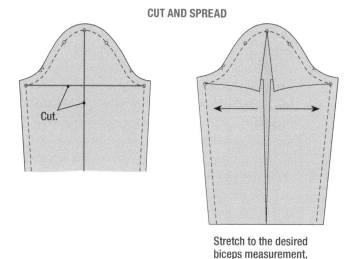

Cut.

Stretch to the desired biceps measurement, plus ease.

INCREASE SEAM ALLOWANCE

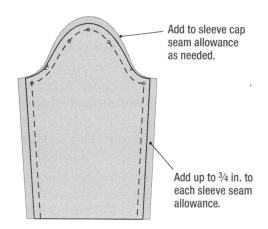

Add to sleeve cap seam allowance as needed.

Add up to ¾ in. to each sleeve seam allowance.

MAKE VERTICAL CUTS

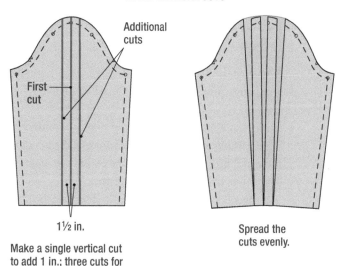

Additional cuts

First cut

1½ in.

Make a single vertical cut to add 1 in.; three cuts for increases more than 1 in.

Spread the cuts evenly.

Fit the Sleeve

In the second two methods, you've increased the length of the sleeve cap seamline. Although this is not a traditional approach, there's nothing wrong with adding to the circumference of the original sleeve cap. Many sewing books warn against changing the cap circumference to avoid sacrificing a smoothly set-in sleeve. However, with the directions that follow, you'll discover a different approach to obtaining a flattering sleeve that affords a comfortable range of movement.

To get the correct cap shaping and a truly personalized fit, it's smart to fit sleeves directly on the person. The cap shaping is usually relatively easy; fitting the biceps is where problems can arise. With a slender or trim arm, the biceps circumference remains relatively small, which means the length of the sleeve cap stays in proportion to the circumference of the armscye. When the biceps circumference is full, spreading the sleeve to accommodate the fuller upper arm also lengthens the sleeve cap seamline. This longer sleeve cap can be difficult to set in, but the techniques explained on the facing page make it easy and give you an alternative sleeve that beautifully accommodates a full biceps.

Cut one muslin sleeve from your adjusted pattern piece. Staystitch around the armhole of your bodice muslin along the seamline, and use this row of stitching as a guideline when fitting the sleeve. Position the sleeve as if to set it in, but sew only the underarm 1 in. on either side of the side seam to anchor the sleeve. The rest of the sleeve will be custom-fit. Try on the bodice and sleeve. Start by pinning the center shoulder mark on the sleeve to the shoulder point on the bodice, then study the drag lines.

Analyze Drag Lines

Drag lines form when fabric is forced to stretch, indicating that the garment is too tight, or when fabric near a mound of flesh requires more contouring. Learning to read a drag line is one of the keys to successful fitting. On a sleeve, one end of the drag line always points to the problem area.

If there is not enough cap height, drag lines form diagonally from somewhere near the center top of the sleeve toward one or both sides of the sleeve. If this occurs, release the pin at the shoulder point and lower the sleeve cap, allowing the fabric to relax until the drag line disappears. The cap may need to be lowered only a slight amount (¼ in. to ½ in.), but if it needs to be lowered enough that bare skin shows at the shoulder, patch over the exposed skin by adding extra fabric as needed to the sleeve cap seam.

When excess fabric forms wrinkles that look like a cowl neck or smiles of fabric down the arm, smooth those wrinkles by pulling the sleeve cap up into the seam.

Once the sleeve has been fitted to remove drag lines or wrinkles, the original center point of the sleeve may no longer match the shoulder seam. Now that all of the drag lines are settled, mark the new shoulder point on the sleeve cap. Although this may feel like you're breaking the rules, what you're achieving is a custom fit.

The Sleeve Cap

Fit the sleeve cap to your bodice, with the muslin still on the body. Since the staystitching on the bodice follows the natural contour of the arm, pin the cap along this line of staystitching. To do this, fold the seam allowance to the inside of the sleeve and pin it into the armscye, making sure there is enough ease across the biceps and that no drag lines form. Ease the sleeve cap fabric with your fingertips as you go; the ease in the sleeve cap forms a very slight air pocket over the top of the arm, which both improves the look of the sleeve and allows greater movement of the arm. The sleeve cap will look like it has tiny little gathers across the top—you'll ease them in later.

Take the bodice off the body, and carefully mark the folded sleeve cap edge where it touches the staystitch guideline. Remove the pins and the underarm stitching, and using a fashion ruler, draw a new, smooth sleeve cap seamline following your marked line as a guide. Rely on the fashion ruler to blend the uneven seamline and to blend the concave and convex curvature, and then transfer this new seamline to your tissue paper sleeve pattern.

Walking the Sleeve

Use the bodice and sleeve pattern pieces to walk the sleeve to the armscye. Start under the arm on the front side seam and compare the sleeve cap stitch line to the armscye stitch line, moving toward the shoulder seam. When you reach the shoulder point on the bodice, place a mark on the sleeve cap. Then repeat the same process starting under the arm on the back side. Then measure the distance between the two marks on either side of the center top of the sleeve cap. This is the amount of ease you'll need to manage when setting in the sleeve.

If the distance is ¾ in. to 1¼ in. or less, which is normal, you are lucky. Even on difficult-to-handle fabric, this amount of ease is not hard to control. If the distance is closer to 2 in. to 2¼ in., you'll have to distribute this abundant ease more creatively. With a larger amount of ease, distribute it between the notches, and in some cases, below the notch toward the underarm seam. This breaks another rule (easing below a notch is usually not recommended), but the technique works well when you're developing a fitted sleeve for a fuller biceps.

Test your muslin sleeve cap by sewing it into your muslin armscye. If you can ease it successfully in muslin, it's likely to cause you no problems in other fabrics. The fabric you use in the final garment affects how much fabric you can successfully ease. Wool eases beautifully, and you can even shrink out some of the ease with steam. Dupioni, on the other hand, is usually difficult to ease. If you can't distribute enough ease to result in a smooth, gather-free sleeve, then an alternative sleeve style will solve the problem.

Altering for a Full Upper Arm

An effective way to bridge the flesh of a full upper arm is to put a seam from the shoulder point down the arm, splitting the sleeve in half. Using this method, the biceps is easily increased without affecting the length of the cap seamline at all. In a typical one-piece sleeve, the underarm seam is the only place to increase the circumference of the sleeve. By adding a seam to the outer arm, you build in an opportunity to alter the fit in another area of the sleeve.

Creating a seam on the outside of the arm also allows you to make a fitting adjustment where it's needed. Often, the fullness of an arm is on the outside of, not under, the arm, and an outside seam allows you to reduce the amount of fabric under the arm, resulting in a more flattering silhouette with air space between the arm and the body.

1. Cut the sleeve pattern in half along the center sleeve line.

2. On both sides, at the point where the center sleeve line intersects the biceps, add half the distance of the increase. Use a fashion ruler or hip curve to draw a gentle curve from the shoulder point through the biceps, tapering back into the original line below the elbow.

3. Add seam allowances.

ALTERING FOR A FULL UPPER ARM

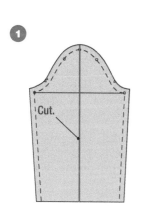

1 Cut.

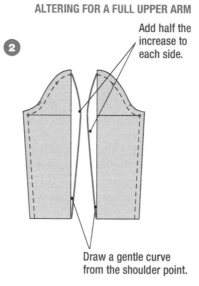

2 Add half the increase to each side.

Draw a gentle curve from the shoulder point.

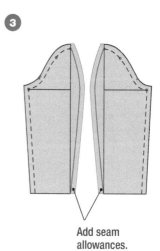

3 Add seam allowances.

How to Set In a Sleeve

The length of a fitted sleeve cap's seamline is always longer than the armscye's seamline. This requires you to ease the sleeve cap into the armscye—a process of shrinking the longer length to fit the shorter one without any gathers showing. The process is easier when you understand how to manage three basic sewing elements: bias, edges, and curves.

WORK WITH THE BIAS

Most of a sleeve cap's edges/seams are on the bias. The beauty—and frustration—of working with the bias is that it can easily be made to stretch or shrink. For example, if a bias strip is stretched lengthwise, the narrow dimension becomes narrower. However, the opposite is also true: If the width of the strip is stretched, the length becomes shorter. The latter is key to setting a sleeve by enabling you to shorten the length of the sleeve cap. You can ease a sleeve cap without using gathering stitches at all (in many cases, sewing the gathering stitches can actually stretch the bias portions of the sleeve cap). Instead, use your fingers to manipulate the sleeve cap fabric into the armscye.

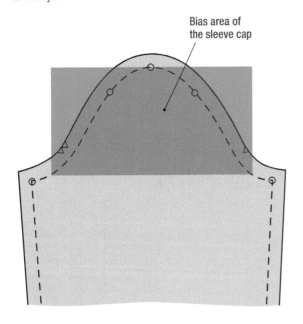

Bias area of the sleeve cap

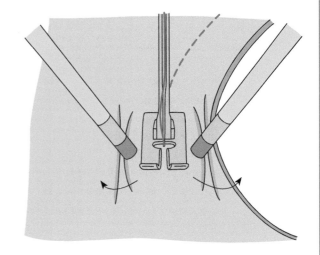

KEEP EDGES ALIGNED AND SEW IN ONE STEP

Align the key marks (shoulder point, underarm seam, notches, and circles if present) as you position your right-side-out sleeve inside your wrong-side-out armscye. Start sewing at the underarm seam with the armscye on the bottom. Gently turn the fabric, keeping the edges aligned and the fabric in front of the presser foot smooth and flat (preserving the curvature of the armscye). To facilitate shrinking the bias portions of the sleeve cap, gently pull either side of the sleeve cap seamline in a direction perpendicular to the stitching line on both sides of the needle and just in front of the needle. You'll get the best results by using your fingers to manipulate the sleeve cap fabric and guide the work all at once, but two pencils with erasers facilitate the pulling action that shortens the bias.

HOW TO SEW CURVES

Resist pulling the curves of the armscye straight in order to place what's about to be sewn directly in front of the presser foot. This practice reduces the length of the armscye (a straight line between two points is shorter than a curved line), and a shorter armscye only makes it more difficult to ease in the sleeve cap. Instead, drive into the curves in small increments and as smoothly as possible, thus preserving the intended length of the armscye.

Using Ready-to-Wear for Fit

Sewers often complain that they can't get their set-in sleeves to fit. This is because almost all ready-to-wear jackets and blouses have lower armholes and wider sleeves than the typical pattern. It's also common for patterns to be wider across the back than comparable ready-to-wear. The most useful place to start solving a sleeve-fitting problem is with a bit of "research" shopping: Try on similar garments until you find one that fits the way you want in the sleeves and shoulders.

Measure a Garment That Fits

Once you've located your Holy Grail set-in sleeve, jacket or blouse, measure it carefully (including the garment's upper back, which controls the freedom of movement), then make sure your future garments with similar sleeves have the same measurements.

On the Sleeve

1. **Cap line circumference:** Measure around the sleeve horizontally at the underarm level.

2. **Cap height:** Measure from the cap line vertically to the top of the armhole.

On the Body

1. **Armhole:** Measure the armhole seamline. (This is optional; use it only for comparison when trying on garments and to see how close your starting pattern is to your idea.)

2. **Shoulder width:** Measure the back horizontally from the end of one shoulder seam to the opposite end. Divide the measurement in half, then compare it to the pattern.

3. **Upper back width:** Measure the back horizontally from armhole to armhole, about 8 in. down from the shoulder. Divide the measurement in half, then compare it to the pattern.

4. **Back width:** Measure the back horizontally from underarm to underarm. Divide the measurement in half, then compare it to the pattern.

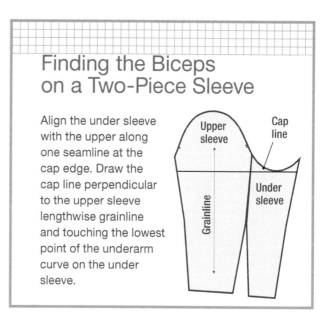

Finding the Biceps on a Two-Piece Sleeve

Align the under sleeve with the upper along one seamline at the cap edge. Draw the cap line perpendicular to the upper sleeve lengthwise grainline and touching the lowest point of the underarm curve on the under sleeve.

ON THE SLEEVE

ON THE BODY

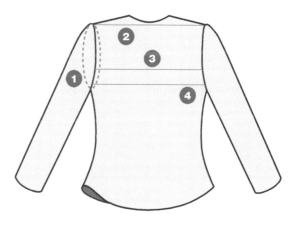

Correct the Pattern

With the measurements you just took, you can adjust a pattern to provide a comfortable, flattering fit.

SLEEVE CAP HEIGHT

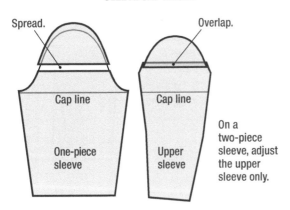

The Sleeve Cap Height

Before you begin, find the ease allowance in your original pattern by subtracting the length of the sleeve cap seamline from the length of the total armhole seamline. All diagrams shown in this section, are without seam allowances.

Slash the sleeve cap horizontally above the notches. Spread or overlap the pieces by the amount needed to make the cap height match the measured garment cap height. Blend the curve across the gap or overlap to create a smooth seamline. Measure the corrected seamline.

The Back

Compare all three garment back measurements with your pattern; alter all three areas with a single adjustment.

To make the back uniformly wider or narrower: Slash the pattern vertically from the midpoint of the shoulder seamline to the hemline. Spread or overlap the pieces. Blend the shoulder seamline across the gap or overlap, and then alter the front shoulder seamline to the same length by extending or reducing it at the armhole (see the left drawing below).

To make the back progressively wider or narrower: Slash the pattern vertically from the midpoint of the shoulder seamline to the hemline. Pivot the side-back piece from the shoulder or hemline as needed to adjust the width of the opposite edge. If pivoting from the hemline, blend the shoulder seamline across the gap or overlap, and then alter the front shoulder seamline to the same length by extending or reducing it at the armhole (see the center drawings below).

To make the back selectively wider or narrower: Use or create a seam at the center back or use a princess seam to subtract or add width selectively across the back but not at the shoulder or the hemline (see the right drawings below).

If you discover that your pattern is more than an inch or so off from your measured ideal, use a closer size, as this method is not meant for resizing a whole pattern.

THE BACK

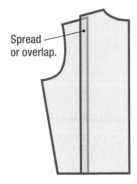

Make back uniformly wider or narrower.

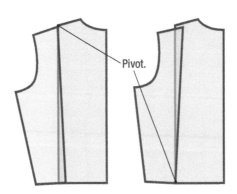

Make back progressively wider or narrower.

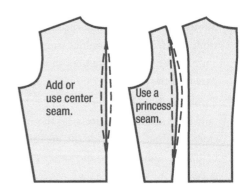

Make back selectively wider or narrower.

The Armhole

Alter the armhole by raising or lowering the under-arm seamline by the same amount you add to or subtract from the sleeve cap height, as shown in the top right drawing.

1. Measure and mark the amount of your alteration on the side seam. Find the section of a designer's curve that matches the armhole curve at the underarm.

2. Slide the designer's curve down, without pivoting, to reposition the armhole shape at the marked point on the side seam. Draw the new seamline.

3. Use other sections of the designer's curve as a guide to blend the new seamline upward into the existing seamline. Then, check that the new armhole seamline length equals the new sleeve cap seamline length minus the original ease allowance.

The Biceps

Before you begin, measure the width of the sleeve on the hemline.

1. Slash the sleeve from the hemline to pivot positions on the cap seamline above the notches as shown at right. On a two-piece sleeve, adjust the upper sleeve only (see "Finding the Biceps on a Two-Piece Sleeve," p. 67).

2. Spread (or overlap) the sections equally at the hemline until the cap line is equal to your measured garment cap line.

3. Redraw the underarm seamlines, tapering equally, to return the hemline to its original width. Draw a straight hemline across the spread (or overlapped) sections.

4. For a two-piece sleeve, slash each outer section on the cap line, leaving a hinge at the outside edge, and pivot the lower portion to abut the inner section at the bottom edge. Redraw the hemline.

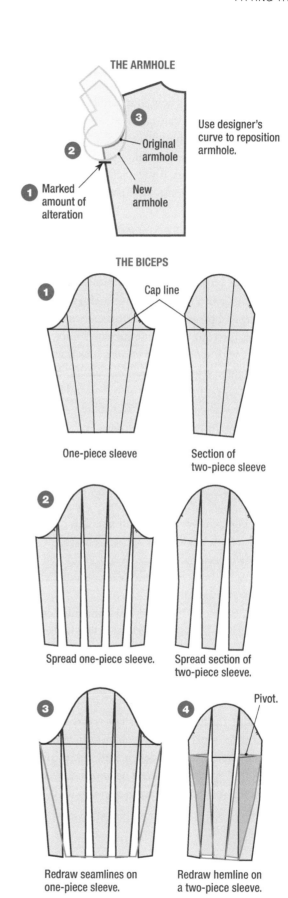

THE ARMHOLE

Use designer's curve to reposition armhole.

3 — Original armhole

2

1 Marked amount of alteration

New armhole

THE BICEPS

1 Cap line

One-piece sleeve

Section of two-piece sleeve

2 Spread one-piece sleeve.

Spread section of two-piece sleeve.

3 Redraw seamlines on one-piece sleeve.

4 Pivot.

Redraw hemline on a two-piece sleeve.

Fitting the Abdomen

A wide waist affects how your clothes fit in more areas than just the waistline itself. For instance, jackets and tops won't button across the front, but the shoulders and neckline might need another person to help fill them out. If you encounter such problems in commercial patterns, there are simple ways to fix them.

When your tummy is proportionally fuller than the rest of your figure, getting the right silhouette requires a two-part fix: first for comfort and then for style. The waistline influences almost everything you wear, but you can change darts, inject extra fabric by cutting and pivoting patterns, make design changes such as inserting panels, use stretchy fabrics, or fool the eye with accessories to create a look that flatters your figure. When you adjust patterns for both fit and style, you make clothes that look and feel fantastic. And with a few design tricks, all of your clothes can be comfortable and flattering.

Altering a Pattern for a Full Abdomen

Full abdomens get a pretty bad rap. This figure characteristic can just as easily appear on young people of average or less-than-average weight. A full abdomen is, in fact, a body type, which exercise and dieting can't always change.

This body type carries several distinguishing aspects. The hips are usually less than 8 in. larger than the waist. The derrière is often flat, and the hips don't extend from the sides. The legs are usually narrow, and the torso is columnar, barrel, or apple shaped.

Fitting the full abdomen is not as easy as buying a garment or pattern large enough to fit your waist circumference. All that does is throw off the fit in the rest of the garment. You end up with excess length, extra fullness through the shoulders, or bagginess in the seat.

Start, instead, with patterns that fit through the shoulders and hips, and alter them to fit the waist. This figure type frequently requires a combination of alterations, depending on the amount of abdominal fullness. Solutions for many of these problems start right here.

Cut and Spread Patterns

To properly alter jackets and tops, start with a pattern that fits through your bust and shoulders, and then adjust the front pattern piece.

Calculate the difference between your waist measurement (parallel to the floor) and the pattern waist measurement. If your pattern size calls for a 28-in. waist and yours is 32 in., that's a 4-in. difference. Divide the difference by 2 (because you're working with a half pattern). Then divide by the number of available seams or feasible opportunities to add extra fabric in the front of the garment. You can add about ½ in. to each seam before distorting your pattern. While you can also spread your pattern to add fabric, sometimes you'll have to combine these alterations in the same garment to add the required amount of fabric to satisfy your needs.

Use one or more of the three methods shown here to increase the abdomen girth of your pattern.

TIP Tops are a necessity, and a jacket is the full midsection's best friend. On a full abdomen, jackets look best when the front opening falls straight and doesn't fan apart. Don't try to fix this problem by adding fabric or otherwise extending the center front of a jacket. A gaping center front is the symptom, but the fix is usually in the side seams or the body of the pattern.

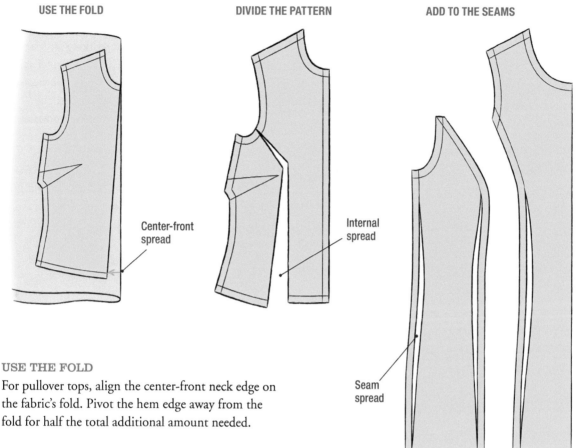

USE THE FOLD

DIVIDE THE PATTERN

ADD TO THE SEAMS

Center-front
spread

Internal
spread

Seam
spread

USE THE FOLD

For pullover tops, align the center-front neck edge on
the fabric's fold. Pivot the hem edge away from the
fold for half the total additional amount needed.

DIVIDE THE PATTERN

Add fabric to center-front-opening jackets in the body
of the front pattern piece. Cut the pattern as shown
above, and pivot the side section toward the side seam.

ADD TO THE SEAMS

Princess-style patterns provide extra seams for alterations. By adding ½ in. to the front-side seam allowance and to both princess seam allowances on your
pattern, you can increase the total front width by
3 in.

 To avoid getting a pattern that is out of
scale with the rest of your figure, don't
choose a pattern size based on the
circumference of your waist. Instead,
select a smaller size representative of
the rest of your figure, based on your
bust or hip circumference. Then add
more room where you need it.

ALTERATIONS USING MULTISIZE PATTERNS

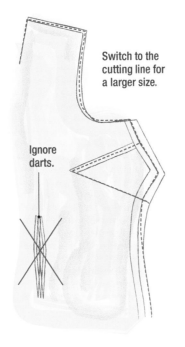

Switch to the cutting line for a larger size.

Ignore darts.

Use a Multisize Pattern

Multisize patterns allow you to shift cutting lines within a single garment. When working with a top pattern, just move the cutting lines to a larger size to accommodate a full abdomen. To get more wearing ease so the garment can fall smoothly over the stomach, don't sew the torso darts; they constrict the fabric over the abdomen.

CHANGE SIZES BETWEEN PATTERN PIECES

If you have too much fabric in the back leg and not enough in the front over the tummy, cut a larger front and a smaller back. Be sure to mark the same waistline height and pocket notches so your side seams stay the same length and the pockets will match correctly.

FRONT

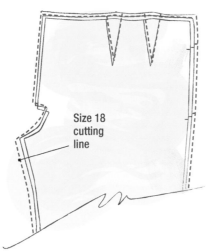

Size 18 cutting line

BACK

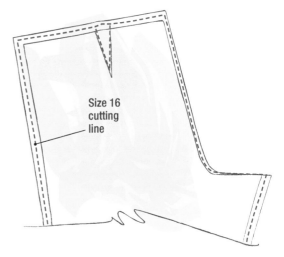

Size 16 cutting line

Move Bust Darts

This slash-and-pivot method takes the excess fabric that gets folded into a standard bust dart and sends it to the abdomen. Here's how to do it:

1. **Draw guidelines:** On the pattern front, draw a line parallel to the grainline from the hem to the bust point and from the lower dart leg at the side seam to the bust point. Cut along both guidelines, leaving a little hinge of paper to pivot at the bust point.

2. **Close the bust dart:** Rotate the pattern section on the hinge until the bust-dart legs meet. When you bring the dart legs together, the fullness of the dart transfers to the tummy area.

3. **Close the dart entirely or partially:** Decide how much room you need to add over the tummy. If you split the difference, you can opt to keep a small bust dart and add less at the tummy.

4. **Finish by adding length at the front hem:** Add about 1 in. to the center-front hemline, tapering to zero at the side seam. This extra length offers more coverage over the vertical fullness of the abdomen.

MOVING BUST DARTS TO ADD FULLNESS TO ABDOMEN

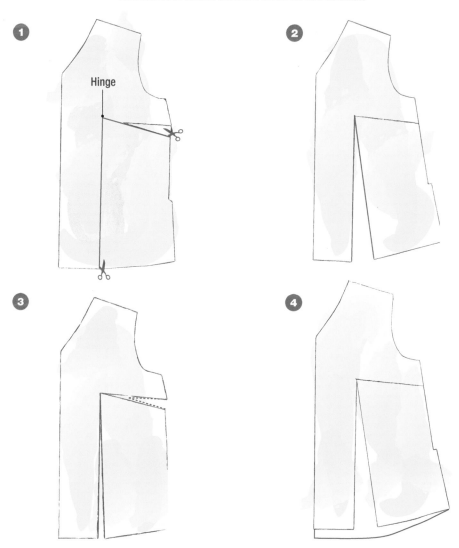

**ADDING PLEATS OR GATHERS FOR
GREATER WIDTH ACROSS THE ABDOMEN**

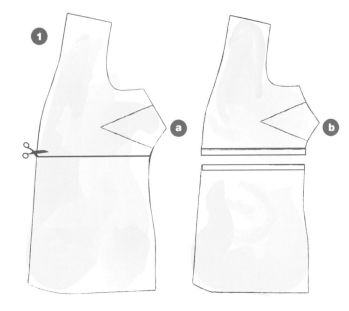

Add Width with Pleats or Gathers

Adding width so you get the right fit is sure to make your garment look better and feel more comfortable. To add fullness, add gentle gathers.

1. Divide the blouse front pattern just below the bust dart (**a**). Add seam allowances to both sections (**b**).

2. Divide the lower blouse section into five equal parts (**a**), and cut the fabric to this shape. Spread them evenly apart for a new pattern (**b**). Gather or pleat the lower section of the blouse to fit the bodice top (**c**). For a smooth, flowing panel, use a soft fabric that does not have much bulk.

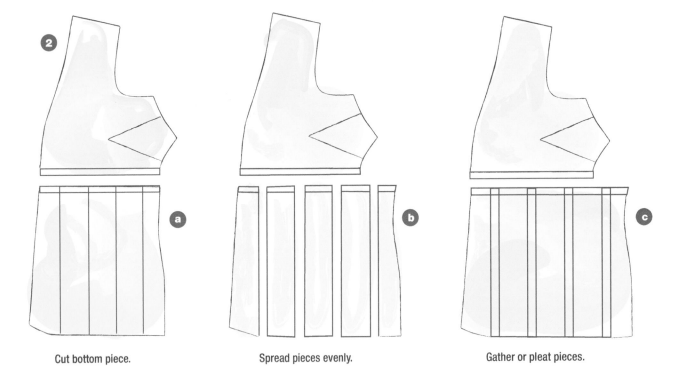

Cut bottom piece.   Spread pieces evenly.   Gather or pleat pieces.

Fitting the Back

Two common fitting problems in the back of a garment are a tight back that restricts movement and a back neckline that rides up or slides back over a curved upper back. Learn how to spot these postural or figure challenges and how to adjust patterns to accommodate them.

Fixing a Tight Back

Fitted and semifitted garments with fitted sleeves sometimes limit your reach, especially if you need to reach forward and/or up. To resolve this issue, you can change the design, use fabric with give or stretch, or make a combination of various adjustments to improve your range of motion.

You can make pattern changes in the back, sleeve, or armhole—adjusting the fit to supply more room—without causing the jacket or blouse to appear too bulky. This problem is difficult to tissue-fit, so make a muslin and recruit a fitting helper.

Fit the garment as usual, with arms lowered, but during the fitting, check for adequate reach room by giving yourself a hug. If the garment is too tight across the back, remove the stitching around the back armhole seamline and hug yourself again. Get your helper to measure the gap that forms between the original seamline and use that distance to establish the amount you pivot the armhole when you adjust your pattern.

After you adjust the back pattern, lay it under the front pattern piece and trace the new shape and length of the side seam to the front side seam. It is not necessary to swing out the armhole on the front as you did on the back, since arm movement is forward. This adjustment does not change the circumference of the armhole, so no alteration is required on the sleeve.

Now alter the pattern.

1. On your back pattern, draw a horizontal line from the underarm point toward the center back. Draw a line from the shoulder point along the arm seamline to intersect the first line. Cut the L-shaped line.

2. Slide the armhole pattern section out using the shoulder point as the pivot. This increases the underarm width the necessary amount—usually ½ in. to ¾ in. Or use the gap measurement you took during fitting.

3. Draw a curved line from the expanded underarm down the side seam 3 in. or 4 in. This graceful curve creates a flattering, shapely silhouette that's missing in most patterns and ready-to-wear garments because they have a straight side seam. The gentle curve from the bust level out to the underarm adds extra reach room. It works like a pseudo gusset to provide more reach room.

FITTING A TIGHT BACK

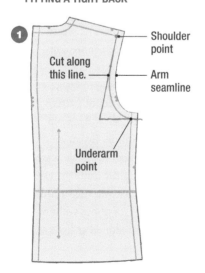

① Cut along this line. — Shoulder point — Arm seamline — Underarm point

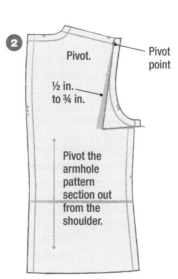

② Pivot. — Pivot point — ½ in. to ¾ in. — Pivot the armhole pattern section out from the shoulder.

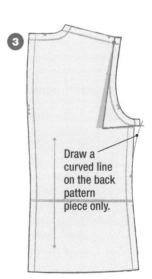

③ Draw a curved line on the back pattern piece only.

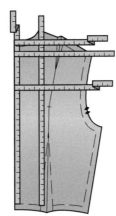

Measuring to Fit a Curved Upper Back

Use these positions for both rounded upper back and dowager's curve. Position horizontal measurements to coincide with the area of roundness; take as many measurements as needed in that area to plot the changes accurately.

FITTING A ROUNDED UPPER BACK

PATTERN WITH SHOULDER DART

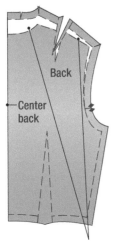

Back

—Center back

Cut just inside neck and shoulder seamline (and armscye if needed) and raise measured amount.

PATTERN WITHOUT SHOULDER DART

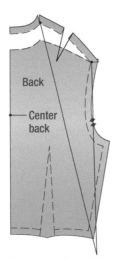

Back

—Center back

Cut as for pattern with shoulder dart but also cut through middle of shoulder seamline.

Fitting a Curved Upper Back

If you find that tops and jackets pull up at the lower back, or the neckline falls to the back, you may have a curved back.

Before proceeding, take your back measurements as shown at left.

A Rounded Upper Back

A rounded upper back presents a more-than-average outward curve across the entire upper back. The distance between the neck and the midback increases by 2 in. to 4 in., and sometimes more. This may also include a width increase as the shoulders move forward.

The fitting problems created by a rounded upper back are the result of insufficient fabric length and/or width across the entire upper back area, causing garments to pull up at the back waistline and feel tight over the upper back. Tight diagonal wrinkles may form between the base of the neck and the armscye. The neckline is generally pulled back and down, cutting into the neck in front. In a jacket or vest made of firm fabric, the back hemline will poke outward.

Garments need more fabric length and curved shaping to accommodate the rounded upper back. When more than 3 in. extra is needed, a single altered seam may not be sufficient, and you may need a change in style to facilitate the alteration. A bodice with a shoulder yoke in back will provide two more seam allowances to distribute the needed length. Additional fullness in the way of gathers or pleats can also be added to the yoke line for a more comfortable fit.

To alter for added length and shaping in back, place the pattern on top of a large sheet of pattern tissue paper, then cut the neck and shoulder seam allowance free just inside the seamline. If you've measured an increase in width across the back as well, continue to cut the seamline along the armscye, as far down as the increased width occurs. Altering in this way will not distort the pattern. Grainlines will not be changed, and seamlines will be altered as little as possible.

Cutting through the middle of the shoulder dart—to but not through the tip—allows the shoulder dart to widen as the seamline is raised, increasing the curved shaping of the upper back. The dart will also lift into a position better able to accommodate a higher, fuller shoulder blade. The dart tip should extend to about 1 in. from the fullest curve of the shoulder blade (see the bottom left drawing on the facing page).

If a shoulder dart is not present, clip through the seam allowance in the middle of the shoulder seamline, creating a space for a dart. When you've shifted the seam and dart as needed, tape it to the paper underneath, and fill in the dart end (see the bottom right drawing on the facing page).

A rounded upper back generally produces variations in the bodice front, specifically a shallow and narrow chest. Measure the front as well, and alter it using the same technique of pivoting the seamlines.

A Dowager's Curve

In contrast, a dowager's curve develops high on the spine, involving the top three to five vertebrae at the base of the neck. The top of the spine at center back curves outward more than average. Fatty tissue deposits may occur in the same area. This figure variation

may become more pronounced with age and may be related to osteoporosis. It may or may not occur in combination with a rounded upper back, a forward head and neck position, a high neck base in back and low in front, and possibly a shallow chest.

The fitting problems this causes result from insufficient fabric length and inadequate shaping high in the center-back area, causing a horizontal wrinkle at the back armscye. As with a curved back, the waistline may pull up at center back as the back neckline rises. The shoulder seam may pull slightly to the back at the neckline, forming a circular wrinkle around the neckline in front, possibly cutting into the neck in front. The garment needs more length and dart shaping transferred to the neckline to better accommodate the dowager's curve. Some additional width may be needed as well to allow for the size of the curve.

To alter for added length, added width, and a shifted dart, place the pattern on top of the pattern tissue, and cut free the seam allowance at the neck, the shoulder, and possibly some of the armscye, as described on the facing page for a rounded upper back. Cut through the middle of the neck seam allowance, then down into the pattern, so you can pivot the shoulder dart to the neck where it's needed. As you raise the seam allowance the measured amount at center back, allowing it to taper to nothing at the armscye, the newly positioned neckline dart will automatically open to accommodate the greater curve in that position. If there's no shoulder dart, the space created in the middle of the neckline allows for a dart to be added. Tape the shifted seams and dart in their new position, and fill in the dart end (see the drawing at left).

FITTING A DOWAGER'S CURVE

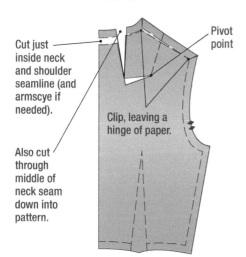

Cut just inside neck and shoulder seamline (and armscye if needed).

Also cut through middle of neck seam down into pattern.

Clip, leaving a hinge of paper.

Pivot point

Other Solutions for the Curved Back

Clothing styles that require little or no alteration for the rounded upper back or dowager's curve feature dropped necklines, an open neckline or collar in front, and a loose fit across the back. Camouflage the variations with textured fabrics and small-scale all over patterned fabrics; collars that stand away from or fill in the neck area, such as a flat or partial-roll, cowl, back-bowed, or ruffled collar; and layered necklines and collars. Scarves or shawls that cover or fill in the upper back also serve to camouflage. Design details at the waist or below can distract attention away from the upper back area. Custom-made shoulder pads can be shaped to straighten the look of the neck and back.

Using a Yoke to Fit Back and Shoulders

When fitting the back and shoulders, additional seams provide additional opportunities for customizing a garment's fit. For that reason, a yoked shirt is ideal for a figure with a rounded back and square shoulders: The yoke provides two seams for adjusting the fit at the shoulders, not just one. First, deal with the square shoulder issue, then alter for the back curve. You can accommodate a narrower shoulder width in front than in back, since this is common with a rounded back.

To understand how to approach the fitting solution, begin by looking at "Shaped Yoke Seams," below, which shows how the dart on a fitted but yokeless shirt or blouse back is converted to a curved yoke seam on the back piece when a fitted yoked pattern is designed. On loose-fitting or unfitted garments, you may find a yoke that is simply a style feature, with straight seamlines on both the back and the yoke. On garments like this, the yoke seamlines can be placed anywhere on the back pattern (by the designer), and may be many inches below the neckline, nowhere near the curved area of the back. But if the back/yoke seamline is curved to provide shaping, the yoke seamlines will typically fall near the neck and most curved portion of the back.

Begin with a pattern that has a curved seamline on the top of the back. Most square shoulders can be accommodated with a simple change to the angles

Shaped Yoke Seams

These drawings demonstrate how a yoked shirt pattern is derived from a basic back pattern with a shoulder dart.

A. Slash from the hem to just below the shoulder dart.

B. Pivot and tape the dart closed.

C. Draw the yoke line perpendicular to the center back after pivoting.

D. Cut off the yoke.

E. Pivot the shirt back to close the hem dart. Then, smooth the yoke seamline into a curve.

Yokeless back with shoulder dart

Shoulder dart pivoted to hemline

Pivot point

Yoke

of the front/yoke seamlines. Probably the easiest way to determine the angles you need is by pin-fitting a muslin shirt front to a muslin yoke. Cut both with extra-wide seam allowances at the yoke seamlines, then (wearing a T-shirt so you'll have something to pin the pieces to) arrange the front smoothly in place with its center front centered and vertical, and place the yoke on your shoulders. With the yoke piece over the front, fold and pin the yoke's front seam allowance at an angle that looks good to you (using its existing position on the neckline), then trace this edge onto the muslin below to create its seamline. Compare the new seamlines with the original pattern (adjust so the difference is equally divided), and then raise the front and back armhole seamlines at the side seam by this adjusted amount to make up for the changes, as shown in the top drawings at right.

To alter the yoke seamline in back to accommodate a rounded back, first measure your waist-to-neckline distance at the center back and compare this to your pattern; you'll be longer, due to the increased curvature. Add the difference as shown in the center drawing at right , which will increase the amount of dart control provided by the yoke seamline on the back piece.

Align the three pieces and draw a new armhole, as shown in the bottom drawing at right. You'll be able to adjust the relative widths of the front and back at the shoulders by altering the position of your new armhole, using your own width measurements in these areas. A flexible ruler (available from art and drafting stores) is a handy tool for adjusting and drawing armhole curves without changing the overall seam length.

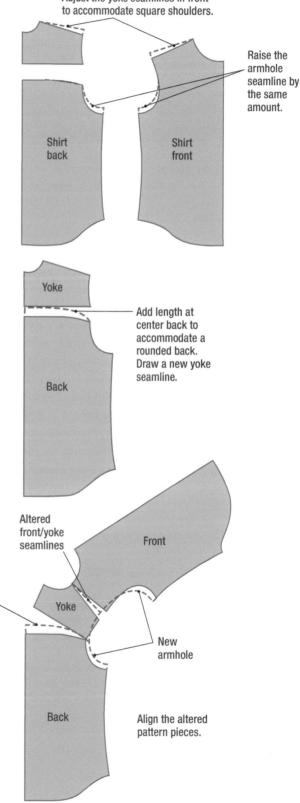

FITTING A YOKE

Adjust the yoke seamlines in front to accommodate square shoulders.

Raise the armhole seamline by the same amount.

Shirt back

Shirt front

Yoke

Back

Add length at center back to accommodate a rounded back. Draw a new yoke seamline.

Altered front/yoke seamlines

Front

Altered back seamline

Yoke

New armhole

Back

Align the altered pattern pieces.

Fitting the Neckline

A neckline or collar should fit without choking and without unwanted looseness or gaping. Even if your pattern fits beautifully everywhere else in the bodice, it's possible that the neckline will require tweaking.

Eliminating Neckline Gapes

Gaping at the neckline can be the result of any combination of factors. We address them below.

A Stretched Neckline

A stretched neckline is the easiest to solve and can sometimes be corrected on finished garments and ready-to-wear. It is particularly a problem with deep V or scoop necks because of the bias grain of these necklines. If the garment fits correctly 2 in. or 3 in. away from the neckline, and the gaping is only at the edge, you are probably dealing with a stretched neckline.

Stabilize the neckline with twill tape or narrow ribbon before attaching the facing or lining. With the garment on the body, pin one end of each of two lengths of the tape to the center front. Pin the other ends to opposite shoulder lines at the neck, adjusting each tape so it lies against the body and both adjusted tapes are the same length. Take off the garment and pin the neckline to the tape, easing in any fullness

so that the neckline lies flat against the tape. Steam to shrink the eased fullness, stitch the tape to the fabric, and complete the neckline as usual.

On a completed garment, use a narrow satin ribbon in a color that matches or complements the garment. Pin it to the inside of the neckline, adjusting it to fit the figure as just described. Hand-sew the ribbon in place, catching both edges to the facing or lining. Steam the neckline to set the eased fabric.

Excess Garment Width

When the front shoulder area of the garment is too wide for the body (an issue with forward-thrusting shoulders), gaping can occur. Keeping your posture relaxed and natural, measure across the back from the left to the right shoulder end point—this is the bone at the end of the shoulder where the arm joins the shoulder. Now measure across the front shoulders from the same points. If your natural posture is very erect the front and back shoulder measurements will be equal. Usually, the front measurement is less than the back, indicating a forward thrust to the shoulders, and requiring that the back of the garment be wider than the front in the shoulder area. (The difference in length is compensated for by the back shoulder dart.)

Measure your pattern from the center front to the shoulder end point on the shoulder stitching line. If the pattern exceeds your measurement, redraw the pattern to correspond to your measurement, as shown in the left drawing below. You should also

REMOVE EXCESS CHEST WIDTH

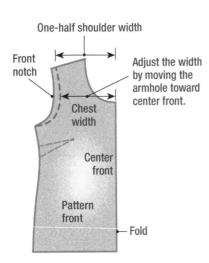

One-half shoulder width

Front notch

Adjust the width by moving the armhole toward center front.

Chest width

Center front

Pattern front

Fold

ADJUST FOR SHOULDER PADS

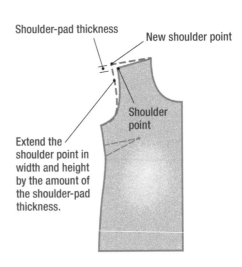

Shoulder-pad thickness

New shoulder point

Shoulder point

Extend the shoulder point in width and height by the amount of the shoulder-pad thickness.

take the chest-width measurement, across the front of the pattern, from one front notch to the other front notch. Compare this to the pattern and adjust the armhole as needed. After adjusting the bodice front, measure the armhole length and correct the sleeve cap seam length as needed.

If the garment has shoulder pads, adjust it as if it did not have pads, then add width and height at the shoulder point to equal the thickness of the pad, as shown in the bottom right drawing on the facing page. If the garment is to be sleeveless, or will have full, capped sleeves, the shoulder should end ½ in. inside the front and back shoulder measurement.

A Concave Chest

To determine whether the chest is concave, place a ruler against your shoulder, and rest the other end at the fullest part of the bust. If the ruler doesn't touch the body through its entire length, there is a concavity, as shown in the top drawing at right.

When a V or deep scoop neck is cut in the pattern without accounting for this natural contour, the neck will gape instead of lying flat. The deeper the neckline, the more of a problem this can be. Ideally, this should be corrected at the patternmaking stage by adding additional dart control. Dart control, also called dart value, is the amount of fabric the dart takes up to build shape. Compare your fitted jewel-neckline sloper to the deep-neck pattern you wish to use. If the total dart control of the pattern does not exceed the dart control of your sloper, you should subtract the neckline length with darts. Slash the pattern through an existing dart, then fold out a ¼-in. to ½-in. dart at the neckline edge. This dart should end at the bust point. The slash will open slightly, making the existing dart larger (see the bottom drawing at right).

Keep in mind that not all patterns include stitched darts. The dart control may be there in the form of gathers, pleats, or tucks, or as extra fullness added into the armhole or to the waist. If a V or deep scoop neck is on a garment that is too long in the chest area, gaping will also occur. Compare your shoulder-to-bust measurement with that of the pattern and adjust the pattern length in the upper chest area if necessary. This will also shorten the armhole, so fit the armhole and possibly make adjustments to the sleeve pattern before cutting the sleeve.

ADJUST FOR A CONCAVE CHEST

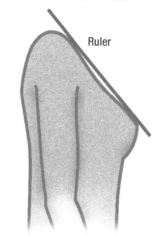

Ruler

If a ruler placed on the shoulder with the other end resting on the fullest part of the breast doesn't touch the body anywhere else, the chest is concave.

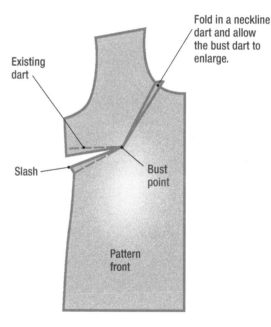

Existing dart

Slash

Fold in a neckline dart and allow the bust dart to enlarge.

Bust point

Pattern front

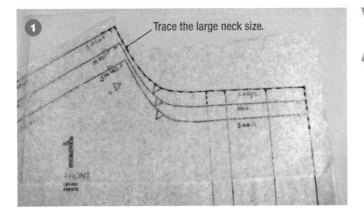

1 Trace the large neck size.

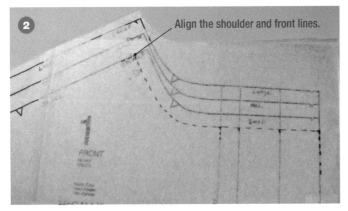

2 Align the shoulder and front lines.

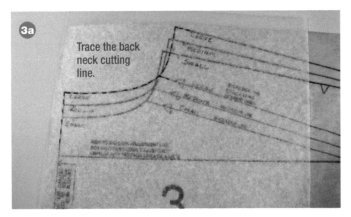

3a Trace the back neck cutting line.

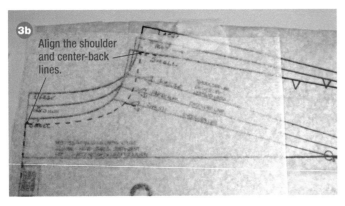

3b Align the shoulder and center-back lines.

Fitting Shirt Collars

To ensure that the collar of a traditional shirt—one with a collar stand—fits properly, you need to adjust three elements: neckline, collar band, and collar. The following technique takes about 10 minutes and yields perfect results every time—regardless of whether you're enlarging a neckline or reducing it. You need only alter the front and back pattern pieces. Neither the collar nor the collar-band pattern pieces are updated.

Begin with a multisize pattern that includes both the neck and body sizes, or purchase two separate patterns: one to fit the body, and one to fit the neck.

Enlarging a Neckline

The multisize pattern shown here is printed with small, medium, and large sizes. For this example, the small-size chest is needed, but to fit a thicker neck, the cutting lines for the large-size neck opening must be strategically superimposed onto the small-size chest's cutting lines.

1. Copy the neckline. Lay a piece of tissue paper over the large-size neck area of the front pattern piece. Trace the neck cutting line onto the tissue paper, and include short sections of the front cutting line and the shoulder cutting line.

2. Shift the tracing and align. Move the tracing to the pattern markings of the desired chest size (in this example, small) as shown at left. Line up the traced shoulder-neck intersection lines and the front cutting line with the corresponding small-size shoulder and front pattern markings, as shown. The traced neckline doesn't overlap any existing neckline at this point. Tape the tracing in place. The large-size neck tracing is the new neck cutting line. Note how the superimposed cutting line of the larger neck "scoops out" the neck opening to accommodate a larger neck.

3. Repeat steps 1 and 2 for the back neckline (3a, 3b). Neither the collar nor the collar-band pattern pieces have to be altered. Just use the existing large-size collar and collar-band pattern pieces. Use the small-size cutting lines for the rest of the shirt.

Reducing a Neckline

For this example, the large-size chest is needed, but to fit a thinner neck, the cutting line of the small-size neck must be superimposed onto the cutting lines of the large-size chest.

1. **Copy the neckline.** Lay a piece of tissue paper over the small-size neck area of the front pattern piece. Trace the small-size neck cutting line onto the tissue paper, and include short sections of the front cutting line and the small-size shoulder cutting line.

2. **Shift the tracing and align.** Move the tracing to the desired chest-size pattern markings (in this example, large). Align the traced shoulder line and the traced front cutting line with the corresponding front and large-size cutting lines, as shown at right. Tape the tracing in place. The small-size neck tracing is the new neck cutting line. The superimposed small-size neck cutting line is outside the printed area of the pattern. Note how it fills in the neck opening to fit the smaller neck size.

3. **Repeat steps 1 and 2 for the back neckline (3a, 3b).** Neither the collar nor collar-band pattern pieces have to be altered. Just use the existing small-size collar and collar-band pattern pieces. Use the large-size cutting lines for the rest of the shirt.

TIP The collar-fitting technique shown here is demonstrated with a man's shirt, but it works just as well with a woman's and can be easily adapted for a roll collar that has no stand as well.

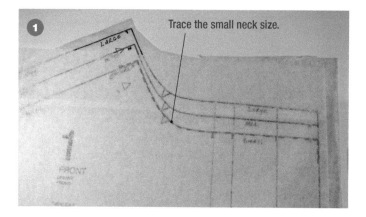

Trace the small neck size.

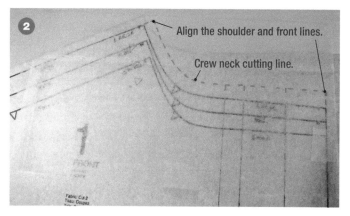

Align the shoulder and front lines.

Crew neck cutting line.

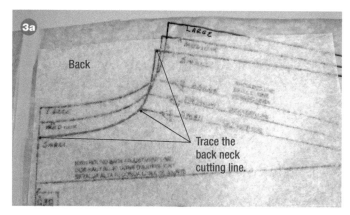

Back

Trace the back neck cutting line.

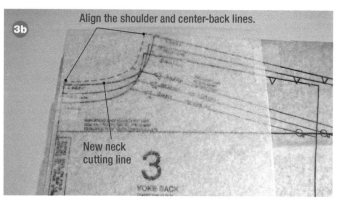

Align the shoulder and center-back lines.

New neck cutting line

Fitting the Bodice with a Muslin

Every fitting process begins with evaluating how the body fills a garment. Understanding how to fit your garment involves understanding that there are three possible fit-problem scenarios: An area is too large, an area is too small, or an area isn't shaped right.

If the garment is too large in one area, reduce the amount of garment fabric in that region; this is "net loss." Next, if the garment is too small in an area, you need to add fabric to that area; this is "net gain." These conditions can exist simultaneously in the same garment, so sometimes you may have to subtract fabric at one location and add it at another; this is "no net change." Understanding this enables you to alter the pattern right at the point of the fit problem by adding or subtracting from the original and adjusting for distortion. A good example of this is correction for a swayback: Since the fabric bunches up at the waist, and the hem rises as well, you have to remove fabric at the waist and add fabric at the hem.

After fitting alterations are made, there may be disjointed seamlines and curves that end up a little too pointed or otherwise distorted that must then be trued. To start this process, make a muslin, put it on, and begin to pin out any fullness and unevenness to form a nice, smooth silhouette. For garments that hang from the shoulders, adjust the muslin from the top down, as lower drag lines often disappear or diminish after the upper adjustments are made. You'll see pattern pieces morph into new shapes that allow for curves and fullness or leanness and length that standard patterns don't. Once you get a feel for it, you'll find this method of fitting patterns an uncomplicated and versatile way to achieve a perfect custom fit that looks like it was draped to your body.

Fitting the Muslin Sleeve

The sleeve on the muslin shown below is too long for the figure. The drag lines cross the arm, indicating the need to fit for a net loss.

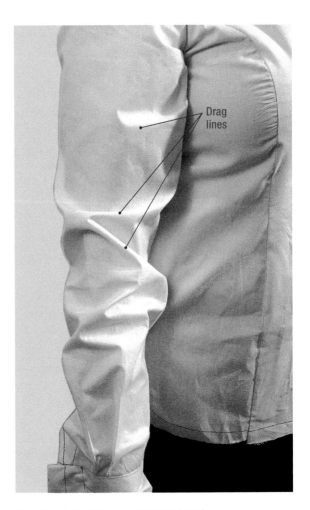

Drag lines indicate too much sleeve length.

1. To remove the excess fullness in the sleeve, fold it out until the sleeve hangs with a minimum of ripples. Don't overfit; you want the arm to have enough room to bend comfortably.

2. Mark the fold on the muslin. Hash-mark across the folded area with a pencil.

3. First, unpin the alteration, and smooth the muslin sleeve out on a table. Measure the distance up from the cuff and then the distance between the hash-mark rows.

4. Transfer this information to the sleeve pattern copy. Fold out the excess area based on your measurement across the pattern. The alteration throws off the seam alignment slightly, which is easily corrected with a ruler. Truing the seam is how you correct for distortion. You can see where area is removed from one side and added back to the other for an overall no net change.

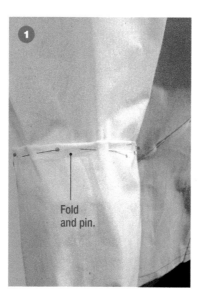

Fold out the fullness and pin.

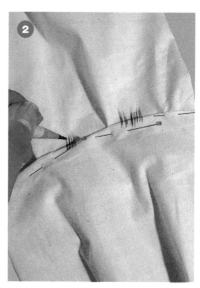

Hash-mark across the fold.

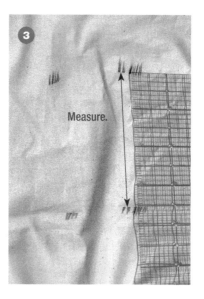

Measure the distance between the hash marks.

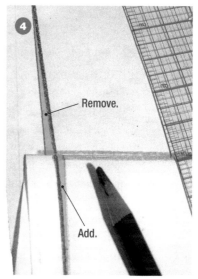

True the seamline to correct distortion.

Fitting the Muslin Back

Horizontal drag lines on the bodice back (see the photo below)indicate that there's too much fabric there. Pin out the excess on the muslin, then transfer the changes to the pattern, as shown on the facing page.

1. Pin the excess into a dart. Begin at the center back, and work around the bodice to the side seam from under the shoulder blades, pinning the excess fabric into a horizontal dart. Then have the subject move her arm to see whether there's still room to raise it. Check the hem to see if it rises with the alteration or if it's level with the floor. If it rises, measure how much, and add that length back at the hem when making the pattern alteration.

2. Mark the folds. As you did on the sleeve, mark the fitting folds with hash marks and a pencil. Then remove the pins.

3. Transfer the information to the pattern. Remove the side-seam stitching from the muslin to make transferring the information to the paper easier. Start with the back side panel; place the pattern copy under the muslin, and align the seamlines and other marks. Pin the muslin to the paper, and use a dressmaker's tracing wheel and carbon to copy the marks from the muslin to the pattern. In some areas, you can dispense with the tracing wheel and carbon entirely and just lay the pattern next to the seam on the muslin to mark the alteration on paper.

4. Remove the excess in the pattern. The shaded area in the photo shows the net loss on the center-back panel. Fold the area closed, and tape.

5. Identify any distortion created by the alteration. In this case, the alteration bent the center-back foldline to the left. To compensate, extend the center-back line below the waist, using the line above the waist for reference.

6. Correct the distortion. Remove the area outlined in blue in the photo from the pattern at the center back, and add it back to the pattern at the princess seam. Extend the hem at the princess seam the same amount as you trimmed off the center back to correct the distortion (no net change).

Once the muslin information has been transferred to the original pattern, you can alter the pattern to add, remove, or reposition fabric. Begin with the easier alteration—the wedge-shaped section of the waist.

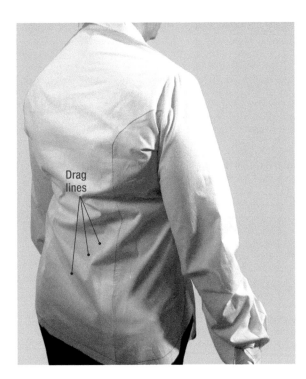

Drag lines across the back indicate excess fabric.

Measure the perpendicular distance from the waistline to the floor at the center front and center back.

Pin out excess at waist.

Hash-mark across the fold.

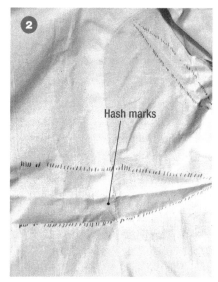

Hash marks

Use a dressmaker's tracing wheel and carbon to copy the marks to your pattern.

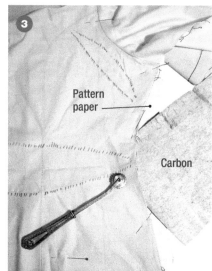

Pattern paper

Carbon

Remove excess in the pattern.

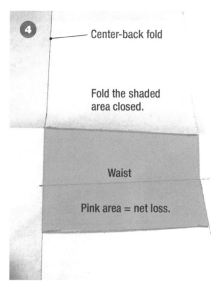

Center-back fold

Fold the shaded area closed.

Waist

Pink area = net loss.

Identify any pattern distortions caused by alteration.

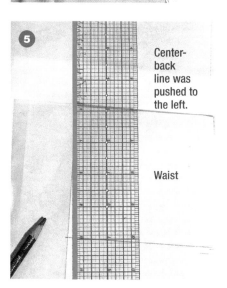

Center-back line was pushed to the left.

Waist

Subtract the correction from center back, and add it to the seam.

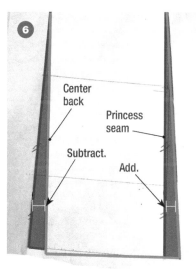

Center back

Princess seam

Subtract.

Add.

Shaping the Side Back

1. Fold out the net loss on the side-back wedge edges. If the wedge edges don't align because one is slightly curved, fold the wedge as close as possible, and then remove the wedge sliver that's left. In the far left photo below, the shaded areas represent the net-loss alterations that were pinned out on the muslin and transferred to the pattern on the side panel.

2. Remove the remaining sliver. After the wedge is folded out, a sliver remains (shaded area). To remove the sliver, cut the paper along the lower curve, as shown.

3. Cover the opening. Mark the original waistline, and rotate the cut edge to cover the sliver, as shown.

4. Correct for the distortion. First, draft a slash line from the waist to the hem. Then, cut the paper on this line all the way up from the hem through the waist.

5. Redraft the hem curve. Slide the side-seam piece down until the original waist point matches the new waist on the pattern. There will be a mismatch at the bottom. To correct for the distortion at the hem, split the difference and redraft the curve for a no net change.

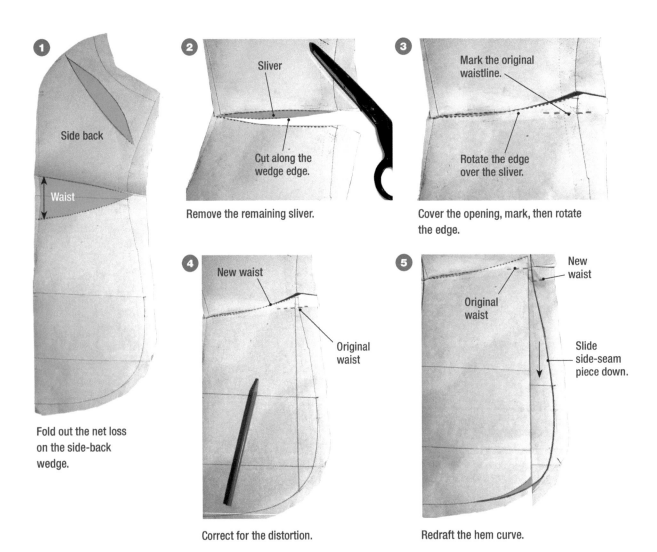

1 Side back

Waist

Fold out the net loss on the side-back wedge.

2 Sliver

Cut along the wedge edge.

Remove the remaining sliver.

3 Mark the original waistline.

Rotate the edge over the sliver.

Cover the opening, mark, then rotate the edge.

4 New waist

Original waist

Correct for the distortion.

5 New waist

Original waist

Slide side-seam piece down.

Redraft the hem curve.

Using a Grid

When the drag line doesn't cross a seam, there's another method of altering: using a grid. It's useful for moving an area from the middle of a pattern piece to an edge. This will be a net loss, and it affects the outline of the pattern when the alteration is finished. Here, the side back panel is altered using the technique.

1. Draw the baseline. Draw a straight line between the endpoints of the marquise-shaped dart.

2. Draw grid lines. Draw grid lines perpendicular to the baseline that pass through the entire marquise shape and extend through the nearest seamline, as shown in the top right photo. The grid lines shown are ¼ in. to ⅜ in. apart.

3. Mark the new stitching line. Measure the length of each grid line inside the dart lines. Then mark that distance in from the stitching line (shown in blue), on the same grid line, toward the dart (**3a**). The direction is shown with the red arrows and marks a dot. Then connect the dots for the new stitching line (**3b**).

4. Compare the new line length. To correct for distortion, measure the original stitching line length and compare it to the new line's length.

5. Correct the distortion. The corrected armhole (shown in red) needs to be brought back to the original armhole length (shown in blue). To do this, find the difference between the two lines, measure that distance in from the princess seam on the original armhole line, and redraft the armhole and princess seams to this point. The green line in the photo represents the correction for distortion (**5a**).

In the completed alteration, the net loss (area removed) is shaded blue (**5b**).

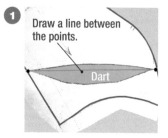

1 Draw a line between the points.

Dart

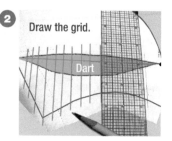

2 Draw the grid.

Dart

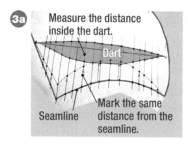

3a Measure the distance inside the dart.

Dart

Seamline

Mark the same distance from the seamline.

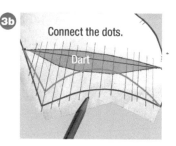

3b Connect the dots.

Dart

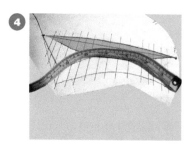

4

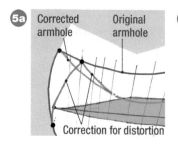

5a Corrected armhole — Original armhole

Correction for distortion

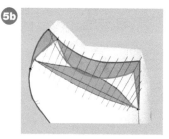

5b

Loss area is removed in the completed alteration.

Fine-Tuning the Bodice Front

Begin by pin-fitting at the shoulder and work down the side seam, taking tucks or releasing seams as needed.

1. Above the bust, there is a vertical drag line that indicates too much width across the upper chest area (**1a**). Under the collar, there is a horizontal drag line, indicating a high shoulder at the neckline (**1b**). Fitting the uppermost alterations first, pin out the two drag lines above the bust (**1c**); both are net loss alterations because fabric is being subtracted.

2. There is also too much fabric under the princess seam on the side panel. Pin the excess out for another net loss alteration to reshape the side-front princess panel.

3. Horizontal drag lines across the bust indicate too little room there (**3a**). To determine the amount of additional fabric needed across the bust for the net gain alteration, cut the muslin vertically (perpendicular to the drag lines) while it's on the body. The muslin will open to form a double-ended dart shape (**3b**). Hold the shape of the opening by pinning a muslin or organza patch over it (**3c**).

4. Diagonal drag lines below the bust indicate a "twist" (**4a**). Twists are typically no net change alterations. Pin out the diagonal twist line (**4b**). Use a pencil to hash-mark across the fold. Use the hash marks to record the shape of your alteration so you can transfer it to the pattern. Use them on all alterations. But for a twist alteration, also draw a horizontal line dividing the dart parallel to the hem (**4c**).

5. Remove the pins. Then measure the distance between the break points (marked with two dots in the photo on the facing page) in the horizontal line. You'll transfer the measurement to your pattern later.

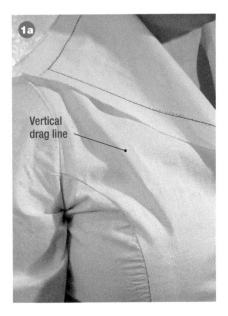

Drag lines indicate too much width across the chest.

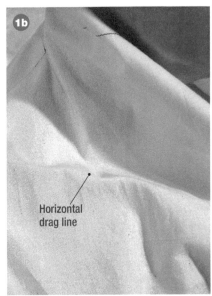

Drag lines under the collar indicate a high shoulder.

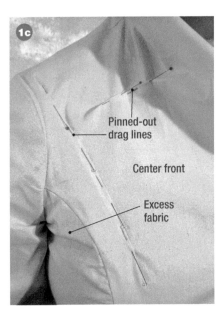

Pin out the drag lines under the collar and at the bust.

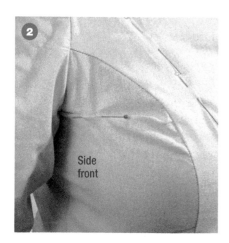

Pin out the drag line under the princess seam.

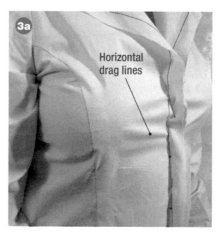

Horizontal drag lines indicate too little room.

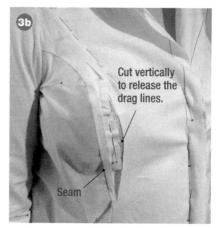

The cut muslin will open to form a double-ended dart.

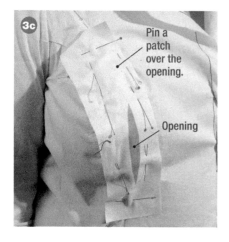

Hold the shape of the opening by pinning on a patch.

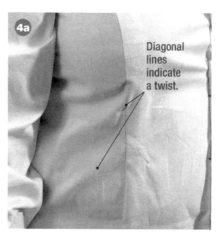

Twists are usually no net change alterations.

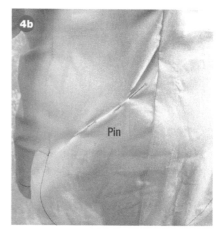

Pin out the twist.

Draw hash marks across the folds.

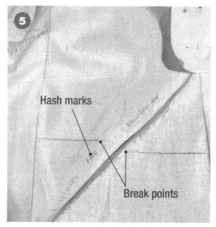

Measure the distance between the break points of the horizontal line.

Transfer Marks to the Pattern, and Alter the Side-Front Panel

Align the side-front muslin over the paper pattern, and transfer the marks to the paper pattern with a tracing wheel and carbon paper. Once you've marked the pattern, make the required adjustments, and then correct for the distortion that occurs when seam lengths no longer match.

1. Because the side-back panel was altered (see p. 88), the side-front and side-back side seams are no longer the same length. Align the waistlines of the side-back panel and the side-front panel. Mark the front side seam so it's the same length as the back side seam.

2. Measure the front armhole length; you'll need this later to correct for distortion. Draft a line (shown in green) from the side-seam mark to the middle of the net loss alteration at the princess seam (**2a**). Cut the line. Pivot the armhole section down (**2b**) to fold out the net loss (**2c**).

3. Redraft the armhole (shown in red) to smooth the change (**3a**). Measure the new armhole; it will be shorter than the original. Extend the armhole at the side seam to make it the original length (**3b**).

Taper the armhole seam down into the side seam from this point.

4. Correct the twist below the horizontal line. First, draw a horizontal line (green) between the two lines that represent the broken horizontal line from step 5 on p. 90 (shown dotted on the facing page). The arrow indicates the direction of the drag line, and shows the direction to move the pattern pieces.

5. Cut the paper along the horizontal line. Slide the pieces in the directions indicated to align the break points. The amount you slide is the same amount you pinned out in the muslin.

6. Once the correction is made, compensate for distortion. Draw a straight line through the jogged pattern piece to make a smooth seamline at each side. Note that the shaded area (pink) removed from one side appears on the other side of each seam for no net change in the pattern.

TIP Consider working with different colored pens or pencils to help keep track of the sequential alterations you make.

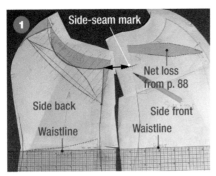

Align the waistlines of the side-back and side-front panels.

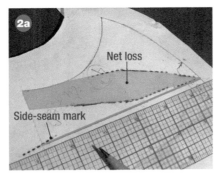

Draw a line from the side-seam mark to the middle of the net loss alteration.

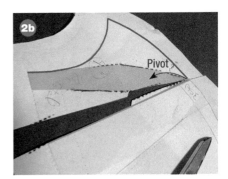

Cut along the line, and pivot the armhole section downward.

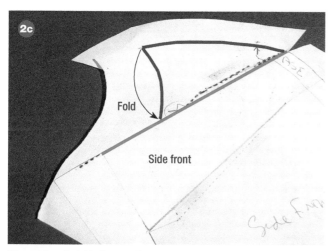

The net loss is folded out entirely.

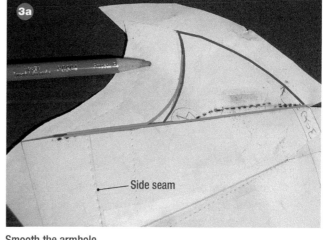

Smooth the armhole.

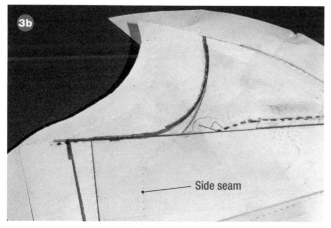

Extend the armhole to its original length and taper it into the side seam.

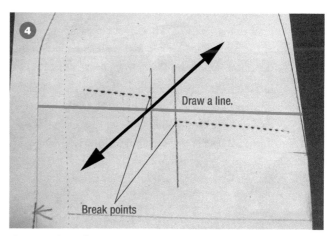

The arrow indicates the direction to move the pattern pieces.

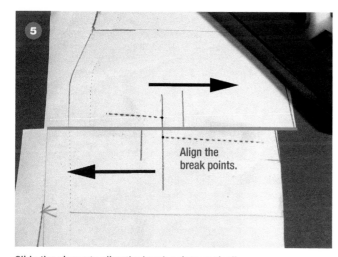

Slide the pieces to align the break points vertically.

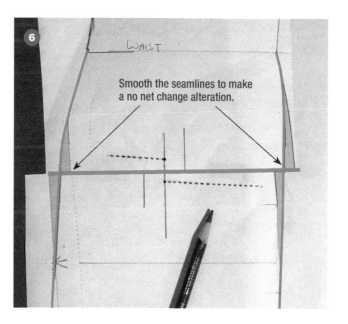

Alter the Center-Front Panel

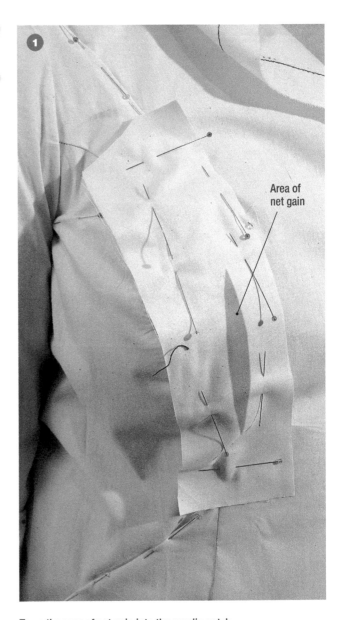

Area of net gain

Begin by transferring the corrections from the muslin alteration to the paper with the wheel and carbon paper. Then make adjustments to the pattern.

1. Trace the shape of the net gain onto the muslin patch that's pinned to the bodice. This will be an area of net gain.

2. Remove the patch. Lay it on the pattern, and use a tracing wheel and carbon to trace the net gain beside the princess seam.

3. Cut along the top edge of the net loss wedge in green. Then pivot the gray area downward to remove that net loss. This pivot closes a portion of the pink-shaded net loss as well. The red line in the photo represents the new shoulder slope.

4. Draw a line from the armhole across the top point of the yellow area of net gain at the armhole to the left edge of the pink net loss area. Then draw a line up to the bottom left edge of the gray-shaded area and back across to the armhole. The net gain and net loss cancel each other out below that line. Cut out this new section.

5. Slide the shoulder segment to the right. Align the right edge of the segment with the right edge of the pink-shaded area to remove that fullness from the pattern.

6. To finish, draft the new princess seam line as shown in red. This incorporates the adjustments made in steps 3, 4, and 5 and divides the yellow area you've added for the net gain.

7. Leave half the yellow section on the front seam and add the other half to the side-front princess panel. The yellow-shaded area represents the net gain as marked on your pattern.

Trace the area of net gain into the muslin patch.

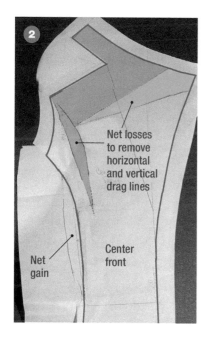

Trace the shape of the net gain beside the princess seam.

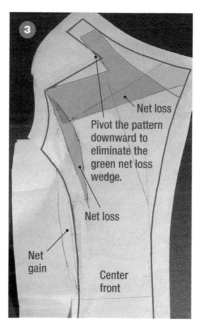

Establish the new shoulder slope.

Draw a line from the armhole across the point of the net gain area.

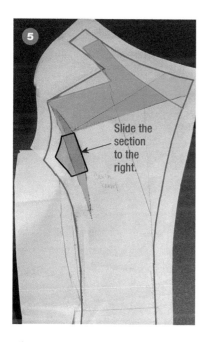

Slide the section to the right so it aligns with the right side of the (pink) net loss area.

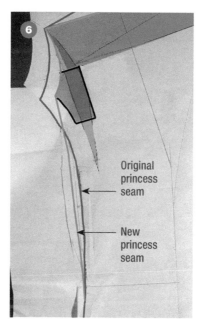

Draft the new princess seam line.

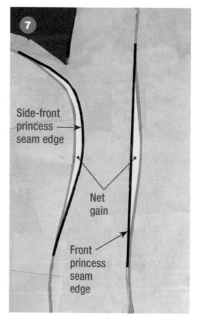

The yellow shaded area represents the net gain.

Fitting Knit Tops

For today's fast-paced lifestyle, knits continue to be fashionable, comfortable, and easy to sew. Knit fabric stretches to fit, making it an ideal choice for many body types. It comes in myriad weights, fibers, and colors to suit just about any style or season.

However, sewing knit garments presents fitting issues that differ from those encountered when you're working with a stable fabric. You may discover that tops and dresses gape and twist. A poorly fitted knit bodice can gape at the armholes, fall incorrectly along the neckline, twist at the torso, and present many other unflattering problems.

It's important to match your fabric's stretch to your pattern and to check your pattern for the fitting details that matter most. Each pattern piece has a specific relationship to the figure, which enables the garment to fit and be worn correctly. Drape-fitting the pattern allows for custom changes and gives you the added pleasure of seeing how the style looks during the fitting process. These simple techniques can be applied to any knit pattern with professional results.

Knit Fabrics and Stretch

Knits are used in a variety of garments, but they must be appropriate for the design. Choice of fabric depends on the particular properties of the knit, including the desired degree of stretch or stability and the type and the design of the garment.

Stretch and Recovery Ratios

A well-constructed knit has stretch and recovery, or memory, to maintain its original shape. Analyze each knit fabric.

An important characteristic of a knitted fabric is its capacity to change dimensions by stretching. The amount and direction of stretch varies according to the knitting process used, the gauge (size of the stitch), and the denier (weight) of the yarn. Knits can be made to stretch in either the course (cross-grain or what is called the weft in a woven fabric) or the wale (akin to the woven straight-of-grain or warp) direction, or both, depending on desired elasticity. This characteristic in knits is sometimes referred to as either a one-way or two-way stretch.

Stretch ratio is the amount of stretch per inch when the knit is stretched to its maximum width and/or length. The stretch factor of knits ranges from 18 percent to 100 percent.

Recovery ratio is the degree to which a knit reverts to its original shape after being stretched. Knits with good recovery return to their original width and length when released. This means they will hold their shape when worn.

Determine Your Fabric's Stretch Ratio

Your fabric's stretch ratio will tell you how much ease (length and/or width) is needed within the pattern. Typically, more ease is used in the pattern width than in the length.

Fold the fabric along the crosswise grain to determine the width ratio or along the lengthwise grain for the length ratio. On the fabric width, measure and mark with pins spaced 5 in. to 8 in. apart. Hold the fabric at the first and last pins. Gently stretch the fabric as far as it will go without distorting the fabric, and measure it. With the fabric relaxed, take another measurement. This indicates the recovery ability.

Analyze the Draft of the Pattern

Most pattern companies drape their knit patterns on a dress form by smoothing out the dart excess at the shoulders, armholes, and side seams. This allows the garment to easily fit the body without gaping, twisting, or needing darts. Most fitting issues occur because the pattern does not have the details listed in "Drape-Fitting a Knit Garment," on p. 99. Because a knit pattern allows for stretch across the body, which eliminates the need for darts, the following details should be double-checked. If these pattern areas are not correct, the finished garment will gape, twist, and/or pitch.

Knit Categories by Stretch Ratio

Below are swatches of four knit types with different stretch characteristics.

	RELAXED	STRETCHED
STABLE/FIRM KNITS These knits have a limited amount of stretch (18-percent or less stretch ratio) and thus maintain their original shape well. They are commonly used in casual day clothing, skirts, and pants. Double knits are also a stable/firm knit.		
MODERATE-STRETCH KNITS These knits combine the characteristics of stable and stretch knits (about 25-percent stretch ratio). They are comfortable to wear and can provide a close-to-the-body fit, such as in a fitted top. These knits are commonly used in casual sportswear and outerwear.		
STRETCH KNITS Knit fabrics such as latex and some spandex knits have a 50-percent stretch ratio. These fabrics are lightweight and work well in body-contoured designs such as swimwear, intimates, bodysuits, and leotards.		
SUPER-STRETCH KNITS These fabrics have a 100-percent stretch ratio. Some common examples are rib knits and 100-percent spandex. These are used for active sportswear, swimwear, and dancewear.		

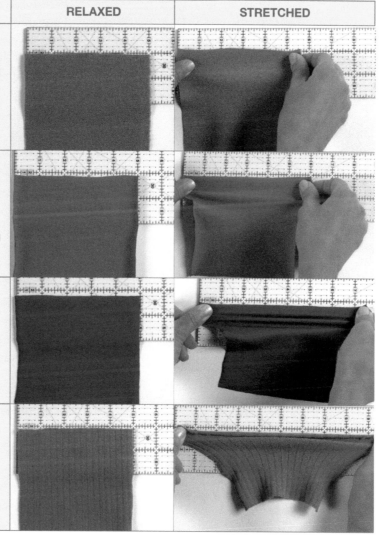

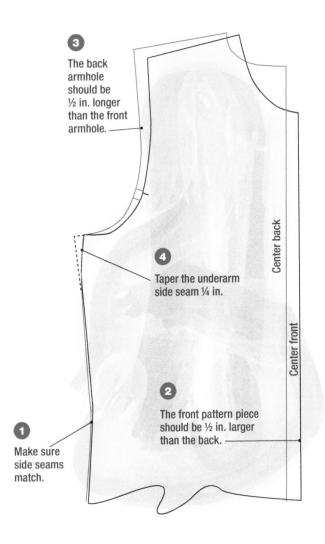

3 The back armhole should be ½ in. longer than the front armhole.

4 Taper the underarm side seam ¼ in.

Center back

Center front

2 The front pattern piece should be ½ in. larger than the back.

1 Make sure side seams match.

 When selecting a pattern size, consider the fabric. You could go a pattern size larger or smaller depending on how much the fabric stretches.

Check the Pattern

Select the correct pattern size by using a full-bust measurement. It will provide the needed amount to go over the bustline. If you use a very stretchy knit, you may want to select one pattern size smaller. If you select a knit with minimum stretch, you may want to select one pattern size larger.

Lay the paper pattern front bodice piece on top of the back bodice pattern piece. Pin the side seams together at the underarm/side seam corner, and pivot the pattern until the center front and center back are parallel.

1. Check the side seams to make sure they match in shape and length. If they don't, divide the difference to make them the same, otherwise the finished garment will twist.

2. Check the front-to-back balance. Make the front pattern piece ½ in. wider than the back pattern piece. If the front is the same size or smaller than the back, the finished garment will twist or pull. The front and back should not be the same because the front needs to be larger to allow for bust shaping.

3. Check the armhole balance. The back armhole should measure ½ in. longer than the front armhole because the distance from the midback to the shoulder is longer than the midfront to the shoulder. If the back armhole is the same as the front, this causes the front pattern to pitch forward and the back shoulder seam to pull to the back.

4. Check the side-seam/underarm shape. To eliminate armhole gaping, taper the side seam ¼ in. toward the body at the underarm area. The tapered stitches should return to the side-seam stitching line within 2 in. of the armhole.

Drape-Fitting a Knit Garment

Once the pattern size is selected and the pattern has been checked for accuracy, fine-tune the fit. Drape-fit your garment using the fashion fabric or one with a similar drape and hand. Then transfer those changes to your pattern for a perfectly fitted silhouette.

Back Shoulder and Neckline

First, prepare the pieces by cutting the pattern out of your desired knit fabric or one with a similar drape and weight. Then baste the side and shoulder seams, and staystitch the necklines so that they don't stretch.

1. Establish the shoulder blade level 5 in. from the neckline, and mark this line. Keep the garment hanging straight from the shoulder blade level line to the floor. If necessary, remove the basting stitches at the shoulder seam. Smooth the fabric from the shoulder blade level up toward the shoulder. If necessary, add fabric to the neckline and shoulder by letting out the seam allowance.

2. Double-check the neckline. If a new neckline is needed, tape extra fabric to the knit design. Then draw the center-back line straight up toward the desired neckline area, and draw a new neckline. Adjust the paper pattern. Transfer all changes to the pattern. Draw a new neckline, shoulder, and armhole from midarmhole if needed. Use a designer's curve to smooth any curves.

 TIP When fitting on the body, distribute your weight evenly on your feet. Shifting your weight causes your shoulders and spine to shift, too.

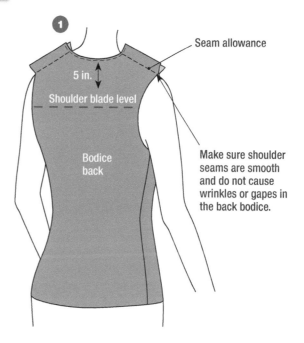

① Seam allowance

5 in.

Shoulder blade level

Bodice back

Make sure shoulder seams are smooth and do not cause wrinkles or gapes in the back bodice.

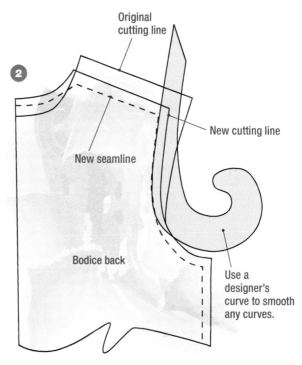

Original cutting line

② New cutting line

New seamline

Bodice back

Use a designer's curve to smooth any curves.

FRONT SHOULDER

Smooth out the excess fabric to eliminate the wrinkle seen on the left side of the neckline.

1

2

Shoulder ridge

3

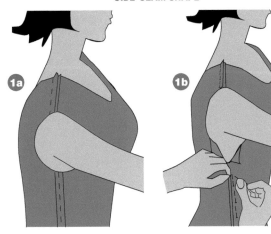

SIDE-SEAM SHAPE

1a

1b

Assess your side seam's contour, and determine if you want to let out or take in any fabric.

Let out the basting stitches, and adjust the seam as necessary.

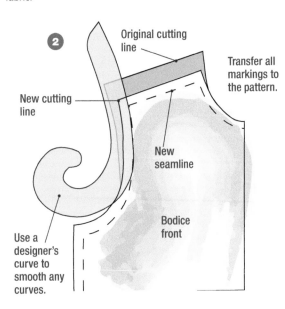

2

Original cutting line

Transfer all markings to the pattern.

New cutting line

New seamline

Bodice front

Use a designer's curve to smooth any curves.

Front Shoulder, Neckline, and Armhole

1. Drape the front neckline and shoulder. Garments hang from the shoulders. Therefore, the shoulder seam must be identical to the body shape. If the pattern shoulder slope is off by just 5 degrees from the body shoulder slope, the garment will drape incorrectly. The neckline should lie flat against the body. Often, there is excess fabric at the front shoulder seam, causing the neckline to gap. Smooth the fabric from the neckline into the back shoulder seam. Pin the front shoulder to match the back shoulder–seam stitching line.

2. Adjust the armhole. The armholes should fit comfortably according to the design (shirt armholes are larger than fitted armholes). Smooth the fabric from the midarmhole area into the shoulder seam. Pin the new shoulder to match the stitching line of the back shoulder seam. Smooth the fabric from the armhole notches down toward the side seam, contouring the armhole at the underarm area.

3. Mark the shoulder ridge. Mark at the bone where the shoulder and armhole meet.

Side-Seam Shape

1. Adjust the side seam. Depending on the desired overall fit, the side seam could be shaped tighter or looser (**1a**). The side seam may also need to be contoured over the waistline and the hip. Release the basting stitches, and repin to the desired shape, keeping the front and back shape the same (**1b**).

2. Transfer all markings. Mark the new stitching lines using a felt-tip marker. Undo all pins and stitching. Transfer all changes to the pattern. Use a designer's curve to smooth any curves, and add seam allowances.

Adjust the Sleeve and Armhole

Once the pattern changes are completed, the armhole circumference must be checked to ensure that each has remained balanced. To be sure that the sleeve fits correctly and drapes over the arm without pulling or twisting, the following three areas also need to be reviewed.

1. Check the armhole. The back armhole should be ½ in. longer than the front. If it is off by more than ½ in., double-check your shoulder fit, and readjust the front and back shoulders. If it is off less than ½ in., reshape the armhole midsection.

2. Check the sleeve-cap seam length. A knit sleeve-cap seam will match the total armhole circumference or have ½-in. ease. The sleeve-cap seam shape may vary, depending on style. Thanks to multisize patterns, if the sleeve is too small, use the next larger size sleeve. If the sleeve is too large, use a smaller size.

3. Adjust for sleeve twists. This happens if the armhole is not balanced (refer to step 1 above) or the sleeve cap is not wide enough in the back. Add ½ in. to the back sleeve-cap seam between the shoulder notch and the back notches. Taper the addition to nothing at the shoulder area and the back notches.

4. Check the sleeve-cap notch. Typically, the center sleeve-cap registration notch (or dot on many patterns) is matched to the shoulder seam. This alignment causes the sleeve to pitch backward and twist. Slide the notch (or dot) ¼ in. toward the front, past the sleeve center.

TIP Pattern pieces relate to the figure. The center front and center back should always be perpendicular to the floor and hang straight up and down. The cross-grain of the pattern should always be parallel to the floor. Otherwise, the garment will drag and pull downward.

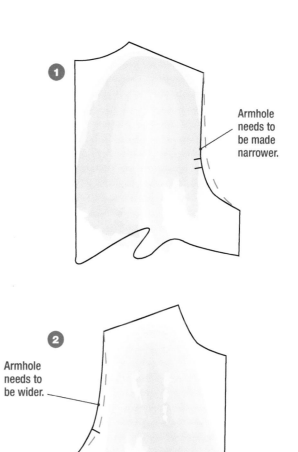

1

Armhole needs to be made narrower.

2

Armhole needs to be wider.

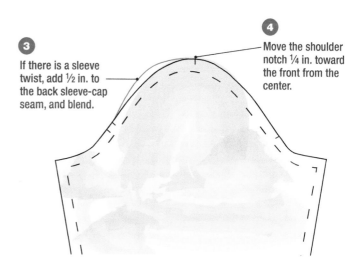

3 If there is a sleeve twist, add ½ in. to the back sleeve-cap seam, and blend.

4 Move the shoulder notch ¼ in. toward the front from the center.

IV

FITTING SKIRTS AND PANTS

Fitting garments at and below the waist is a matter of creating space for the body's fullness, wherever it happens to be, and removing excess fabric where the body is relatively slimmer. Women's bodies vary widely when it comes to the location of curves: You may have a narrow waist and slim hips, but be wide through the thighs; or you may have a fuller abdomen, with padding high on the hip, and a flat seat. Whatever your silhouette, you can fit skirts and pants to flatter.

A standard pattern assumes that the hip measurement is about 9 in. or 10 in. larger than the waist. But if you have a pronounced pear shape, the difference is usually somewhat bigger than that. Conversely, an "apple" body type might have just a few inches of difference. In either case, you'll need to adjust the waist or hip to get the fit you want. Here, you'll learn how to assess your figure and make the needed alterations to accommodate your specific waist-to-hip ratio. These techniques are suitable for both skirts and pants.

Pants present more fitting problems than skirts, as they must fit over and around the seat, encircle the thighs comfortably, and hang properly through the rise. A fuller- or flatter-than-average seat commonly throws off the fit of pants in all these areas, creating drag lines (sometimes called "smiles") at the front crotch or under the seat, or excess vertical folds along the back leg. Simple alterations, either to the pattern or with a fitting muslin, can reposition fabric to the places where you need extra fullness, while removing extra fabric to create slimmer contours.

Finally, one of the best ways to obtain a perfect fit in pants is to draft them to your personal measurements. The technique isn't difficult, and once you've drafted a basic pants pattern, you can change it to create new styles. Further, the drafting process helps you understand why pants patterns look the way they do, and gives you essential information for evaluating commercial patterns.

Fitting the Waist and Hip

Skirts and pants hang from the waist, so perfecting the fit there is essential to a garment that looks and feels great. The technique offered here explains an alternative to the traditional fitting process. It gives you a tool to help handle a variety of fitting issues that center on the waist and on the waist-to-hip area.

Making a Duct-Tape Form

Duct tape can be a sewer's best friend when it comes to solving fitting problems. Duct-tape dress forms are quite common; in the same way, a duct-tape hip mold is an extremely accurate record of the exact shape and position of the wrappee's waistline, hip darts, and side seams. It fits like a glove and, once it's cut apart and flattened, it's a sloper, and can be used just like a drafted sloper as the basis for designing any kind of skirt, as well as the waist-to-hipline position of pants. This sloper is also perfect to use without further adjustment as a pattern for any close-fitted skirts made in stretchy, spandex-blend fabrics.

A duct tape hip mold is an excellent and accurate record of one's waistline, hip darts, and side seams.

Creating the Hip Mold

Start by slipping cotton ribbing tubing over the figure so it covers from waistline to hipline plus a few extra inches above and below. Smooth the fabric (the tubing is stretchy, but sew a seam or add a panel if necessary to fit it to the figure) so it's wrinkle-free in the area to be taped.

What You'll Need

You don't need much to make a duct-tape hip mold, but it does pay to get the best products.

• Manco® (known as Duck Tape, and also packaged as Ace Hardware's Professional brand) is by far the best choice for duct tape; no other duct tape tears as easily, molds as well, sticks as cleanly, lasts as long, and is as stable as the Manco brand.

• ¼-in. white car-pinstriping tape for marking the centers and side seams on your tape sloper. You will have to go to an auto parts store to find this tape, but it will not peel off your duct-tape sloper, even many months later.

• ½ yd. of all-cotton rib-knit tubing (duct tape won't stick to blends or synthetics)

• Enough ¼-in.-wide elastic to go around the waist of the person you're going to wrap

• Scissors

• A fresh, sharp permanent marker

The more contoured the surface being taped is, the narrower and shorter the tape pieces need to be to cover it smoothly. Use full-width tape lengths only on areas that are relatively flat; tear narrower strips for all other areas. Overlap the tape pieces generously, keeping the tape as wrinkle-free as possible. The completed mold should be at least two tape layers thick at all points.

1. Tear a narrow strip of tape (about ¾ in. wide) long enough to surround the waist, and apply it to cover the waistline area so it feels comfortably snug.

2. Cover the hips from the top down using narrow strips. Smaller, narrower strips provide the contouring and shaping needed over the high hip. Increase the strip widths as you approach the hipline area, where full-width strips will work smoothly. Complete both sides before doing the back and front.

3. Move on to the back, again starting near the top and working down to the hipline. Slash or tear tape ends lengthwise if necessary to help them lie more smoothly when they extend into more contoured hip areas. In the same manner, complete the front, creating a smooth and horizontal finish at the hipline.

4. Establish center front, center back, and side seam lines by applying pinstriping tape vertically to the completed tape mold (**4a, 4b**). Use visual clues like the wrappee's nose, belly button, spine, gap between the legs, and side seams on an upper garment as guides, or, if you prefer, use a weighted string to establish a true vertical.

5. To establish the waistline, wrap elastic around the waist and position it exactly as desired by the wrappee, then trace the elastic line onto the duct tape with a permanent marker.

6. Remove the hip mold by cutting through the cotton ribbing exactly along the center of the center-back tape line.

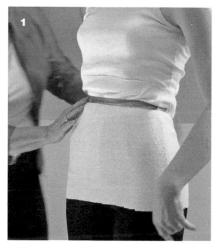

Apply a narrow piece of tape snugly around the waist.

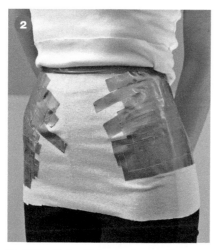

Cover the hips with tape, using smaller, narrower pieces to contour and shape the mold over the high hip.

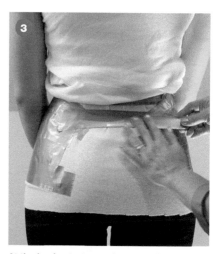

At the back, start near the top and work down to the hipline.

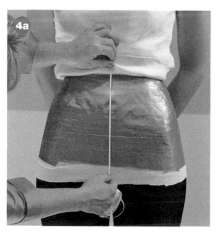

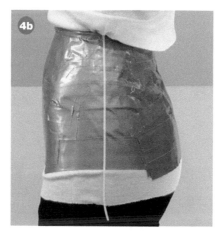

Apply pinstriping tape to mark the center front, center back, and side seam lines.

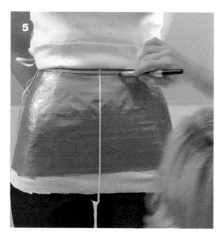

Mark the waistline with elastic, then trace it with permanent marker onto the tape.

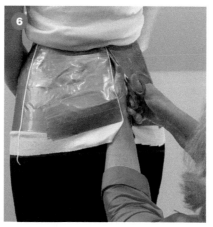

Cut through the cotton ribbing at the center back to remove the mold.

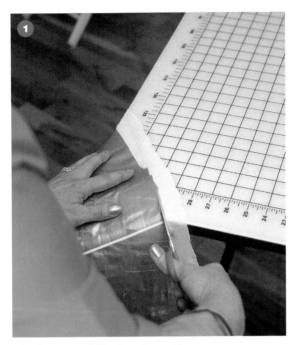

Trim the excess ribbing from the mold.

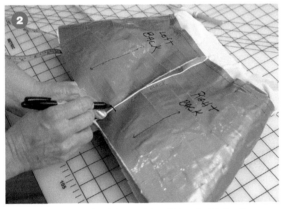

Label the four panels of the mold and the pinstriping lines; add grainlines and alignment marks.

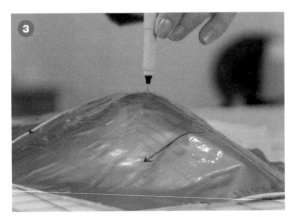

Mark the apex of each panel; these will become dart points.

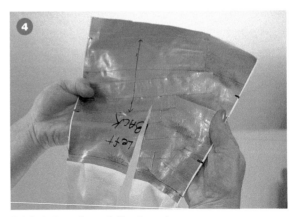

Cut darts from the waistline to each apex.

Cutting Darts in the Mold

If the wrappee's figure is symmetrical, you need to convert only one side of the mold to a darted sloper; save the second half to make a yoked sloper variation. But if the figure is asymmetrical, make a darted sloper for each side.

1. Supporting the hip mold on the end of a table or over your hand, trim away the excess ribbing and smooth out the waistline and hiplines.

2. Label each of the four panels of the mold (right front, and so on) and also label each line on both sides (side seam, and so on). Add grainlines by measuring about 3 in. from each center line and drawing a parallel line. Draw alignment marks across each vertical taped marking line (these will become notches on your pattern), then cut the four panels apart exactly through the center of each line.

3. Emphasize the shaping of each panel by pushing out its center. Find the apex of each panel by placing it tape side up on the table and looking at it from the side. Mark the apex, which will become the dart point.

4. Cut an on-grain dart by slashing vertically from the waistline to the marked apex. If a single slash doesn't allow the panel to lie flat, cut a second, parallel dart slash within about 2 in. of the first, on whichever side seems to have the most remaining shape. If you make a mistake, cover it with more tape and recut.

Adding Ease

For fitted skirts and pants in fabrics without stretch, you'll need to add ease, and you'll want to fine-tune the amount you need with a test skirt made up in a fabric similar to what you'll want to eventually wear. You can start by adding ¼ in. equally from waist to hipline at each hip mold side seam, for a total of 1 in. of ease, which works well with many typical, sturdy skirt fabrics, but the actual amount can vary considerably with different types of fabric. Whenever working with an unfamiliar fabric, cut 1-in.-wide seam allowances at the sides and baste the side seams so you can try on the skirt and adjust the fit. For future skirt patterns, you might want to trace your sloper onto cardboard or tagboard, add ease, and cut it out, so you'll have a properly sized template that can be traced onto commercial patterns.

Creating a Waistline Pattern

As another benefit, since you need only half a complete hip mold to create your darted sloper, you can cut the other half apart horizontally to develop a customized waist yoke or contoured waistband, as shown in the sidebar at right. You can draw in any style of yoke or band you like. Once you get the hang of this easy and intuitive method for taking a mold from any shape, try taping a basic pattern of any hard-to-fit body area.

Using the Sloper to Create Contoured Waistbands

Yokes and contoured waistbands are easy to create from a duct-tape hip mold. Just cut the mold horizontally across the front dart point. Fold out the darts in the yoke section. If the block doesn't lie flat below the yoke or section, slash mini darts into the skirt pieces.

TIP If the figure you are fitting is symmetrical, convert only one side of the mold to a sloper. If the figure is asymmetrical, make a darted sloper for each side.

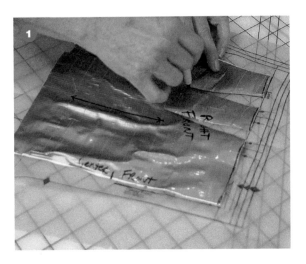

You can use the flattened hip mold to trace a permanent pattern template.

Template pattern traced from the hip mold

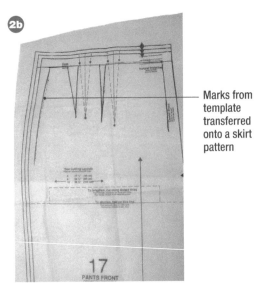

Marks from template transferred onto a skirt pattern

Using the Mold

One front and one back panel of your flattened hip mold makes a sloper that can be used as is to customize patterns for stretch skirts that require no ease. To add ease to your sloper, simply add ¼ in. to each side seam, then cut out your pattern with 1-in.-wide seam allowances and baste it together and check the fit. Choose a pattern that's bigger than but as close to the width of your sloper (with or without ease) as possible. Remember that most patterns are marked only with cutting lines; you must measure in to find the seamlines. For future use, trace a permanent template from your hip mold.

1. Align the sloper panels to the pattern you want to alter at the center front or center back verticals and the waistline at these lines.

2. Trace the corresponding sloper outlines onto the front and back pattern pieces (**2a**). Then, if necessary, adjust the lower portion of each pattern so that its hipline aligns with the sloper panel hipline. Blend or redraw the side seam so it continues from the sloper onto the pattern (**2b**). Note that for the skirt pattern shown here, you need to add seam allowances at the waistline corner and side seams and mark new cutting lines where necessary.

Measuring the Abdomen

Accurately measured waistlines and hiplines are essential for fitting the abdomen.

FIND AND DECLARE THE WAISTLINE

Tie a length of ¼-in.-wide elastic snugly around your bare midsection. Wear it for five minutes of regular activity to "find" your waist.

The elastic will settle into position according to the shape of your midsection.

If the elastic rolls below the traditional waistline, lift it to a more flattering position to establish your declared waistline.

FIND AND DECLARE THE HIPLINE

Mark the widest body measurement below your waistline with a length of nonstretching seam binding that is kept parallel to the floor. This is your hipline. It can range from 2 in. to more than 10 in. below your waist.

Measure the hipline circumference.

Measure the vertical distance between the waist and hipline at the center front, center back, and side seams. Record your measurements to use for altering your patterns.

Fitting a Skirt

To fit a skirt, buy a pattern size closest to your declared hipline circumference and fit it over the abdomen to your declared waistline.

MARK THE NEW WAIST

Before cutting out your pattern, mark a new waist on the tissue.

MARK NEW WAIST

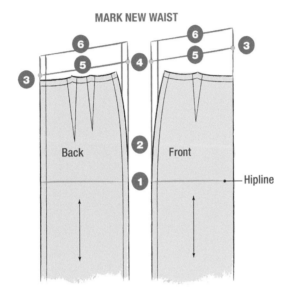

Back

Front

Hipline

SOLVE WRINKLES

ESTABLISH CONTOUR

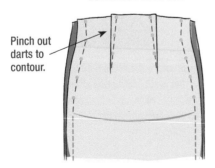

Pinch out darts to contour.

1. Draw the hipline perpendicular to the grainline at the hip mark on the front and back pattern pieces.

2. Draw a new side seam straight up from and perpendicular to the hipline.

3. Measure up from the hipline on the center front and center back to correspond to your center lengths (see "Measuring the Abdomen," p. 109), and mark the pattern.

4. Measure up from the hipline at the side seams, and make a second mark.

5. Connect these two marks.

6. Draw a line 2 in. above that line. Follow this line when you cut your pattern and fabric.

SOLVING WRINKLES

Sew or baste the vertical seams, leaving an opening for the zipper. Try the skirt on, and pin the zipper opening closed. Use your elastic to hold the skirt up. Proceed to fit:

1. Tuck the extra waist fabric under the elastic.

2. Smooth the fabric up from the hipline and out toward the seams and waist.

3. Keep the side seams perpendicular to the floor, and pin them accordingly.

You may have to open the side seams above the hipline to redistribute the fabric properly. It's possible to have more fabric in the seam allowances of the skirt back than the front.

ESTABLISH CONTOUR

It's not enough to alter the distance between the hip and waist or expand the waist circumference of a pattern. To make the fabric contour smoothly to the body, you may need to pinch out evenly spaced darts until the wrinkles disappear and the fabric follows your shape. The original pattern darts may change or disappear altogether. Darts, however, add a flattering design detail and create an illusion of a narrower waist. If the fitting eliminates the darts, consider using a pin tuck sewn to the inside of the garment as a faux dart. When you're satisfied with the fit, mark the new seams, darts, and waistline, and make the changes on the pattern.

Fitting Pants

These alteration options are the easiest because the full-abdomen corrections are made above the hipline and crotch curve using the skirt pattern you fit on the facing page.

USE YOUR SKIRT PATTERN

Position your custom skirt pattern under your new pants pattern, align the hiplines and center front and trace off the properly fit section.

CUT AND SPREAD THE PATTERN

You can work flat and expand your pattern to your measurements as illustrated in bottom drawing at right.

ADAPT A PULL-ON PANTS PATTERN

Elastic- or drawstring-waist pants patterns, known as pull-on pants, provide an easy-fitting option because the waist is the same circumference as the hip. This pants style won't bunch around the full waist as it does on hourglass-shaped bodies. Adapt a pull-on pants pattern with a standard waistband or a faux waistband just across the front. With minor pattern adjustments, you can also fit pull-on pants with a zipper and faced waistline.

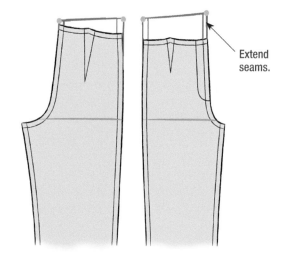

Use your custom-fit skirt pattern to fix the waistline on a pants pattern.

Extend seams.

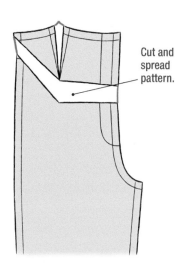

Cut and spread pattern.

You can also solve a pant-fitting problem by cutting and spreading the pattern to fit your abdomen or custom-fit skirt pattern.

Fast Fix for Ready-to-Wear Pants

Buy pants that fit at the waist, then take in the hips and narrow the legs at the side seams. This alteration can interfere with some pockets, but it usually occurs below trouser pockets.

If the pants come with a matching jacket that also needs altering, find extra fabric by converting a double-breasted style to a single-breasted style by moving the buttons. This works in ready-to-wear and on patterns.

TIP Fitting the abdomen from the hipline up is like making a bed. Just align the hiplines on your body, and smooth the wrinkles of your pattern or fabric up and out into the waistband and the side seams.

Adjustable Fit with a Two-Piece Waistband

If you find that pants are difficult to fit through the waist—even when you use a pattern that has worked for you before—this method of reengineering your trousers waistline will make fitting much easier. It calls for a waistband that's installed in two sections, with a seam at the center back.

Start with a pattern that fits well but might need a little fine-tuning at the waist. By using a two-piece waistband, and changing the construction of the pants slightly, you can fit the waistline perfectly when the rest of the pants are nearly complete. You won't need to remove and resew the waistband repeatedly to improve the fit.

This solution is an adaptation of the standard man's trouser waistband. You'll add up to $1\frac{5}{8}$ in. to the new center-back waistband seam allowance and widen the allowance on the back pants seam to match. You'll also need to change the standard construction sequence to sew the center-back waistband seam last. This enables you to try on the almost-completed garment and tweak the fit through the waist and hips by simply adjusting the back seam. This approach works on pants with fly fronts, with side zippers, or with side-front, inside-the-pocket zippers.

Adjusting the Pattern

Before you start adapting a pants pattern, make sure it fits well, and that the waistband equals the body's waist measurement plus 1 in. for ease, plus seam allowances and the closure overlap (if the waistband calls for one).

1. Cut the waistband at center back, and add a $1\frac{5}{8}$-in. seam allowance to both pieces.

2. Add 1 in. to center back at the waist, blending to $\frac{5}{8}$ in. at the crotch curve.

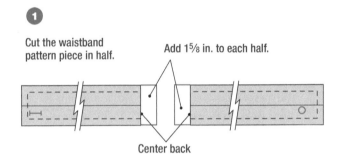

1

Cut the waistband pattern piece in half.

Add $1\frac{5}{8}$ in. to each half.

Center back

2

Center back

Add 1 in. to center back at waist, blending down to $\frac{5}{8}$ in. at crotch.

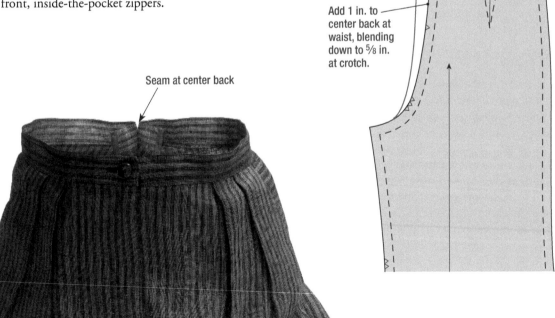

Seam at center back

Sewing the Pants

Sewing the pants really couldn't be easier. You pretty much sew everything by standard plan; the point of departure happens at the crotch, which you sew partially before attaching and finishing the two pieces of the waistband.

1. Sew the crotch seam from front to back, stopping 3 in. beyond the inseam. Attach the right and left waistbands and finish, including closures (a). Pin or machine-baste the center-back seam, matching waistline seams at center back. Try the pants on, and readjust if necessary.

2. Sew the center-back seam when you're satisfied with the fit. If you want to leave a V-notch at the top of the waistband for extra wearing ease, stop the seam ½ in. to ¾ in. below the top of the waistband. Trim the seam allowances as little as possible, leaving them up to 1¼ in. wide at the waistband, and tapering to ⅜ in. at the crotch curve. After you trim the seam slightly, the center-back seam isn't bulky or noticeable when worn.

3. Finish the seam allowances with rayon seam binding. Cut two pieces of binding, each 1½ in. longer than distance from the center-back top of the waistband to the bottom of the zipper. Dampen the binding, then fold it lengthwise, leaving 1/16 in. extending on one side; press. Encase the raw edge of the center-back seam allowances in the folded binding, placing the wider portion of the binding on the wrong side of the fabric; leave ½ in. excess at the top (a). Stitch the binding in place. At the zipper, turn under the excess binding, trim it to ⅛ in., and stitch to the end. Turn under the top of the center-back seam allowance, including the excess binding, and whipstitch it to the wrong side of the waistband (b).

Then, all you have to do is hem the legs, and you're ready to enjoy a comfortable, well-fitting garment. You can also quickly and easily readjust the center-back seam to accommodate any future minor body changes.

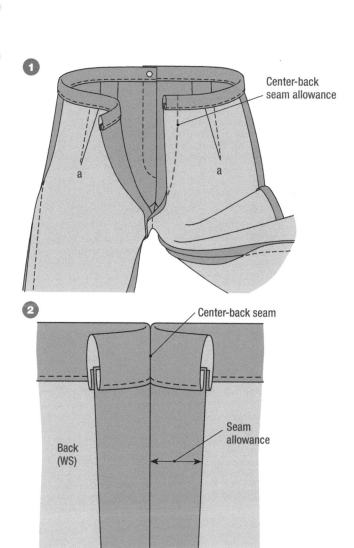

Center-back seam allowance

Center-back seam

Seam allowance

Back (WS)

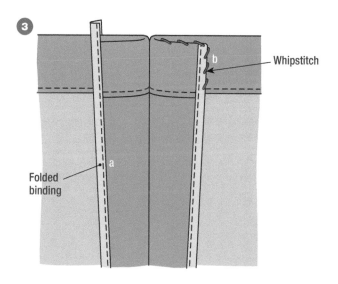

Whipstitch

Folded binding

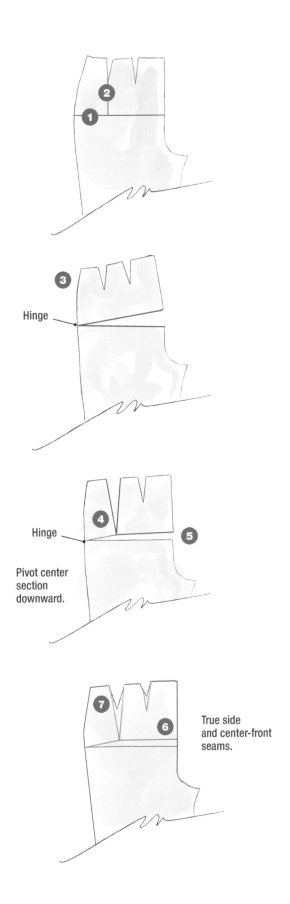

Hinge

Hinge

Pivot center
section
downward.

True side
and center-front
seams.

Fitting a Fuller Abdomen

Pants and skirts can be made to fit a fuller abdomen in a number of ways: by altering the material, changing the waistband, or suspending the waistline.

Slash-and-Pivot Method

With this method, you can make pant and skirt fronts fuller without enlarging the seat and legs.

1. Draw a line perpendicular to the grainline across the tummy on your pattern. Place it at the abdomen's fullest point.

2. Draw a vertical line from the waistline edge where the tummy fullness begins to dissipate down to line 1. You could also run it through an existing dart.

3. Cut from the center-front seam to the side seam. Leave a little hinge of tissue paper for pivoting at the side seam, and lift the upper section of the pattern.

4. Slash through the dart. Cut the vertical line to the tummy line, leaving a second hinge where they meet, as shown.

5. Pivot the center section downward so the horizontal cut edges are parallel from the second dart to the center front. The best way to find out how much to spread the pattern is to make a muslin so you know how the original pattern fits you. This will tell you how much you need to add in width and length over the abdomen.

6. True the side and center-front seams. This pattern-work was done to the front only. You need not do anything to the back. Although the shaping of the side seam has changed, the length of the seam has not; it will fit nicely onto the back side seam.

7. Fit the top of the pants or skirt to your own waistline with custom-pinned darts. Make darts for this figure shorter so they don't extend into the tummy region. You don't want to take away the room that you just created. You may use multiple smaller darts or a simple elastic casing.

Waistband Alternatives

If you have trouble wearing traditional waistbands, here are three creative ways to fix the ring around your middle.

Use a Narrower Elastic

Use 1½-in.- to 2-in.-wide elastic as a facing for a smoother, more modern look (see the top drawing at right). This is also more comfortable because the elastic sits over the curve of the tummy and not at the waist.

- Find a smooth elastic that feels comfortable against your skin.

- Wrap the elastic around your middle so it is comfortably snug. Overlap the ends, and secure them with machine stitching.

- Section the elastic evenly. Align one edge right side up to the right-side-up pants or skirt top seamline, and pin.

- Machine-stitch. Stretch the elastic as you sew.

- Turn the elastic to the inside of the garment. Tack it to the seams.

Use a Fabric Band

A wide, stretchy fabric band hugs the front and back along the tummy and upper hip (see the center drawing at right). Pick a band that has a firm stretch and a fiber content that includes 10 to 15 percent spandex.

- On your pattern or ready-made garment, measure and mark a line 5 in. below the waistline on the front and back pieces. Remove this upper section.

- Cut ⅓ yd. of stretch fabric on the cross-grain. Fold it to a finished height of 6 in. To determine how much circumference to cut, wrap the stretch fabric around your middle—or measure your pants at the 5-in. mark—and cut a width that is 85 to 90 percent of the circumference.

- Sew the stretch fabric into a tube by joining the short ends with right sides together. Fold it into a 6-in.-wide finished piece. Divide and mark the tube and the garment waistline into four equal sections. With right sides together, pin the tube to

the garment. Match the tube seam with the pants' center-back or side seam. Machine-stitch the tube in place, using a long straight stitch and stretching the tube to fit the pants as you sew. Wear the band up as a soft yoke, or wear it turned down a little below the waist. You decide which is more comfortable for you.

Add a Stretch Panel

You can add a stretch panel over the tummy, either at the pattern stage, or by altering ready-made pants with a matching-color fabric (see the bottom drawing below). There are many stretch fabrics that work for this. Look for a single or double knit with spandex.

- Add a horizontal seamline on the pattern just under the tummy. This makes the panel pattern. Allow for seam allowances at the line and a foldover for elastic casing at the waist edge.

- Cut the knit panel to fit snugly—but not tightly—over the tummy. Or, cut a longer stretch fabric to allow for double thickness over the tummy. Sew the panel to the pants front and assemble as usual.

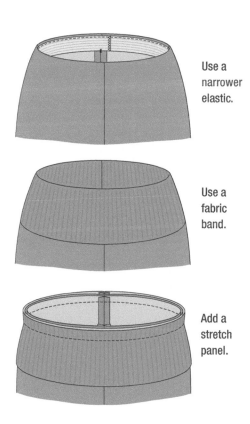

Use a narrower elastic.

Use a fabric band.

Add a stretch panel.

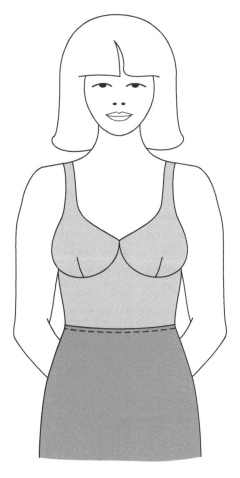

Attach a skirt to a slip to suspend it.

Suspending Pants and Skirts

Some folks cannot have anything press against their tummies, so keeping their pants and skirts up is a real challenge. Hidden accessories can be the answer for those with chronic conditions that make close-fitting waistlines uncomfortable. Remove the darts and the waistband altogether, and try the following solutions.

Use a Slip

Attach the lower section of a skirt to a full slip. Because the skirt hangs from your shoulders, the problem of tipping hems is removed. And, because the skirt does not have to go around the fullness of the tummy, you can wear a pencil skirt that looks like a pencil skirt. Just make sure the hem of the jacket or blouse you're wearing extends at least 2 in. past the seam that joins the slip to the skirt. Use a slip from your own lingerie drawer, or make a simple pullover slip using nylon tricot.

- Put on the slip. Have a sewing buddy draw a line with disappearing ink or chalk around your slip that sits below the fullness of your tummy and runs parallel to the floor.

- Decide the skirt length needed from the chalkline to the hem. Then measure and mark the skirt evenly from the hem up to this distance, and add a seam allowance.

- Attach the skirt to the slip with pins. Make sure the skirt hangs properly. Then hand- or machine-stitch it in place.

 TIP If your shoulders are narrow, or if you work sitting at a desk, suspenders can move and slide onto your upper arms. Prevent this by criss-crossing the suspenders at the back.

Use Suspenders

Most people with round tummies wear their tops untucked over the top of their pants and skirts. Consider wearing a pair of suspenders hidden underneath your top. Suspenders allow you to have a loose fit at the waist. With this tummy-fitting solution, you can choose to remove the waistband, not sew any darts, and finish the pant or skirt waistline with a simple facing. Lingerie elastic has a smooth, silky finish and is comfortable to wear against the skin, so it makes good suspenders.

- Measure the strap. To measure how long the lingerie elastic must be, drape a measuring tape from your back waist diagonally across your back, over your shoulder, and straight down to your waist. Allow for a 2-in. turnover of elastic at each end.

- Sew a simple, flat button to each of the finished ends on the suspenders. Create four buttonholes along the waist edge of your pants or skirt. Fasten the suspenders to the garment through the button-holes.

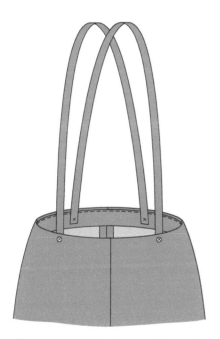

Use suspenders to hold up a skirt or pants.

Tummy-Control Panel for Pants and Skirt

You can easily add a control panel to existing pants or skirts. Just trace the outline of the garment front from the waistline to the desired length of the control panel and from side seam to side seam. Be sure to allow a waistline seam allowance, but make the panel slightly narrower (read on for the specifics) at the side seams so it holds firmly over the body.

To allow for maneuvering, open the front of the waistband on the inside slightly beyond the side seams. Baste the panel to the side seams, and tuck the top seam allowance into the waistband. Try on the garment, and adjust if necessary. Then sew the panel to the side seams, and close the waistband. There's no need to finish the panel's bottom edge unless you're using woven fabric, which can be serged to prevent raveling.

Depending on how much control you need, make the panel from a firmly woven cotton-blend fabric (which has little or no give), a spandex blend, a swimsuit fabric, or a four-way stretch fabric, sometimes called power knit or power net.

You can draft a control panel for your favorite pattern, too. For pants that have a back or side zipper, make the control panel from side seam to side seam. Pin out the darts or pleats on the front pattern piece. Draw around the pattern top edge and down the side seam to the fullest part of the hips. Then cut off ½ in. on each side seam. Baste it in place along the side and upper edges of the pants front after you've sewn and pressed the darts and center-front seam.

If the pattern has a front zipper, simply cut two sections from side seam to center front. Baste the panel to the center-front seam, sew in the zipper, and then baste the panel in place at the top and sides. This prevents the zipper area from pulling toward the back and distorting.

Fitting High Hips or a Swayback

A high-hip curve and a swayback are commonly confused figure variations, because they can exhibit a similar symptom: excess fabric at the back waist. If you have a high-hip curve, this problem occurs on both pants and skirts. In contrast, a swayback causes different problems on pants and skirts.

High-Hip Curves

Most patterns are designed to accommodate the full-hip circumference about 7 in. to 8 in. below the waist. In reality, it may be as little as 1 in. or as much as 10 in. below the waist. A high-hip curve is

HIGH HIP

Hip fullness near the waistline creates waistline wrinkles at the side and side back on skirts, and drag lines from hip to crotch on pants.

Back   Front

ALTERATIONS FOR A HIGH HIP

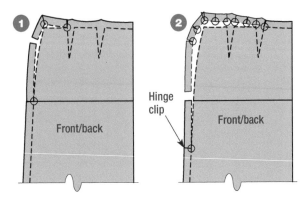

Front/back   Hinge clip   Front/back

generally positioned 2 in. to 4 in. below the waist, with obvious weight deposited just in back of where a garment side seam would be. A high-hip curve often comes in combination with a large abdomen and a flat bottom. A low-hip curve is generally 8 in. to 10 in. below the waist, with weight deposited just opposite crotch level on the side thighs, where a garment side seam would lie, and slightly behind. Some figure types have both high- and low-hip curves, sometimes smoothly curved between, sometimes with a slight indentation between the two curves.

A high-hip curve generally requires both added length and added width: length to go over the curve and width to go around. This repositions the hip curve on the pattern to accommodate the fuller circumference at a higher level. Garment styles can reduce or eliminate the need for alteration for a high-hip curve, depending on the size of the curve. Darts are difficult to fit over a high-hip curve and may be better converted to tiny, straight-hanging gathers, unpressed pleats, flare, or added fullness controlled by elastic. You can also keep the waistband flat in front and eased by elastic across the back or just above the high-hip curve itself. You can also combine flare with gathers or elastic.

To correct for a high hip, place the pants front and back patterns over tissue paper. Alter the front and back equally at the side.

1. Release the side seam allowance front and back by cutting just inside the seamline from the measured hipline to the waist and at the waist from side seam at least to the outer dart. Clip to, not through, the seamlines. You may need to release and raise more of the waistline seam allowance on the front or back for tummy fullness and/or very high hips.

2. Clip across the side seam allowances, and hinge-clip (clipping to, not through, seamlines) at the start and end of the alteration, the side/waist corner, and along the side seam allowances. Pivot the released seams the measured increase needed, and tape the pieces to hold. Convert darts to gathers or elastic (recommended).

Swayback

A swayback occurs when the pelvis is habitually held at an angle, top tilting forward and tailbone tilting back. This results in protruding buttocks and a more indented than usual groin, an increased distance between the fullest part of the buttocks and the inseam or body center, and a reduced distance between hipline and waist at center back just the opposite of the increased length and width at the side seam caused by the high hip.

Pants with a fitted crotch curve will respond quite differently to a swayback than will skirts. On skirts, the fabric will roll or wrinkle at the back waistline, usually without distorting the hip-fitting line, due to reduced center-back length on the figure. You may not see this roll on pants because the increased crotch length can pull it down. When extreme, this variation can even pull the waistband and hip-fitting line down at center back. The skirt requires less length at the back waistline, and the pants require a wider back inseam for increased crotch length. The pants might also need to be lowered at the back waist, like the skirt. This will be obvious if the waist-line roll appears after correcting the inseam. Loose-fitting styles in both pants and skirts may reduce or eliminate the need for alterations to accommodate a swayback.

To correct for a swayback, place the pants or skirt front and back patterns on tissue paper, so you can tape shifted seam allowances in place after altering.

Altering a Skirt for Swayback

Adjust only the skirt back.

1. The waistline seam allowance and darts, hinge-clipping at the waist/side-seam corner and at darts.

2. The released seam and darts, lowering the waist at center back by the measured amount and blending back to the hinge at the side seam. Check or restore dart lengths and positions.

Altering Pants for Swayback

Again, adjust only the back.

1. The waistline seam allowance and the darts, hinge-clipping at the waist/side-seam corner and at darts, then around the crotch curve and down the inseam about halfway to the knee, hinge-clipping at the corners.

2. The crotch curve by the measured amount, allowing the waist and dart to overlap the pants, lowering the waistline, shifting the center-back seam, and slightly spreading the dart. (Although it doesn't show in the drawing and may be equally slight with your pattern, both sides of the dart are cut free and will move when the crotch curve is shifted.) Notice that all seam lengths have remained unchanged, even though they have been repositioned.

SWAYBACK

A tilted pelvis creates center-back wrinkles on skirts and drag lines from crotch to side seams on pants. The pants' waistline may also wrinkle or tilt downward at center back.

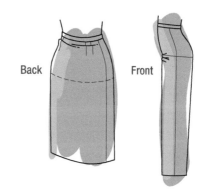

Back   Front

ALTERATIONS FOR A SWAYBACK

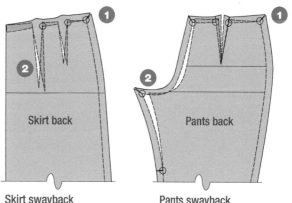

Skirt back   Pants back

Skirt swayback   Pants swayback

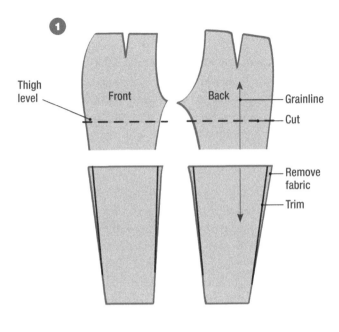

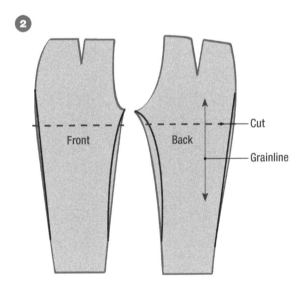

Fitting Wide Hips and Slender Legs

A figure with wider hips doesn't necessarily also have wide legs, and sometimes it's desirable to create a more slender silhouette by tapering pant legs to a narrower size. At first glance, it might seem logical to simply redraw the side seams and inseams to make pants conform to thinner legs, but there's more going on here than a simple change in circumference. At the hips, the body is curving in two directions at once, around the legs and over the seat (and depending on the figure, over the tummy), and the fabric that fits these multiple contours needs to bend similarly. Simply narrowing the thigh area won't help the fabric make a smooth transition from the three-dimensional curves of a wider torso area to a slender leg.

To bend in more than one direction at the same time without producing wrinkles, fabric needs to be darted; this is why there are waistline darts on pants. (Similarly, bust darts on blouses and jackets allow fabric to curve both around the upper body and over the bust.) The more we ask our pants fabric to bend—as the difference between the larger area and the smaller one increases—the bigger the corresponding dart needs to be. In other words, you need to narrow the leg width in such a way that also widens the hip darts. Once this is done, the fabric will make the transition smoothly to your relatively small thigh.

1. Start with a pattern that fits your hips. Cut both the front and back pattern pieces at the thigh level (about 3 in. to 5 in. below the crotchline), so you've got leg and torso sections.

2. Redraw the inseam and side seam equally to fit your thigh and remove excess from the pattern.

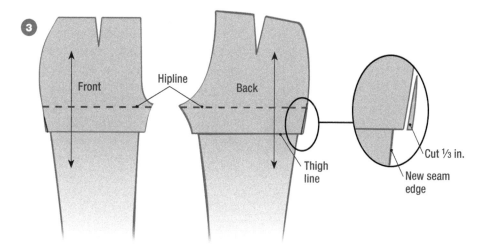

3. To make the torso sections fit the new leg sections, work as follows: Match the grainline arrows on each section, and realign each torso with the corresponding leg. Then mark the new side seam position from the leg onto the torso section. Measure the distance from the mark to the original side seam. Remove one-third of the seam allowance by redrawing the side seam from the thigh to the hip.

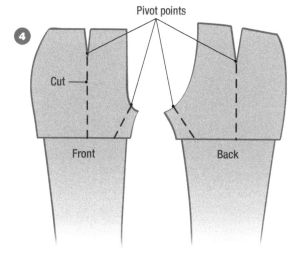

4. Slash the torso sections where indicated by the dashed lines, leaving a paper hinge at each marked pivot point.

5. Pivot each torso pattern, overlapping the edges of each slash, until the lower edge of the torso is the same width as the top of its corresponding leg section. You'll notice how this causes the dart at the waist to widen and also flattens the crotch curve. If necessary, correct the grainline by extending the line on each leg section onto the torso.

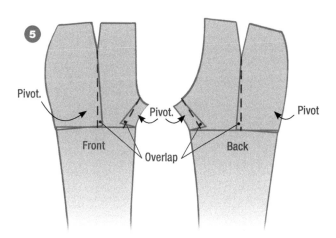

The Pants Pattern

Working with a muslin is one way to develop a well-fitting pants pattern.

Prepare the Muslin

Start with a basic slacks pattern you've made before. In any areas that felt snug when you was last made the pattern, shift the seamlines outward so the muslin version of the pattern will be a little loose all over,

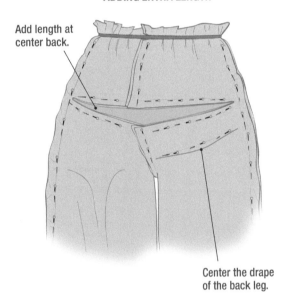

ADDING EXTRA LENGTH

Add length at center back.

Center the drape of the back leg.

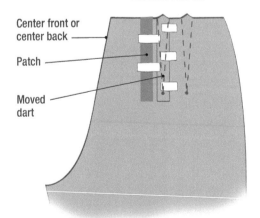

MOVING A DART

Center front or center back

Patch

Moved dart

and add an extra inch or more of seam allowance above the waistline. It's better to start a little bigger because it's easier to pin out extra room than to slash and patch an area that's too small. You can also start with a bigger size than you'd typically use, and extend the waistline seam allowance. If your pattern requires a front pocket piece to create a complete side seam, be sure to tape the pocket piece in place on the pattern before you cut, so your muslin will have a full side seam.

Add or Subtract Length

Some figures require the addition of extra length in back. You'll know you're in this camp if your waistline always pulls down into a V in back, even when you're standing up. Muslins for these figures have to be slashed and patched as part of the pin-fitting process. Slash the muslin from side seam to side seam, spread it to provide the needed length, and fill the gap with scrap muslin. (Then, if the legs are droopy, pin out the excess length with a horizontal dart at the top of the thigh.)

Reposition Darts

Before you cut anything out, check the distance from the center front and center back to the nearest edge of the first or center dart. This should be around 3½ in. on a size 6, 4 in. on a size 8 to 12, and 4½ in. on a size 18 or larger, and you should move the center darts if they're not within this range. There are no rules governing the placement of the side dart; it's a visual decision. To move a dart, simply cut out a narrow rectangle containing the entire dart and shift the cutout as needed, keeping the waistline aligned. Tape it in place along with some scrap paper to fill in the hole it left. This placement is important for establishing the grain on your draped muslin, and it's universally flattering, as well as being a ready-to-wear standard. If there are two darts on the front or back pattern pieces, it isn't necessary to shift the outside one unless you think it will look better.

Cut Out Pattern

Cut out your pattern in any medium-weight to lightweight fabric (avoid stripes or checks; they distract your eye), and sew it with the side and center seam allowances and the darts to the outside so you'll be able to adjust them easily. Leave the opening at the center back. The additional steps to fit the muslin are demonstrated in "How to Fit a Pants Muslin" on pp. 124–125. You'll simply look at the wrinkles and test the wearing comfort to know where to adjust your pattern. It's only necessary to fully pin one side of the figure, unless the two sides are noticeably different.

Using the Muslin

When you're completely happy with the fit of your muslin, take it off and carefully mark the corrected seamlines on it, then take it apart without undoing the horizontal darts created in the pin-fitting process or removing any inserted patches. As long as both sides of your fitted muslin are the same, you can apply all the following steps to the front and back pieces of a single leg.

- Trim each seam allowance to a uniform distance from its seamline—⅝ in. is a good choice if you'll be using the muslin to correct a lot of commercial patterns.

- Draw a grainline/crease line perpendicular to the hemline from the bottom edge to the tip of each waist dart; use the inside one if either piece has two darts.

- Compare your corrected waistline seam length with the original pattern and add or subtract length from the original waistband pattern by the same amount.

Your muslin is now a corrected version of the pattern you started with, and you can cut from it directly, or trace it first onto paper or card stock. If you want to make basic darted slacks with different leg widths or pocket details, transfer these details onto a tracing of your corrected pattern, preserving the shape and darts from the crotch level up. The only dimension that may need tweaking is the circumference, so it's a good idea to cut an extra ¼-in. seam allowance width at the side seams and pin-fit these when you're working in an unfamiliar fabric.

Correcting a Pattern with the Muslin

Use the muslin to correct patterns with different dart styling or dart alternatives at the waist, including pleats or yokes.

- Pin out the darts on your muslin piece.

- Fold out or pin together the new pattern's darts or equivalent details (and include any pocket details needed to provide a complete side seam).

- Place each pinned muslin piece on top of the corresponding pattern piece with the crotch level and inseams near the crotch aligned.

- Trace the muslin's outline onto the paper pattern above the hipline, including the center seams, waistline, and side seams.

- This ensures that no matter what details provide dart shaping at the waist on the new pattern, when they're constructed, the fit of the pants above the hips will be essentially the same as on your muslin.

**USING A MUSLIN
TO CORRECT A PATTERN**

Align crotch level and inseams near crotch of pattern and muslin.

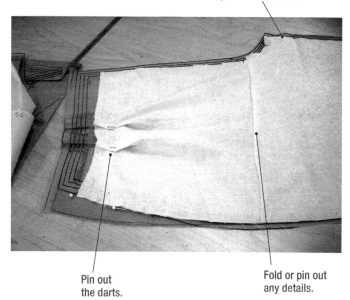

Pin out the darts.

Fold or pin out any details.

How to Fit a Pants Muslin

A. EVALUATE THE FIT
AND POSITION OF THE WAISTLINE

From front or back, the crotch on these pants is too long, the legs are too loose, and the back legs are drooping. The wearer should pull up or down on the waistline to position the crotch depth comfortably.

Adjust the waist level and upper side seams on both sides to secure the preferred position. On this model, the center back seam is a little long; it will be corrected later. However, if the back seam is too short (causing the back waist to pull down in a V), that correction should be made now, as shown in the top drawing on p. 122.

B. ADJUST THE LEG
AND CHECK THE SITTING COMFORT

Pin the side seam to correct the hip and leg circumference as needed. Pin to the hem on one side only, folding up the hem to allow the fabric to drape smoothly to the foot. Pin the opposite side seam to match from the waist to at least the midthigh so the seated comfort can be evaluated. Sit down to check the fit, then readjust the waist or legs if needed.

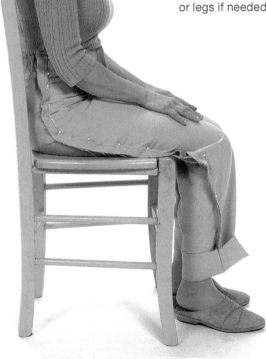

C. ADJUST THE LEG DRAPE AND DART LENGTHS

To smooth the wrinkles in back, pinch the center-back seam horizontally, level with the fullest part of the rear, creating a dart that tapers to nothing at the side seams. Pinch out as much as is needed to create a smooth fall from this dart to the hem. Pin the dart from the center to both side seams. Check the vertical darts to see that they end near the apex of the contours they fit, pinning or releasing them as needed. Most darts are too short. Repeat these steps in front if necessary.

D. CHECK AND ADJUST THE CROTCH CURVE IN BACK

Wrinkles from excess room below the crotch curve in back are a common problem, as shown at right. Correct this by pinning the center-back seamline closer to the body below the horizontal dart until the wrinkles smooth out. The same problem can occur in front.

E. MARK THE WAISTLINE AND EVALUATE THE RESULTS

Tie a narrow elastic around the waist and position it at the preferred waistline, then trace it with a marker to create a final waist seamline. Evaluate the drape of the fully pinned leg from front and back and tweak your pins as needed. Finally, it's a good idea to take off the tweaked pants and stitch each pinned alteration, so you can remove the pins and test the fit with freedom to move, sit, and stretch.

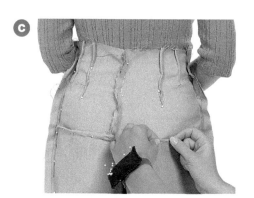

Fitting a Full Seat

The fundamental problem with fitting a full seat isn't the hip/derrière measurement, but the difference between the hip and waist circumference. The more prominent the seat, the more fabric you need to cover it. Accommodating the derrière is a matter of increasing both the pants width and the length between the crotch point and the waistline. With these adjustments, you'll make comfortable, flattering pants every time.

MEASURE YOUR BODY

Take measurements of the areas on your body indicated by red lines in the "Measurement Comparison" chart below. You will adjust only the back pattern piece, so take the measurements around the back only from side seam to side seam. Copy the chart and write the measurements in the "Body" column.

MEASURE THE PATTERN

If the pattern doesn't include seamlines, add them inside the cutting lines. Next, draw the lines shown on the pattern in the right drawing below. Then, measure the pattern along those lines, omitting the seam allowances, and write down the measurements in the chart in the "Pattern" column.

To fit the pants back pattern, follow the step-by-step instructions on the facing page.

FIT THE WAIST

Once you've added the extra fabric for a full derrière, you need to refine the fit for your narrow waist and adjust the waistband.

- Custom-fit the darts. Don't stitch the darts until the side, front, and back seams are in place.

- Put on the pants and pin the darts to fit. You may wish to reposition and lengthen them. If you need to take up a lot of width at the waist, increase the number of darts to two or three per side. This creates a smoother transition from the full derrière to the waistline.

- Adjust the waist treatment. If necessary, redraft the waistline or waist facing to reflect the changes you've made by fitting the darts.

MEASURING YOURSELF

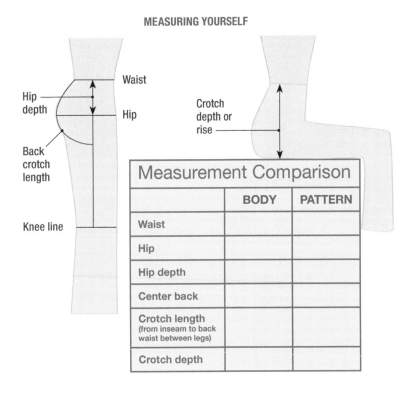

Measurement Comparison		
	BODY	**PATTERN**
Waist		
Hip		
Hip depth		
Center back		
Crotch length (from inseam to back waist between legs)		
Crotch depth		

MEASURING YOUR PATTERN

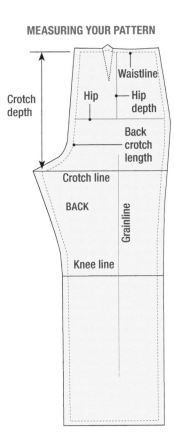

Altering a Pattern for a Full Seat

In the method shown here, the pattern is cut into pieces and "stretched" to add length and width where it's needed. Add all of the length but only half of the width since you cut two back pattern pieces from the altered pattern. The width is added to the hip, and the length is added to the center-back seam and crotch curve. All the corrections are made to the back pattern only.

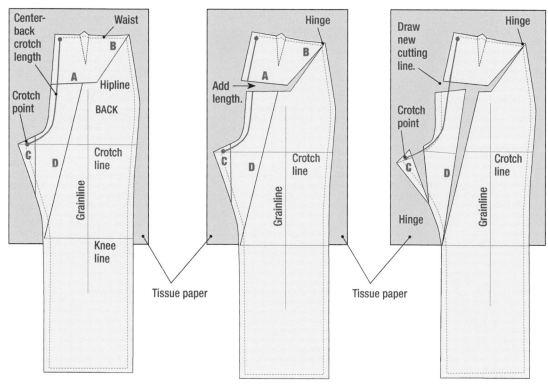

STEP 1
Mark cutting lines. Follow the diagram above to draw slash lines on the pattern. You don't have to measure—just place the lines approximately where the width and length are needed most. Label the lines as shown. Slide a sheet of tissue paper under the pattern.

STEP 2
Lengthen the center-back seam. Cut along line A and diagonally along line B. Leave a paper hinge at the waist seamline. Spread the pattern vertically, as shown, to increase the center-back crotch length (CBCL). Subtract the pattern CBCL from your personal CBCL. You will add 1 in. to 1½ in. to the crotch point in step 3. Add the remaining length at line A. Tape the top section of the pattern to the tissue paper.

STEP 3
Extend the crotch point and widen the hip area. Cut lines C and D, and leave a paper hinge at the inseam seam allowance. Spread line D toward the inseam to create half the desired back-hip measurement from side seam to center-back seam. Tape this section to the tissue. Extend the crotch point outward to increase the center-back crotch seam length by 1 in. to 1½ in. Tape the crotch point to the tissue. Using a fashion ruler or french curve as a guide, connect the broken seamlines smoothly, then draw corresponding new cutting lines.

127

Fitting a Flat Seat

Tucks are the key to getting flat-seat issues behind you: First, pin a long vertical tuck down the back of the leg or a horizontal tuck across the seat. You may need one or the other or both to get your fit right. Next, move those tucks into the pant seams or waistband to remove the excess fabric.

REMOVING EXCESS LENGTH
When the seat is sagging, it usually indicates that there's too much length from the back waistline to the crotch.

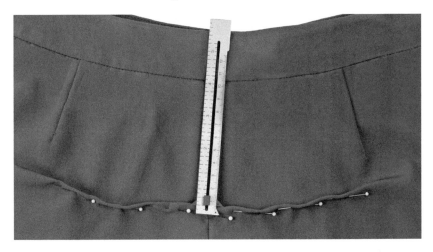

1. Pinch a horizontal tuck across the pants back until the seat and legs hang straight. Taper to nothing just before the side seams.

2. Measure the tuck width at the center-back seam (two times the distance from the pin to the fold).

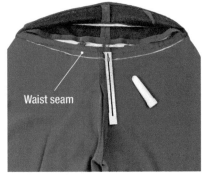

3. Open the back waistband seam between the side seams.

4. Transfer the tuck depth measurement to just below the waist seam, and mark it with chalk or a disappearing marker. Remember, the measurement will diminish to zero at or just before the side seams.

5. Position the waistband's original stitch line along the new chalkline. Pin in place, stitch, then topstitch. (*Note:* In some cases, you may first have to take in the pants back circumference by shrinking it with steam or enlarging the darts.)

REMOVING FULLNESS

A vertical tuck down the back of the pant leg removes excess fabric in that area.

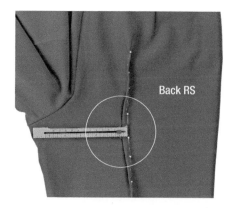

1. Pinch out excess fabric with a tuck running from the seat (or above it, as shown here) to the knee. Taper from as much as 1 in. of fabric at the seat to nothing at the knee.

2. Measure the width of the tuck across from the crotch point (two times the distance from the pin to the fold).

3. Open the inseam of the pants from the knee to the crotch.

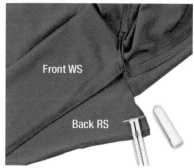

4. Transfer the amount of the tuck width with chalk to the back inseam.

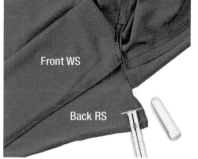

5. Lay the front leg's original seamline along the new back inseam line. Pin the two layers together. Sew the seam following the front-seam track. Trim and serge or otherwise clean-finish the raw edges.

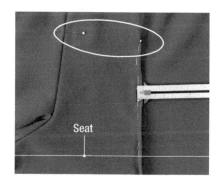

6. If your tuck goes above the seat, you'll need to remove excess fabric from the center-back seam. Pin-mark how high your adjustment goes on the center-back seam.

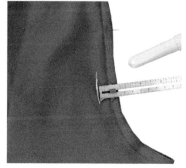

7. Transfer the tuck amount to the center-back seam.

8. Taper the new seam at the beginning and end into the original seam and stitch along the chalkline. Trim and clean-finish the seam allowance.

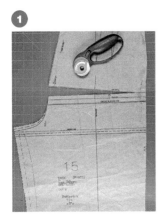

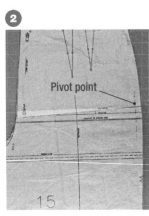

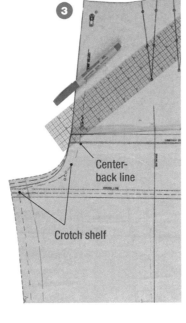

Crotch point

Draw in tuck width.

Draw in new seamline.

Pivot point

Center-back line

Crotch shelf

Altering a Pattern for a Flat Seat

If you're sewing pants from scratch, you can alter a pattern for a perfect fit through the derrière.

For Fullness

1. Sew test pants from your pattern in an inexpensive woven fabric. Then pin out the excess fabric as described on p. 129. Transfer your pin-fitting adjustment to the pants pattern inseam. Draw a point along the center-back seam ½ in. to 1 in. in from the crotch point equal to the tuck width.

2. Draw a new seamline from the revised crotch point to the inseam. Reshape the new inseam using a curved ruler to fine-tune the fit. For thin inner thighs, draw the seam curved toward the leg and then adjoining the inseam, as shown. If in doubt about the seam shape, mirror the original pattern inseam at the new location.

For Length

1. Sew test pants, then pin out the needed horizontal tuck as described on p. 128. Cut the pattern through the center-back seam all the way across to, but not through, the side seam allowance. Leave a tiny hinge of pattern paper at the side seam.

2. Pivot the upper section of the back down by the tuck amount.

3. Redraw the center-back line so that it meets the crotch shelf line smoothly. It is now straighter and less angled for a better fit.

Drafting a Custom Pants Pattern

Nothing flatters like a good fit. And you can take the guesswork out of fitting pants by custom-drafting your own pattern from the start. It sounds complicated, but with a few simple measurements, a ruler, pattern paper, a pencil, and the diagrams shown here, it's as easy as working a crossword puzzle. You just draw a line, and, along it, mark points that correspond to your body measurements; then square the lines. (Squaring means drawing a line at 90 degrees to the line containing a referenced point.)

After drafting the pattern according the instructions that follow, trace the draft to make your first pattern to test the fit. Add seam allowances and a hem allowance. Cut an inexpensive, stable fabric to test, and perfect the pattern on your body. Correct your pattern from this fitting, and you'll have a master pants pattern that can be modified for style changes.

Measuring for a Custom Draft

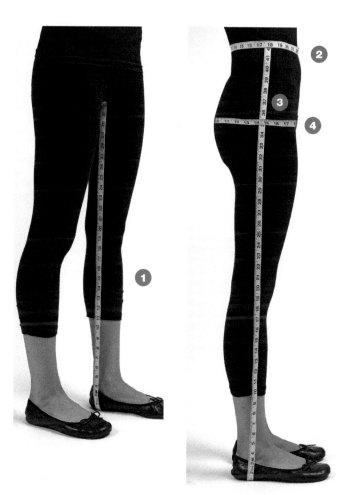

Exact measurements are the building blocks for your pattern. Wear only undergarments or a leotard.

1. **Inseam:** Stand on 1 in. of the tape measure with the heel of your foot, and measure to the crotch. Subtract the 1 in.

2. **Waist:** Measure your waist circumference.

3. **Side seam:** Stand on the tape measure with 1 in. under your foot, and measure up to your waist. Subtract the 1 in.

4. **Hip circumference:** Measure the fullest part of your hip.

5. **Crotch depth:** Tie a piece of elastic around your waist. Sit on a firm, level surface, and use an L-square or a ruler to measure from the elastic to the surface. Add 1 in. for ease.

Ankle: Measure the hem circumference of your favorite pants.

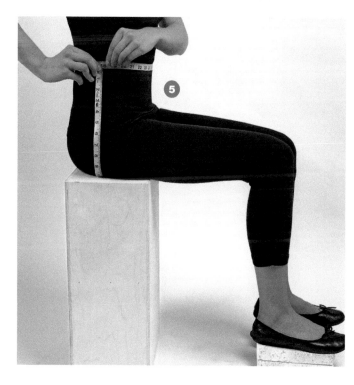

131

Drafting the Front Pattern

Start with a vertical line drawn at least 4 in. from the left edge of the paper and several inches longer than the side-seam length. Label a point at the top of the line as "A." Measure down the seam length plus ⅝ in., and mark a second point labeled "B." (This is the hemline.)

1. MARK POINTS

- From point A, measure down ⅝ in., and mark point "1." This is the waist.

- From point 1, measure down the crotch depth, and label point "2."

- Mark point "3" halfway between points B and 2.

- From point 3, measure up one-tenth of your inseam length, and mark point "4" as the knee position.

- Take one-tenth of half your hip circumference, and add 1¼ in. Mark that distance up from point 2 as point "5." This is the hipline.

- Square lines out from points 1, 2, 4, 5, and B.

2. ADD CIRCUMFERENCE MEASUREMENTS

- From point 5, measure out one-fourth of the hip circumference minus ⅜ in., and mark point "6." Square a line up and down to lines 1 and 2.

- Mark the intersecting points "7" and "8" as shown.

- Fix point 6a from 6 by dividing half your hip circumference by 10 and adding ¼ in.

3. ESTABLISH THE CREASE LINE

- Center a mark between 5 and 6a. Label it point "9."

- Square a line through point 9 up to the waist and down to the ankle. This is the crease line.

- Mark points "10," "11," and "12" as shown at the crease line intersections.

1 **MARK POINTS**

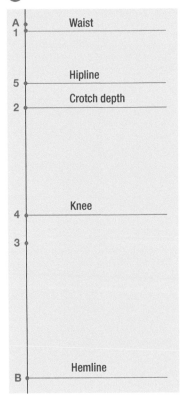

2 **ADD CIRCUMFERENCE MEASUREMENTS**

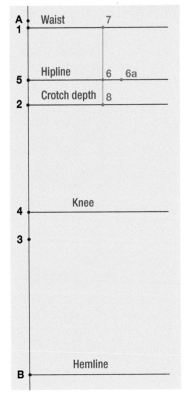

3 **ESTABLISH THE CREASE LINE**

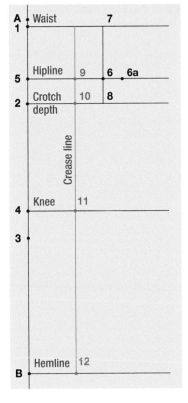

4. SHAPE THE LEG

- Transfer your favorite pant leg width to your draft by marking one-fourth of the hem circumference minus ⅜ in. on each side of point 12. Label these points "13" and "14," as shown.

- With dotted lines, connect 13 to 5 and 14 to 6a. Find the center between 2b and 8, and mark it "2c." Using the same measurement, make a point "8b" toward 6.

- Draw a line from 8b to 2b.

5. ADJUST FOR THE STOMACH

- For an average stomach, work from point 7.

- For a flat stomach, mark a new center-front point ¼ in. to ⅜ in. left of point 7. Label it "7a."

- For a protruding stomach, mark a new point ¼ in. to ⅝ in. to the right of point 7. Label it "7b."

- On the hipline, mark a point called "6b" ¼ in. to ⅜ in. right of point 6. Draw a straight line between 6b and 7, 7a, or 7b (whichever is right for your draft).

- To complete the rise, draw a line curving gently to 2b, incorporating the angle created earlier.

6. CURVE THE WAISTLINE

- On the waistline from either point 7, 7a, or 7b, measure one-fourth of your waist circumference plus 1 in. for the dart width, and draw a gently curved line from the crease line connecting to point A. The shape of this line will be finalized in the fitting.

- One inch from point A, curve a side seam to the hipline at point 5.

- The crease line is also the dart's foldline. Mark ½ in. for dart depth on each side, and mark the dart point 3½ in. below.

4 SHAPE THE LEG

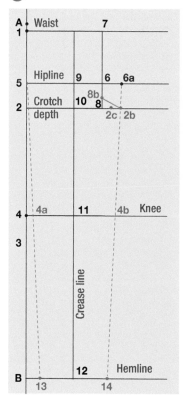

5 ADJUST FOR THE STOMACH

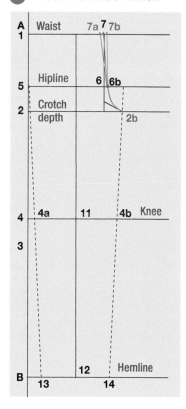

6 CURVE THE WAISTLINE

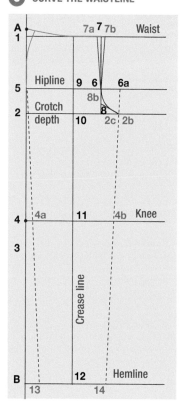

Drafting the Back Pattern

Draft the pants back over the pants front. You can draw right on the front in a different color and trace copies later to use as patterns, or you could tape paper you can see through over the front draft.

1. FIND THE CENTER BACK

• Extend line 5 (hipline) on both ends.

• Mark a point ¾ in. to the right of point 9 on the hipline. Label it "15." Draw a dotted line from point 15 to point 11 (this becomes the crease line for the back of the pant leg).

• Divide the hip circumference by 4, and add ⅜ in. Then take one-fourth of this measure, and mark this distance along the hipline to the right from 15. Label it "16." Typically, point 16 falls inside the body of the previous pattern piece.

• For the next step, mark point "17" up from point 2 on the side seam. But first assess the shape of the derrière: For a normal/average seat, measure up 1⅝ in.; for a flat seat, measure up 2 in.; for a protruding seat, go up ⅞ in.

• Join 17 to 16 with a straight line. At point 16, square a line up past the waist and down to line 2. This is the center-back (CB) line.

2. SHIFT THE HIPS

• From point 16, measure one-fourth your hip circumference plus ⅜ in., and mark point "18." From point 18, draw a line parallel to line 17-16. Mark point "19" where it intersects CB.

• Measure the distance from 18 to 15, and mark that length from 15 to the right on the hipline. Label it "20."

• Measure ¾ in. outside points 13, 14, 4a, and 4b, and draw dotted lines to connect the points from the ankle to the knee on both sides.

• From the knee, take the inseam line straight up to point 20. On the side seam, extend the line through the hipline point 18 and past the waistline. Label it "21."

1 FIND THE CENTER BACK

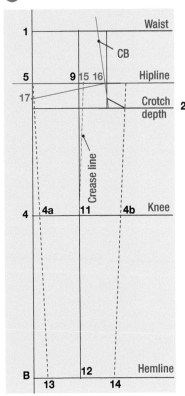

2 SHIFT THE HIPS

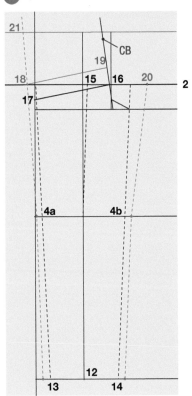

3. FIND CENTER BACK AGAIN

- Measure from point 21 to point 11, and mark point "22" that length from point 11 to the CB line.
- The front inseam length from the knee to 2b is the same on the back minus ¼ in. Label that point "23."
- At point 22, go in ¼ in. to ⅜ in. Label that point "24."
- Draw a line from point 24 to point 19. Curve a line gently from point 16 to point 23 for the back crotch.
- From point 24 to 21, find one-quarter of your waist minus ¼ in., add the desired dart depth, and mark as "25." From this point, gently curve to point 18.
- Add seam and hem allowances to the pattern before using it.

3 FIND THE CENTER BACK

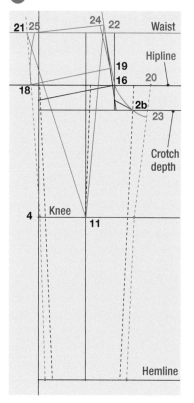

Tools for Drafting Patterns

Investing in some pattern-drafting tools will make the drafting process easier and more accurate.

- Mechanical pencil
- Pen
- Highlighter
- Metal square
- Triangle
- See-through drafting ruler
- Designer's curve

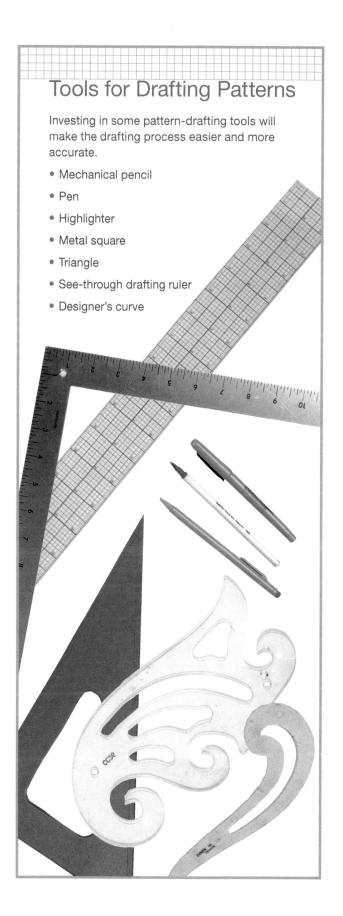

SPECIALTY FITTING TECHNIQUES

Depending on your fitting challenges, your level of skill as a patternmaker and sewer, and the type of garment you're trying to fit, you may find that general fitting techniques aren't producing the results you need. If so, read on to learn some alternative approaches that might just be the answer to your prayers.

Sometimes, a commercial pattern simply can't be made to fit your figure. In that case, consider making your own custom-fit pattern. You can do so by draping a basic pattern and restyling it to suit your fashion needs or by making a direct copy of a garment that fits you well. These methods take some time, but the improved fit will be its own reward, and you'll find yourself using these perfected patterns over and over.

Most sewers with a few years of experience are aware that their figures change over time. Sizes and styles that were once easy to fit and flattering are more difficult to find, and the adjustments that were automatic and straightforward no longer solve your fitting challenges. Understanding the most common body changes can help you target the unfamiliar pulls and puckers that you see. If you're losing or gaining weight, learn to sew garments that are quick to take in or let out—so you can make the most of your sewing time.

A well-fitting bra can substantially improve the fit and appearance of blouses, dresses, jackets, and coats. If, like many women, you're dissatisfied with the fit of a purchased bra, or can no longer find your favorite size and style, consider making your own. You'll be pleasantly surprised at how easily this can solve an assortment of fit and comfort problems, not just in the bra itself, but in all the garments you wear over it.

Draping the Bodice

Draping is the perfect way to get your proportions right and turn pattern fitting into a breeze. We are all uniquely shaped. Standard commercial pattern companies just can't make enough sizes to fit all of us. Draping puts you in the driver's seat for altering commercial patterns or making your own.

By draping, you can put your energy into one master fitting that allows for your personal lumps, bumps, and slopes that no commercial pattern can account for. Here, you'll learn the steps of draping a bodice and then transferring the information to paper. When you're finished, you'll know how to make a bodice pattern block—sometimes called a sloper—that basic, close-fitting pattern with minimum wearing ease that just might change your relationship with patterns. From this bodice block, you will be able to design tops, vests, jackets, and coats in different styles that will automatically fit you. Your own custom block enables you to work on design without all the fitting concerns.

Preparations for Draping

You will need a sewing friend, 2 yd. to 3 yd. lightweight fabric, and the ability to stand for about one hour. Wear your best-fitting foundation garments and a close-fitting T-shirt, one that can be used to pin the draping cloth to. Wear shoes to ensure that your posture is the same as when you're dressed to the nines. If you have a custom dress form, you can drape it to get an accurate fit as well, but pad it first to build in some room for breathing. Otherwise, the resulting pattern will be too tight.

PREPARE THE MUSLIN

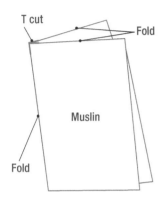

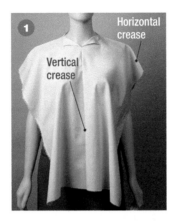

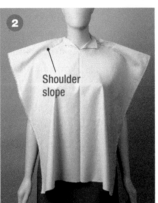

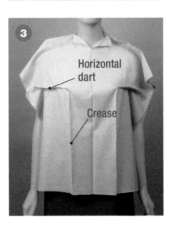

PREPARE THE MUSLIN

You will need one piece of muslin the right length and width to cover your body. To calculate the length of your muslin, measure from the top of your shoulder to your hip. Add 5 in. to this measurement, then multiply by 2. To calculate the width of your muslin, divide your body's largest circumference by 2 and add 5 in.

Rip the muslin, then fold it in half, first lengthwise and again on the crossgrain. Press a sharp crease along both folds. Cut a T at the intersection of the folds just large enough to fit over your head, as shown at left.

PIN IN THE SHAPE

1. Pull the muslin over your head, and balance the hems evenly from front to back. Place the vertical crease accurately over the center front and center back of the body.

2. Smooth the fabric over the body and systematically pin excess fabric into darts, tucks, and seams as needed to define the figure. Keep two rules in mind:

   • Always keep the crosswise grain that sits at the bustline and across the shoulder blades parallel to the floor.

   • Below the bustline and shoulder blades, the straight of grain (center-front and center-back creases) must fall at right angles (perpendicular) to the floor. Pin along the top of the shoulder following the contour and keeping the muslin smooth and undistorted, but leave a little excess fabric sitting above the shoulders for fine-tuning later. For women with sloped shoulders, wear a light shoulder pad to create a more balanced proportion, especially in a full figure.

FIT THE BUST

3. Smooth the muslin across the chest to make the crosswise grain parallel to the floor. A natural dart starts to form from the bust point and falls at an angle toward the side seam. Pin out the natural dart wedge, taking in enough fabric to lift the hem edge until it is parallel to the floor. The muslin should hang like a box from the bust points.

4. Crease the muslin vertically with the grain from the bust points straight down to the hem edge. Pin out the excess fabric along these creases into vertical torso darts on both the front and back. As needed, you can tie a narrow elastic around the waistline to hold the muslin to the body and facilitate pinning.

ESTABLISH THE SIDE SEAMS

5. Pin the side seams as close as you can to the body without distorting the muslin. Trim the excess fabric along the side seam. Use your fingers to feel and "trace" how close you can safely pin up to the armhole. A ruler held high into the armpit helps you locate where the armhole sits and the side seam ends.

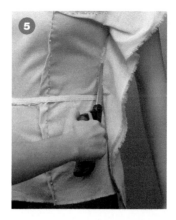

Go back, double-check, and pin the side seam again, getting close to the body and keeping the seam perpendicular to the floor. Mark the seam with a felt pen when you are confident the side seams are accurate.

ADJUST THE ARMHOLE

6. Use your fingers to guide the shape, and mark as you go. Clip into the fabric to allow it to shape nicely. If you clip too far, tape the fabric back together. Trim the muslin around the armhole to show the shape you want.

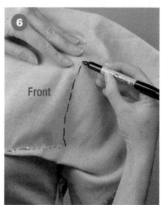

7. To solve for gaping at the back armhole, pin a horizontal dart from the armhole to the shoulder blade.

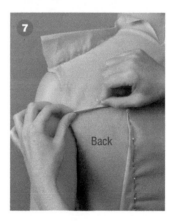

MARK SEAMS AND EDGES

Check the darts, side seams, and armholes, then make sure the seams sit nicely on the shoulders. Establish ease between the muslin and the body by sliding your fingers under the fabric and resetting the pins; set them as close together as possible.

8. Now you're ready to mark seams and edges. Tape the T slits closed just below the neckline. Use your fingers to feel the outline of the neck while marking the fabric. When you are satisfied with the muslin's overall fit and smoothness, mark it with key points such as shoulders, neckline, armholes, darts, bust points, shoulder-blade apex, waistline, and side seams.

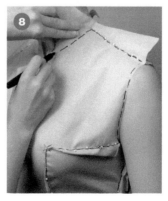

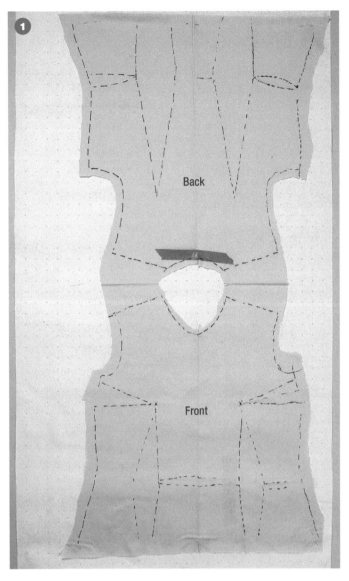

Create a Paper Pattern

Asymmetrical figures need right- and left-side pattern pieces. However, a symmetrical figure can work with just one side of the muslin.

1. Remove the pins and lay the muslin out flat over pattern tracing paper. Secure with weights and use an awl or pinwheel to punch the key lines you've marked. Begin with the center-front and center-back lines, which are also your straight-of-grain references. Seam allowances are not included.

2. Lift the muslin off the pattern paper, and mark all the punch holes with a pencil. Use a ruler or curve to make smooth lines.

3. Using a ruler, define the torso darts. Keep the vertical lines directly under the bust point on the front and the shoulder-blade apex on the back and perpendicular to the floor.

4. Temporarily tape the bust dart closed. Lift the pattern into a bowed shape to tape the dart without distortion. Once the dart is closed, lay the back side seam along the front side seam from armhole to waist.

   Ensure that the front and back side seams are the same length and shape. For a length adjustment between waist and hem, add the difference at the hem. Adjust waist-to-armhole lengths at the armhole.

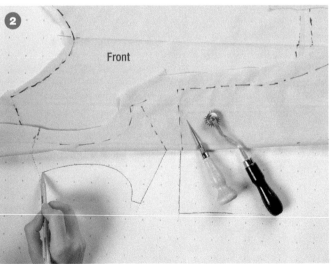

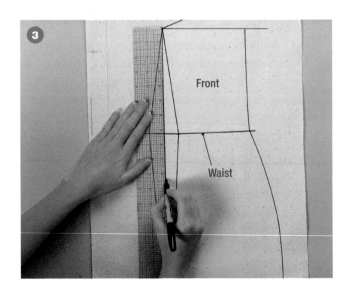

5. While the bust dart is taped shut, trim along the front side seam to remove the seam allowance. Carefully remove the tape from the bust dart. Compare the seamlines. The front and back shoulder length should match. Make corrections until corresponding seams are the same length.

6. If you pinned a back armhole dart, close it and rotate it to the shoulder before you shape the back armhole. Draw a line from the shoulder-blade apex to a midpoint on the back shoulder seam. Cut along the line. Place a small piece of tape on the pattern at the shoulder-blade apex. From the armhole to the apex, cut along one leg of the armhole dart.

Close the armhole dart by pivoting the shoulder out and down until the dart legs meet. This step opens a new dart at the shoulder. Tape the armhole dart closed. Use a french curve to shape the back armhole, then trim away the excess paper around the armhole.

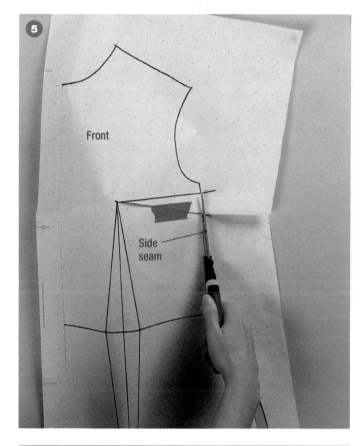

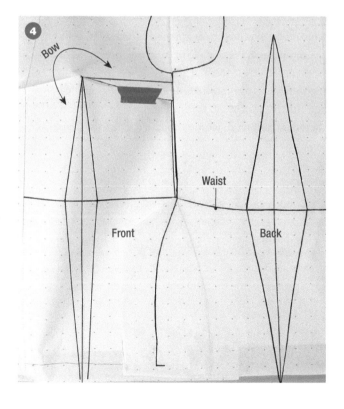

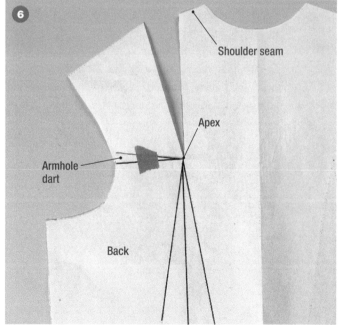

The Bodice Block

A block is meant to duplicate the body as closely as possible. When you design a garment from a block, you will incorporate more wearing and design ease.

The test garment allows you to fine-tune the smoothness and fit of your block. Whatever adjustments you make to the fitting muslin, transfer them to the pattern block. Label the front and back bodice blocks with your name and measurements, and the date. Trace the pattern onto tagboard. Label the test garment as well, and store it in a zip-top bag with your block.

Drafting a Sleeve for a Bodice Block

A tight sleeve is annoyingly uncomfortable, but when you enlarge a sleeve pattern to fit, it often doesn't ease into the armscye properly. Sleeve fitting has always been tricky business. In many cases, it's just easier to create a custom sleeve from scratch.

Once you've draped a custom-fit bodice, as described in the previous pages, you'll want to add a sleeve. Although you can drape a sleeve on the body, it is faster and more accurate to draft one using measurements from the arm and the armhole that it will fit into. A sleeve block is used like a template. The beauty of having your own block is that all the fitting adjustments are built in. Since it already fits, you can get right to the design process.

Using your bodice block, your measurements, and several simple formulas for drafting the right amount of ease, you can finally get the sleeve fit you want and use it in everything you sew. Here you'll learn how much ease to add as you walk through each step.

The Tapered Sleeve

This simplified method produces a fine-fitting one-piece tapered sleeve. You can use this draft to make an endless variety of sleeves by adding an optional elbow dart. As with all sloper or block patterns, this sleeve is drafted without seam allowances.

To get started, you'll need the bodice pattern you draped earlier (see pp. 137–141) and a few arm and armhole measurements. Be sure your bodice block fits you nicely, particularly through the shoulder and armhole. You'll want the edge of the armhole to come right out to the shoulder point and curve smoothly around your arm with no restrictions or binding. If you draped your bodice on a dress form, it may be necessary to drop the armhole a little for ease of movement. Usually ½ in. out and ½ in. to 1 in. down along the side seam is enough to give ample room (see the left drawing below).

Plan ahead for shoulder pads if you wear them. These days, shoulder pads are used primarily to define the shoulder and create a slimming proportion. Many women don't wear them at all. But if you have sloping shoulders, you may like shoulder pads; a shoulder pad that is about ½ in. thick creates a natural-looking shoulder contour. To accommodate the padding, raise

THE TAPERED SLEEVE

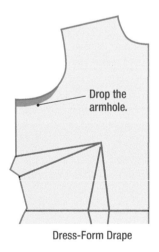

Drop the armhole.

Dress-Form Drape

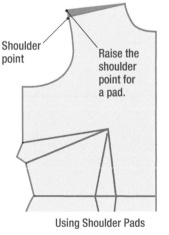

Shoulder point

Raise the shoulder point for a pad.

Using Shoulder Pads

the shoulder at the armhole by the same amount on both the front and back pattern pieces, tapering to zero at the neck (see the bottom right drawing on the facing page).

MEASURE THE ARM

Your arm and armhole measurements plus a few calculations determine the proper sleeve dimensions. Reference the drawing at right when taking the following arm measurements.

- **Biceps circumference:** Measure easily, not tightly, around the fullest part of the arm, about 4 in. below the shoulder.
- **Arm length:** With the arm bent slightly at the elbow, measure from the shoulder bone at the top of the arm, passing over the elbow, down to the wristbone (above the little finger).
- **Length to elbow:** Measure from the shoulder as above but just to the point of the elbow.
- **Elbow circumference:** Bend your arm. Measure around the expansion at the elbow. This tells you what the minimum width can be at the elbow.
- **Wrist circumference:** Measure around the wrist. Insert one finger between the wrist and the measuring tape. (The wrist measurement is used if you design a sleeve with a cuff.)

ADD EASE

Add ease to your raw measurements. A sleeve has three kinds of ease:

- One is created by gathering stitches along the length of the sleeve cap to shorten the length and also help the fabric mold around a shoulder.
- Wearing ease is the difference between the completed sleeve measurement (typically a width measurement) and the dimension of the arm.
- For further comfort, movement, and style, sleeves are designed with added fabric, also called style ease.

Patternmakers know the minimum amount of ease to use for various garment sections. The following formulas explain where to add these minimum amounts. Style ease is added later when you design your block.

- **Width of the sleeve under the arm formula:** Biceps circumference plus 2 in. to 3 in. for ease. (The fuller your biceps, the more ease you need.)
- **Width of the sleeve at the elbow formula:** Elbow circumference plus 1 in. to 2 in. for ease.
- **Wrist circumference formula:** Circumference plus 1 in. for ease.

MEASURE THE SLOPER

Take the armhole depth measurement from your pattern by squaring a line on the front and back bodice pattern pieces from the straight of grainline to the underarm point at the side seam. Measure from the shoulder point straight down to the underarm line. Add the front and back measurements and divide that by 2.

MEASURING THE ARM FOR A SLEEVE

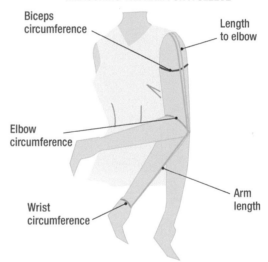

Biceps circumference

Length to elbow

Elbow circumference

Wrist circumference

Arm length

MEASURE THE SLOPER

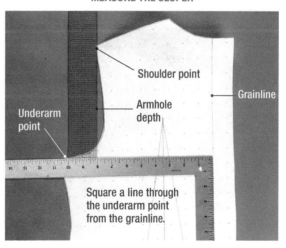

Shoulder point

Grainline

Underarm point

Armhole depth

Square a line through the underarm point from the grainline.

Block In the Sleeve Draft

Begin with a sheet of pattern paper about 20 in. wide by 30 in. long. As you go along, the draft is drawn on a fold, so use half the adjusted measurements discussed on p. 143 with the ease added in.

1. Fold the paper in half lengthwise.

2. Along the foldline of the paper, mark points indicating the length of your arm from the shoulder point (top) to the wrist.

3. Square a line at the top point.

4. From the top, measure down and mark your armhole depth (measured from the bodice).

5. Square a biceps line out from the armhole depth that is half your adjusted sleeve width (biceps circumference plus 2 in. to 3 in., divided in half).

6. Measure down the foldline and mark your elbow point.

7. Square a line from the elbow point, and mark half your adjusted elbow circumference.

8. Square a line at the wrist point from the fold.

9. Mark half the adjusted wrist circumference on the wrist line.

10. Draw the underarm seam by connecting the adjusted sleeve width and elbow circumference points in a straight line that crosses the wrist line.

11. Turn the folded edge of the paper to the underarm seam. Crease the paper to create a one-quarter division line, then open.

BLOCK IN THE SLEEVE DRAFT

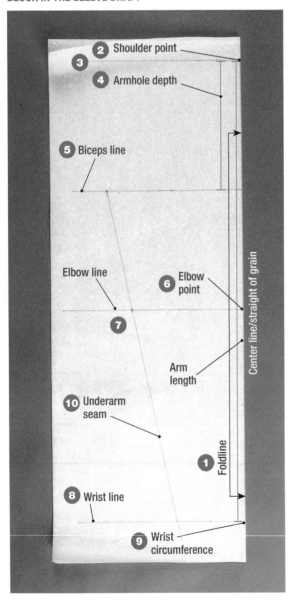

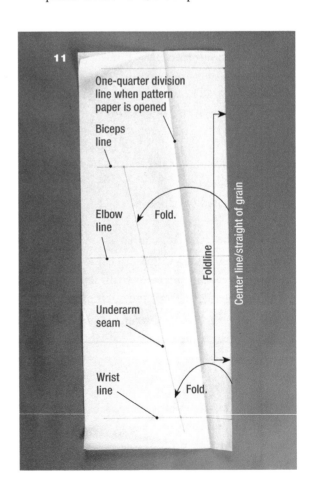

DRAFT THE CAP

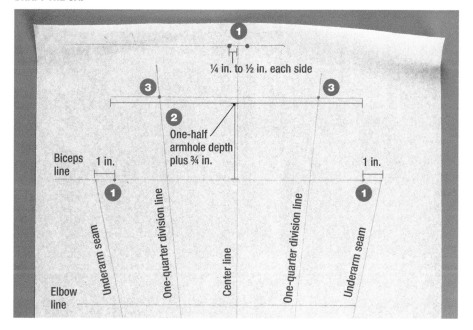

Draft the Cap

After establishing the basic shape of the sleeve, draw the top portion known as the sleeve cap. This fits into the armhole and bends the sleeve around the shoulder.

1. Place marks ¼ in. to ½ in. on each side of the center line at the top of the sleeve and 1 in. inward from the underarm seam on the biceps line.

2. From the biceps line, measure up the center line one-half the armhole depth plus ¾ in. and mark a point.

3. Square a guideline through the mark across the sleeve and then mark line intersections.

4. Connect the pairs of points with straight lines to form the sleeve-cap guidelines.

5. Mark a halfway point on each of the sleeve-cap guidelines.

6. Using a designer's curve, connect the dots with a smooth, continuous curve. The dots are merely guides. You do not have to touch each one with your curve. The aim is to have no sharp points.

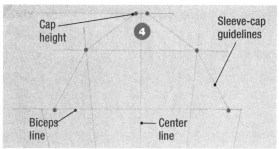

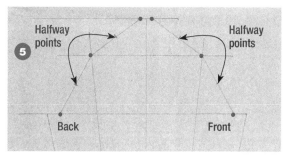

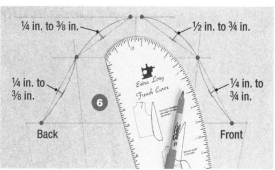

Notch the Cap

Notches aid in positioning the sleeve into the armhole. You will have to place the notches on both the sleeve cap and the garment's armhole. Fold the shoulder point to the biceps line along the center line and crease the fold. Use this new crease line (as shown in the top drawing below) as your guide to place the front and back sleeve notches. Draw a double notch on the back sleeve and a single notch on the front sleeve. The shoulder dot is placed later when we "walk" the cap around the bodice armhole.

Shape the Wrist Edge

Finish the wrist edge by adding a little length at each of the quarter points. Connect the dots using a designer's curve, as shown in the bottom drawing below. Adding this length is optional, but if you've ever been annoyed at the way a sleeve draws up at the underarm seam, you will appreciate this addition.

NOTCH THE CAP

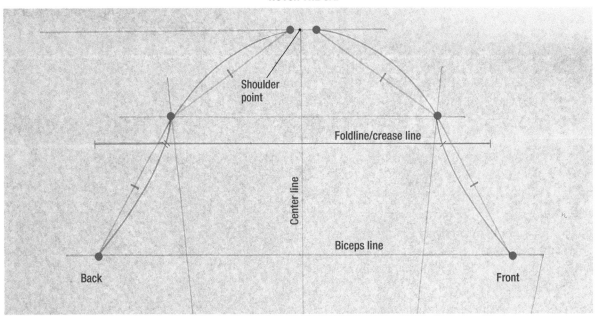

SHAPE THE WRIST EDGE

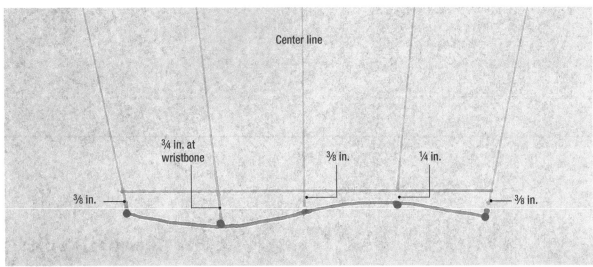

Add the Elbow Dart

For added comfort and improved smoothness in fit, add an optional elbow dart. With a dart, you add ease for the elbow as well as smooth some fullness away from the forearm. Create a dart using a simple slash-and-pivot technique.

1. Start by marking the sleeves with balance points along the underarm seam. Place the points 3 in. above and 2 in. below the elbow line along the underarm seams. You will use these marks as notches when sewing later.

2. Mark the pivot point at the intersection of the elbow line and the center grainline. Reinforce the pivot point with a piece of Scotch tape.

3. From the back sleeve seam, cut along the elbow line all the way to the pivot point.

4. From the wrist edge, cut along the center line, stopping at the pivot point. Leave a tiny hinge of paper so you can pivot the lower section of the sleeve.

5. Pivot and overlap along the wrist edge until you have an opening at the elbow that measures ½ in. to 1 in. Secure the overlapped section with tape.

6. Typically on pattern blocks, we do not finish darts with stitching lines. But as a note for later, the open dart at this stage is not what you will sew. You can either ease the fullness or stitch in the dart. If you want to sew the dart, stitch the shape shown in red in the bottom right drawing that comes to a point at the first quarter line of the sleeve, leaving the remaining fullness as wearing ease.

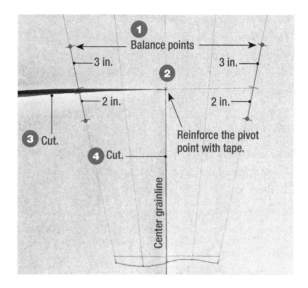

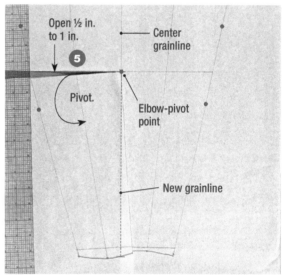

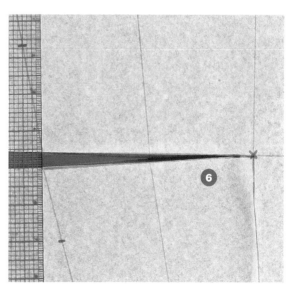

Walk the Cap

The next step is to transfer the sleeve-cap notches to the bodice armhole and position the shoulder notch on the sleeve cap. To determine these locations, use a process called "walking" the cap.

1. Beginning at the side seam, align the sleeve back edge to the bodice back armhole edge.

2. Keep the edges flush, and carefully inch the sleeve-cap edge along the armhole edge. Use a pin as a pivot to align the edges as you walk the curve.

3. Continue walking the cap to the shoulder, and mark a temporary shoulder notch on the sleeve.

4. Repeat these steps with the bodice front, walking the sleeve cap along the armhole and marking the armhole with a single notch and a second temporary dot at the shoulder on the sleeve. You now have two temporary dots on the sleeve-cap edge.

5. Measure the distance between these two dots; this is the ease amount in your sleeve cap. Divide this cap ease in half and mark the sleeve shoulder notch.

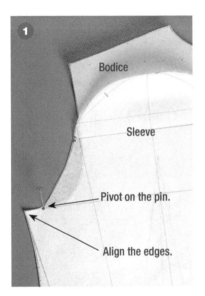

Bodice

Sleeve

Pivot on the pin.

Align the edges.

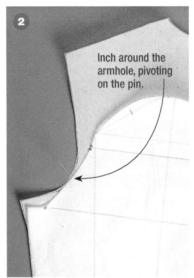

Inch around the armhole, pivoting on the pin.

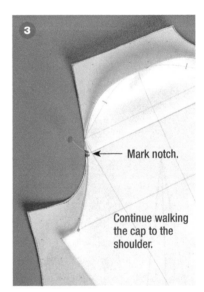

Mark notch.

Continue walking the cap to the shoulder.

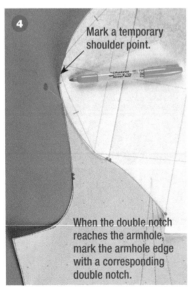

Mark a temporary shoulder point.

When the double notch reaches the armhole, mark the armhole edge with a corresponding double notch.

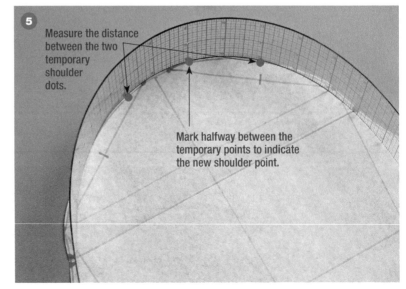

Measure the distance between the two temporary shoulder dots.

Mark halfway between the temporary points to indicate the new shoulder point.

Find the Percentage of Difference

Check the cap ease by measuring your cap length and armhole circumference and then calculating the percentage of difference. The sleeve-cap length should be from 5 to 10 percent larger than the armhole. Anything more makes it difficult to set a smooth sleeve.

You can reduce the ease by shaving the height from the cap. Do this in very small increments; measure and calculate the percentage before shaving more. A higher cap is more comfortable. The garment style plays an important role, too. A set-in sleeve needs a higher cap, while a dropped-shoulder garment needs a flatter cap.

Also, your fabric affects ease. An allowance of 10 percent looks nice in a wool tweed, but may be too much in a cotton poplin. For this reason, don't shave the cap on a sleeve block. Wait until you're creating the design to make the decision.

Test the Sleeve

Use your new sleeve pattern to cut out a muslin copy, adding seam allowances along the cap and side seams. Close the elbow dart, and stitch the underarm seams together. Pin the sleeve into the bodice armhole, placing the pins along the seamline as if it were a sewn seam.

Make sure the sleeve hangs smoothly on the arm. As you pin it into position, rotate the sleeve a little back and forth until you find a smooth drape. Mark the new notch positions with a different color felt-tip pen and transfer the new marks to your pattern blocks.

Once the sleeve block fits and hangs smoothly, trace your working copy onto heavy paper. Do not add seam allowances to the block pattern. Label it with your name and measurements, and the date.

Cut out a muslin and pin it to the bodice armhole to test the sleeve pattern.

Draping a Skirt Sloper

A skirt is the simplest garment to drape. You'll need a sewing friend, 3 yd. to 4 yd. of light- to medium-weight muslin fabric, and the ability to stand for about one hour. Wear the shoes you would with a skirt and your best-fitting foundation garment. The shoes ensure the same posture that you'll have when you're dressed in finished garments.

If you have a dress form that matches your size and shape perfectly, you can drape that for an accurate fit as well. But be aware that a dummy may need a slight layer of padding first so you can build in some breathing room; otherwise, the resulting pattern may be too tight.

In the end, you'll have a basic skirt sloper that can serve as groundwork to design other skirts. You can be assured that every skirt you design from it will fit and hang beautifully.

Prepare the Muslin for the Skirt

It is important to cut the fabric straight on the lengthwise grain and keep the waist and hem edges square. Press and align the fabric. Then use your measurements to figure out the size to cut your muslin.

THE SKIRT FRONT

- Place a pin or otherwise mark a side seam position on your clothes or body so you're sure to measure to the same side seam location.

- Measure across your fullest horizontal circumference—either the hip or tummy—from center front to side seam marker. Add 2 in. to 3 in. to this measurement for ease and seam allowances. Multiply the total by 2 to establish the width to cut your muslin fabric skirt front.

- Cut the muslin piece 5 in. to 6 in. longer than your desired skirt length. Along the lengthwise grain of the fabric, identify and mark the center grainline with a felt-tip pen.

THE SKIRT BACK

The skirt will have a center-back seam, so plan to cut two pieces of fabric.

- Measure across the fullest part of your hip from center back to side seam. Add 3 in. to 4 in. to this measurement for ease, plus 1 in. for the center-back seam allowance.

- Cut two pieces of fabric for the back, with each the width calculated above and the same length as the front piece you cut earlier.

- Machine-baste the front to the backs along the side seams. Baste the center-back seam, leaving 12 in. open at the top.

Fit the Muslin

1. Tie narrow elastic comfortably around the waist. With the seam allowances to the outside, pull on the skirt muslin and tuck it under the elastic.

2. Arrange with the center-front and center-back lines aligned on your body. Throughout the draping, keep the center lines positioned properly on the body and perpendicular to the floor.

3. Stand straight with your weight equally on both feet while your friend adjusts the skirt until it hangs evenly. Begin adjusting from the top, using the waist elastic to hold everything in place. Move the skirt up and down under the elastic until the side seams and the center-front and center-back seams hang perpendicular to the floor.

4. Once all vertical lines are hanging correctly, make sure the hem is parallel to the floor. Adjust as necessary.

5. The fabric above the waist elastic may not be even—that's okay. What's important is that everything below the waist hangs smoothly and evenly.

FIT THE MUSLIN

5 It's okay if the top isn't straight.

3 Adjust from the top and keep seams perpendicular to the floor.

1 Tie narrow elastic around the waist.

2 Keep the center-front and center-back lines perpendicular to the floor.

4 Keep the hem parallel to the floor.

SMOOTH WRINKLES INTO DARTS

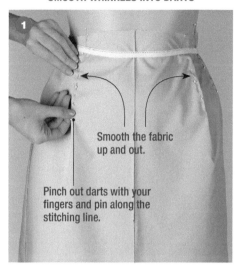

1

Smooth the fabric up and out.

Pinch out darts with your fingers and pin along the stitching line.

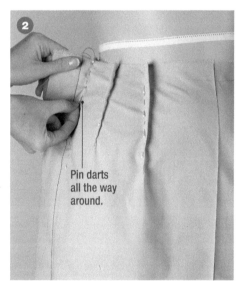

2

Pin darts all the way around.

Smooth Wrinkles into Darts

1. Lift the waist elastic and pinch out the excess fabric that forms between the hip and waist. Smooth the fabric across the tummy and hip level. You want it to drape smoothly from the most prominent point of the figure. Typically, you should position one dart below the bust point on the front or shoulder blade on the back, then another halfway between the side seam and first dart. Allow the figure to direct where and how many darts to use. Curvaceous figures need more darts than straighter figures.

2. Pin darts all the way around the skirt. As you work, make sure the skirt remains straight and smooth with side seams perpendicular to and the hem parallel to the floor. When pinning each dart, let a ¼-in. space float between the skirt and body for ease. Keep the dart points above the fullest part of the tummy or hip.

MARK THE MUSLIN

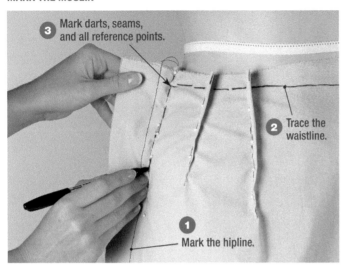

3 Mark darts, seams, and all reference points.

2 Trace the waistline.

1 Mark the hipline.

CONVERT THE MUSLIN TO A PATTERN

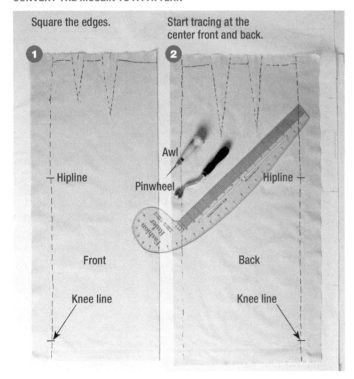

1 Square the edges.

2 Start tracing at the center front and back.

Awl

Pinwheel

Hipline

Hipline

Front

Back

Knee line

Knee line

Shape the Side and Back Seams

Along the side seam, outline the hip curve with pins, leaving ½ in. to 1 in. of ease on each side. The ease amount is a personal preference and also determined by body type. A fuller hip and tummy need more ease. Remember that you must have enough room to sit without straining seams or creating tight stretch lines.

If there is a dip at the center-back seam, you can pin that in as well to shape the seam to an accurate contour of your body. (Note that you should keep the elastic in place as you pin the side seams.)

Mark the Muslin

If you have an asymmetrical figure, creating a separate pattern for the right and left sides of the body can be a benefit. However, if your figure is reasonably symmetrical, one side of the muslin is all you need to make a conventional pattern that is cut on the fold of a double layer of fabric.

1. Mark the hipline and the kneeline at the side seam.
2. Dot marks around the waist using the elastic as your guide. Mark above the elastic.
3. Using the pins as your guide, mark the darts and seamlines and add the notches.

Convert the Muslin to a Pattern

Remove the muslin. Double-check that all pins have been marked using a felt-tip pen. Remove the pins. An old piece of foam core under your pattern paper makes recording your marks safe and easy. You won't have to worry about marking your table.

1. Smooth the muslin and square the edges. Use an awl and pin-tracing wheel to punch the key points into the paper right through the fabric.
2. Begin with the center-front and center-back lines. These lines will be your straight-of-grain references. After you've traced all lines, lift the muslin from the paper.

Use a ruler, L-square, and curve to connect the punched "dots" to finish your pattern. Remember, your sloper does not include seam allowances.

Expect to see uneven punched lines. These won't provide a good pattern and must be straightened.

Square the Corners

Beginning at the center front, draw a straight line connecting the waist point to the hem edge by following the punches. Use this line as the squaring-off point for the remainder of the pattern. Work with an L-square to complete these steps.

- Square the hem from the center-front line.
- Square the side seam and center-back seam from the hem up to the hip curve or center-back indentation.
- Along the waistline, square 1 in. out from the center-front line.
- Draw the grainline on the skirt front and skirt back parallel to the center lines and perpendicular to the hemline.

To finish the waistline edge, shape the darts by bringing the dart legs together and folding the dart as you would if sewing. Then fold the dart toward the center front. Cut the pattern along the waistline, following the curve of the waist to give your dart the correct shaping at the waistline edge. Remember, there are no seam allowances on a sloper pattern. Label your pattern pieces with your name, date, waist, and hip measurements.

The Personalized Sloper

When you look at the completed flat pattern, it's interesting to see how your figure emerges. It may not look like the typical commercial pattern. Don't be surprised to see your curves sitting higher or lower than the standard. Notice how your waistline is shaped. It's common to see dipping from back to front, and your darts may resemble the shape of a wineglass rather than a straight wedge. All of these nuances in shaping guarantee a finer fit.

TIP You can go through a lot of paper in the drafting process. Try using newsprint on rolls, which you can obtain from your local newspaper-printing outlet. This paper is inexpensive and plentiful for preliminary drafts. When your pattern block is perfected, trace a final copy onto a resilient, nonacid paper.

Copying Existing Garments

If you've been lucky enough to stumble upon a ready-to-wear garment that fits just the way you like, you don't have to anticipate with fear the day it wears out. Instead, make a pattern from it, so you can duplicate its size and shape as often as you want. Here, you'll find two methods for copying a garment. In the first, you trace the garment onto pattern paper. The second involves applying a layer of tape to the entire surface of the garment to duplicate the shape of each section, and using the resulting tape units as a pattern. Choose your technique based on the size and style of the garment (a voluminous overcoat might be too large to tape, for example), its details, and its fabric.

This method allows you to make a pattern from a beloved garment without having to rip it apart to do so. The garment itself becomes your guide as you trace each piece of it onto sturdy-but-soft pattern material.

For this example, we will be tracing a pair of pants. If you are new to the patternmaking game, start with simple, unlined, flat-front pants with a waistband. As you become used to pinning and tracing the pattern as described, you can progress to more complicated garments.

Typically, it's best to choose a fabric for your new garment that has the same weight and drape as the original. This ensures a similar fit. Choosing a heavier or lighter fabric requires some troubleshooting. In the case of these pants, for instance, using a thicker wool might require adding circumference in each leg to accommodate the fabric. If you go this route, add 1 in. to the side seams.

Materials and Supplies

The right tools make copying your garments easy and ensure the accuracy of your new pattern.

PATTERN MATERIAL
The pattern material should be easy to manipulate, resistant to tearing and stretching, and easy to write on.

A favorite material is Tru-Grid® by Pellon®, a nonfusible interfacing material with 1-in. gridlines printed on it. The lines take the guesswork out of grainline placement, and the 1-in. markings are a great help when verifying lengths and widths. Tru-Grid is 45 in. wide, so you'll need about 1½ yd.

Lightweight nonfusible interfacing also works well when placed over a cardboard grid surface. Woven fabric such as muslin is acceptable as long as it isn't too flimsy. Avoid tissue paper, which tears easily, and other types of paper, which are usually too stiff.

MARKING TOOLS
Choose a tool that writes easily and leaves clear marks on your pattern material.

Charcoal and graphite pencils are suitable because they don't tear patterns or fade. Have a pencil sharpener on hand to keep the point sharp.

Avoid disappearing ink or standard pens and markers that can stain your original garment.

OTHER ESSENTIALS
- Seam gauge
- Designer's curve
- Clear ruler or yardstick
- Straight pins
- Tape measure

Find the Grainlines

To ensure that your knockoffs fall correctly on the body, you need to identify and follow the grainlines on every piece.

1. To identify the grainlines on the original pants, flatten one leg right side out, matching the side seam to the inseam. Pin the seams together up to the crotch curve. The fold created on the front and back of the leg is your grainline. Pin along the fold, as shown. Above the crotch curve, look closely at the fabric weave to find the grainline to the waist.

2. Draw the grainlines on the Tru-Grid. Remove the pins that secure the side seam to the inseam. Reposition the pants so they lie flat as you would wear them. On the Tru-Grid, draw a straight line 4 in. longer than the pants. Place the pants grainline along the drawn grainline. Pin the pants to the Tru-Grid along the grainline, up to the crotch.

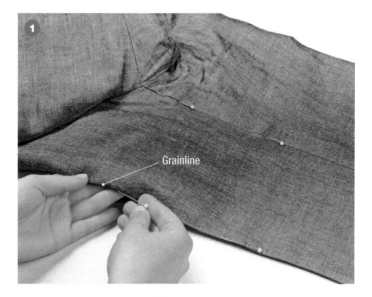

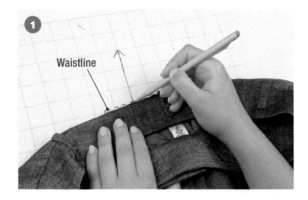

Waistline

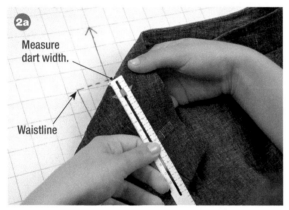

Measure dart width.

Waistline

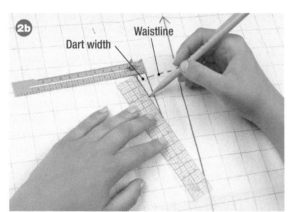

Waistline

Dart width

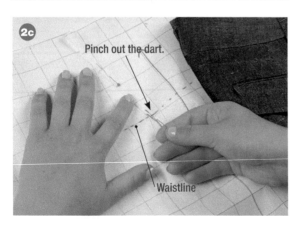

Pinch out the dart.

Waistline

Draw the Pieces

The order in which you trace your seamlines is important. Use dashes to represent the seamlines so you won't confuse them with cutting lines.

1. Begin with the pants back. With the grainline still pinned to the Tru-Grid, rearrange the pants to trace off the waistline seam just below the waistband. Make sure that the grainline is aligned at all times. Fold the pants back, and mark the top of the center-back seam. Then mark the waistline to the first dart.

2. Copy each dart. Fold back the pants, and draw the dart stitch line from waist to tip this becomes the new dart's fold line. Measure the dart width with your seam gauge (**2a**). Double that amount, and center that measurement over the first line to draw the dart legs (**2b**). Pinch the dart closed on the Tru-Grid, and pin (**2c**). Smooth the pants back over the pinched dart, trace the waistline to the second dart (if there is one), and repeat. Then trace the rest of the waistline seam.

3. Working along the waistline, add notches for pockets or other details. Without shifting the pants, remove the grainline pins. Place your hand inside the pants, and repin the bottom layer only along the grainline.

TIP Draw an X where seams intersect. This provides a reference point to go back to if the garment accidentally shifts.

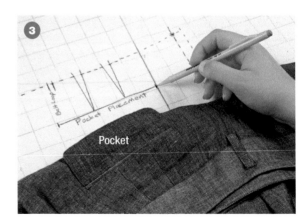

Pocket

4. To trace the center-back seam and crotch curve, rearrange the pants to expose that seam. (Always keep the grainline aligned.) Pin the crotch seam to the Tru-Grid: Put the first pin 3 in. or 4 in. down from the waistline, and then trace it (**4a**). Remove the pin, and then repin the next couple inches of the curve. Trace, and repeat this process to the inseam (**4b**). You can also tuck the unpinned leg inside the leg with the pinned grainline to access the crotch curve.

5. Render the side seams. Unpin the crotch from the Tru-Grid. As with the other steps, make sure that the pinned grainline hasn't shifted. Then roll the leg over to the side seam. Flatten it with your fingertips, pin it down, and trace the seamline.

6. Copy the inseam. Unpin the side seam from the Tru-Grid. Roll the leg over to the inseam. Pin it down, and trace. Unpin it, and draw in the pants hemline.

To copy the front of the pants, unpin the pants, flip the leg over, and repeat the above steps. For side front pockets, mark the point where each end intersects the waistline and side seam. The pocket pieces will be drafted in "Copy Key Details," on p. 158.

TIP To make copying the crotch curve and inseam easier, rip out the stitches at the inseam, and open up the pants; the pants will lie flatter on the Tru-Grid. After you've traced the areas, simply restitch the inseam on your sewing machine.

4a Center-back seam

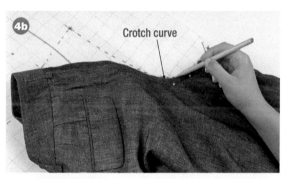

4b Crotch curve

5 Side seam

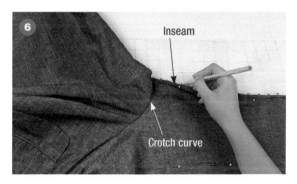

6 Inseam

Crotch curve

Fly facing

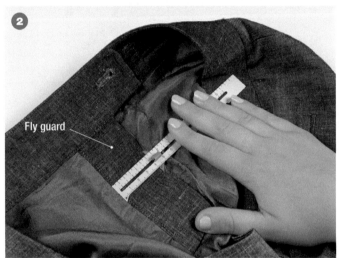

Fly guard

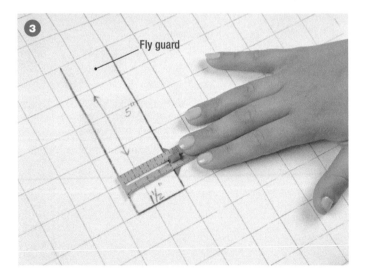

Fly guard

5"

Copy Key Details

Smaller pieces can either be traced or measured separately and drawn freehand on Tru-Grid.

FLY FRONT

1. Measure the facing on the fly side.

2. Measure the guard on the other side.

3. Using your measurements, draft the fly front freehand on Tru-Grid.

TIP If the waistband is straight, there is no need to trace. Just measure its width and length, and then draft it with a ruler.

POCKETS

1. Recreate the pockets. Pocket flaps can be measured and drawn as rectangles and then curved at the corners.

2. For the pocket bags, turn the pants inside out to access their correct size and shape.

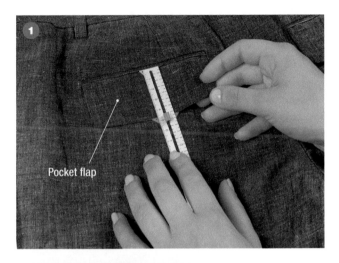

Pocket flap

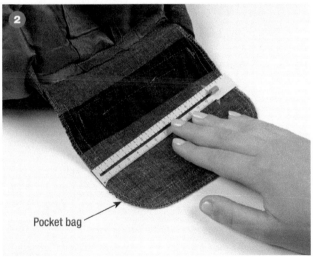

Pocket bag

WAISTBAND

1. Place the center front of a curved waistband on the lengthwise grain. Pin it down, and draw the outer curve of the band as shown.

2. Unpin the waistband, and remove the pants. To draw the other long end, measure the band on the pants with a seam gauge; then measure, and draw it on the pattern. Repeat for the back waistband, aligning the center back on the grainline. (Note: The right and left side of the front band will have the same curve but may be different lengths to accommodate the closure.)

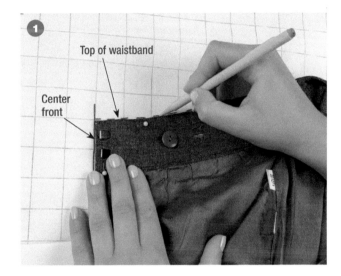

Top of waistband

Center front

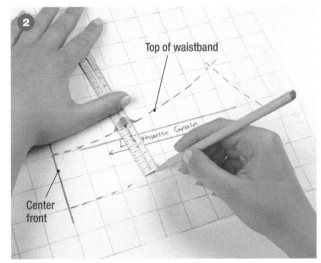

Top of waistband

Center front

Verify the Results

Check your work against the original pants.

1. Mark and measure the pants in intervals.

2. Compare the pants to your pattern draft. This is where Tru-Grid really comes in handy! If adjustments are needed, cross out the incorrect line, and redraw it using the 1-in. grid marks as your guide.

Finish the Pattern

Once you have verified all stitching lines, prepare the pattern for production.

1. Using a clear plastic ruler, add seam allowances around all of the pieces. Make them ½ in., ⅝ in., or 1 in.—your choice.

2. Label the pattern pieces. Write the name of each pattern piece in big, clear letters (2a, 2b). Add notes, such as how many pieces to cut. If desired, also jot down the seam allowance width as a reminder.

To double-check the fit, cut the pattern out in an inexpensive muslin fabric, and baste the seams together. There's no need to sew all the details at this point unless you want to double-check their positions, too.

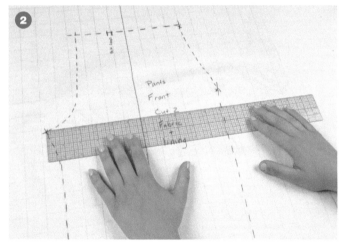

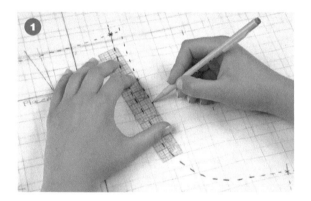

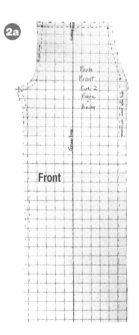

Front

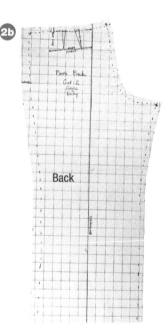

Back

Making a Pattern with Masking Tape

A fast and easy way to make a pattern from a ready-to-wear garment, without snipping any stitches, is to copy the garment with tape. The technique is shown here by copying a simple pair of pull-on pants. However, you can copy any garment: a blouse, jacket, coat, or even your sofa upholstery.

The process isn't hard: Tape an outline of the seams, fill in the void, transfer the taped shape to your pattern medium, and then add the hem and seam allowances.

Most of the time, it's best to work from the inside of the garment so you can see the exact stitching lines. But you can take a pattern from the face of the garment as well, which is necessary for lined garments.

Gather the tools listed below, then turn your garment inside out, and lay a strip of tape inside the hemline to test the fabric and tape compatibility. You don't want to tape an entire garment and then discover that the tape pulls out the metallic thread. Tuck one leg inside the other and position your pants inside out, with the back crotch on top and fully exposed. Now you're ready to start taping.

Matching Tape to Fabric and Other Supplies

Base your choice of tape on the weight and drape of the garment's fabric. For lightweight and medium-weight fabrics, including lightweight silk, rayon, slinky knit, and similar fabrics with a delicate hand, use either masking tape or medium-tack painter's tape. Medium-tack tapes release more easily, but they can also separate easily. Heavier and denser fabrics like denim, Ultrasuede®, heavyweight corduroy, and twill may require duct tape (Duck Tape by Manco is recommended) for a substantial and firm transferring medium.

Always test your tape/fabric compatibility before covering your garment with tape. And never leave any tape on your garment for more than an hour or two.

Opt for the nonwoven, interfacing-type pattern papers because they are strong, soft,

and easy to handle. Muslin also makes an excellent transfer medium. Pattern tissue works, but it isn't as forgiving and sometimes adheres to the tape before you want it to.

Have the following tools available:

- ⅝-in.-wide tape measure
- Pins
- Permanent, fine-point pen
- Scissors
- Yardstick
- Designer's curve and/or hip curve (optional)

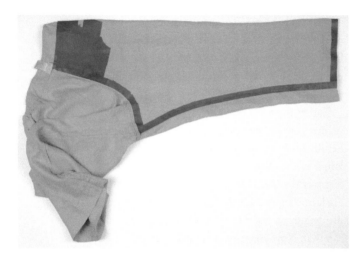

Outline the seams with tape.

Fill in the outlines.

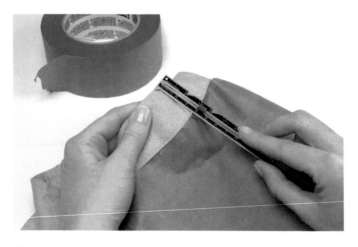

Measure the waistband casing.

Outline the Seamlines

Use ¾-in.- or 1-in.-wide tape torn into strips about 1½ in. long, and abut the long edge of the strip along the stitching line of the crotch seam as shown in the top left photo at left. Then overlap the strip ends so they'll hold together when you remove them later as one piece from the garment.

Tape up to the seamline but not onto the seam allowance. Once you've outlined the crotch seam, proceed down the inseam in the same manner. When you reach the hemline, tape horizontally against its edge. Continue taping along the seamlines until you've built an outline of the leg's pattern piece.

Fill In the Void

Once you've outlined the seams, fill in the leg with 2-in.-wide tape, starting horizontally at the hemline (see the center photo at left) and ending at the waistline. Overlap each 2-in.-wide strip and the outline tape to ensure that your taped shape won't pull apart when it's removed from the garment. As you fill in the leg with tape, pull out the other leg to keep your fabric flat. Make sure to smooth out the wrinkles as you affix your tape horizontally from the hem up to the waist.

As you work your way up the leg and approach the crotch wedge, use narrower tape or tear your 2-in.-wide tape in half if needed to accommodate the smaller area.

Tape the Waistline

At the waistline, stretch out the elastic where it gathers the fabric so you don't tape in wrinkles or pleats. You can do this by pulling the pants over an ironing board or recruiting an extra pair of hands to help hold the elastic taut until you capture the desired shape. Tape up to the base of the elastic. Then, measure the width of the elastic and the amount of fabric turned over for the casing, and make note of this distance to use later (see the bottom photo at left).

If your pants have a waistband instead of a folded casing, tape an outline of the waistband in a later step. If your pants have a dart, see "How to Copy Darts and Pockets" on the facing page.

How to Copy Darts and Pockets

You can use this same method to copy garments that include details such as darts and pockets.

COPYING A DART
Tape the section containing the dart while the garment is on your body or dress form. Mark the dart line on the tape. Cut along the dart line after you separate the tape from the garment. When you flatten the pattern, the dart will appear.

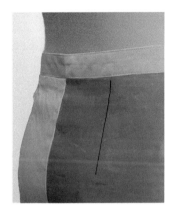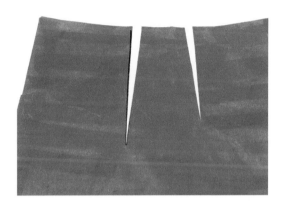

COPYING A PATCH POCKET
Follow the same steps as for a full pattern piece, using smaller pieces of tape. Pull the tape off from the top. Apply it to the pattern paper, and add seam allowances.

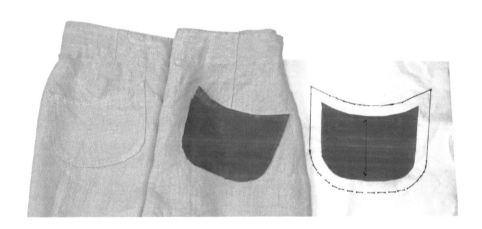

COPYING AN INSET POCKET
Copy the leg from the outside of the garment and the pocket from the inside.

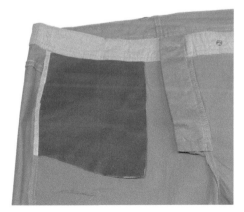

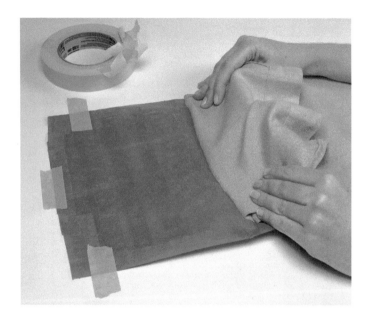

Peel the garment off the taped shape.

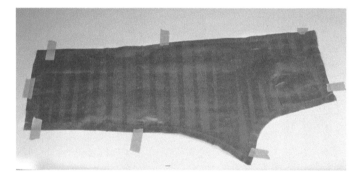

Secure the taped shape to the table, temporarily.

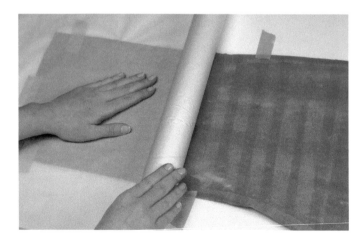

Lay pattern paper on the taped shape.

Remove the Tape

Once your first pattern section has been outlined and filled with tape, it's time to remove the taped shape from the garment. First, make sure you have established complete tape cover. Fill in any missing areas and check for ample tape overlap. As an extra precaution, especially if you've used medium-tack tape or masking tape, you can apply a strip of duct tape down the length of the pant leg to prevent the taped shape from tearing apart.

Prepare a clear table space large enough to accommodate and transfer your pattern. Place the leg with the adhesive side of the tape facing up, and the smooth side of the tape against the table. Gently lift the pants hem edge and start separating it from the taped shape at the hemline (see the top photo at left). As you separate the pant leg from the taped shape, use small pieces of tape to hold the edges to the table and prevent it from shifting (see the center photo at left). You don't want the taped shape to fold over onto itself by accident. Continue lifting the fabric by rolling the pant leg out of the way to release the entire taped shape.

Transfer the Tape to a Pattern

Cut your pattern paper 6 in. longer than the length of your pant leg, which allows ample extra length for hem and waistline considerations. Roll the pattern paper lengthwise. With several inches of tissue extending below the hemline, carefully unroll the paper and attach it to your taped shape (see the bottom photo at left). Go slowly and unroll only an inch or so at a time, smoothing the paper before proceeding until the entire taped shape is transferred to the pattern paper. When you've covered all of the tape, gently lift and turn the pattern paper over to see your captured pattern shape.

Now that you have finished taping and transferring the leg back, replicate the leg front following the same process. If you are copying a garment other than pants, the method is the same: Outline the seams and fill in the void with tape, transfer the taped shape to pattern paper, and proceed to the next pattern piece. A sleeve requires taping in the round, which is simplified by placing a sleeve board inside the sleeve.

Mark the Pattern

After you've transferred the leg front and back, compare the side seams and inseam lengths, and if they aren't the same, correct them as needed. Extend the waistline twice the width of the elastic and mark that amount above the tape shape along the waistline (see the top photo at right).

Treat the hemline like the waistline, adding the same amount of hem allowance used on the original garment. Before drawing in the seamlines, fold over your pattern paper along the hem and waistline so that you retain the correct shape when you add seam allowances. Tape the folded edge down. Many tape measures are ⅝ in. wide. To simplify marking a seam allowance, just lay one edge against the side of the leg seamline and draw in your seam allowance along the opposite edge.

Add seam allowances to all sides of the pattern (excluding the waistline and hemlines), as shown in the center photo at right. Cut the folded hemline and waistline seams on the new cutline you established by adding the seam allowance.

Add Grainlines

Fold the pant leg in half, aligning the inseam and side seam from the hemline to the knee, and then crease the leg to form your grainline, as shown in the bottom photo at right. Realize as you crease the grainline that it only lines up and matches below the knee. Don't try to make it line up any higher because many times it won't.

For other garments, you can identify many of the pattern grainlines by locating the center-front or center-back lines. But if you're copying a pattern piece that doesn't have an obvious grainline—such as the side-front panel of a princess-style jacket or dress—try to identify the grainline on the original garment and mark it on the tape while it's still affixed to the garment.

Add Notches

Pin the front and back side seams together, and mark both pieces at the waistline, hipline, knee, and hemlines. Use these marks to make notches to aid sewing accuracy during construction. And mark your pattern pieces as front and back to avoid confusion.

Now that you understand the simple steps, you can repeat them for copying more complicated patterns.

Measure and mark the waist casing on the pattern paper.

Add seam allowances.

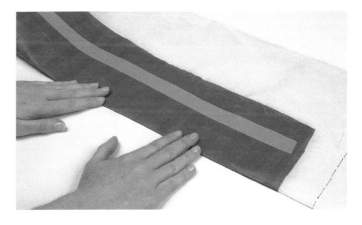

Fold the leg to establish the grainline.

Sewing for a Changing Figure

The passage of time, along with life changes, ensures that your figure won't remain the same from year to year. The beauty of sewing your own custom clothes is that you can always have clothes that fit and flatter, no matter how your silhouette alters.

Choosing a Pattern to Take In or Let Out

Some patterns are better suited to taking in or letting out. Consider these points when making your selection:

- If you gain or lose inches equally on the top and bottom, one-piece sheath dresses are fine; if not, opt for two-piece outfits.

- Keep style lines simple, focusing details around the neckline, where alterations aren't needed as often.

- Avoid fussy details at sleeve cuffs, in the waist area, or near the hem—they complicate adjustments.

- Faced waists are easier to alter than elastic waists or structured waistbands.

- Sleeveless garments can be taken in more than those with sleeves. Use sleeve facings rather than bindings.

- Sleeves with a lower sleeve cap, which can be set in flat (before sewing the bodice side seam), are easier to adjust.

- Put zippers or other closures in the seam you're least likely to alter, and choose invisible back zippers over fly fronts.

- Omit pockets when you can—the alteration process makes it hard to keep them appropriately positioned.

Weight Change

Most dedicated garment sewers enjoy wearing clothes that are stylish, unique, and definitely well fitted. When you're actively working to trim down, this can give rise to a fitting dilemma: You'd like your clothes to reflect your ever-svelter shape, but you don't want to invest hours in sewing garments that will look oversize in a month's time. You deserve a flattering wardrobe throughout your weight-loss journey—consider it one of the rewards for approaching your healthiest weight.

To achieve this, you don't have to sew a new set of clothes every few weeks. Try the approach described here for making garments that can shrink along with your measurements. (And if you put back on a few inches, the clothes can be adjusted, too, as long as you leave wide enough seam allowances.) You'll learn how to select pattern styles and fabrics that are visually slimming, and—even more important—you'll learn some special construction techniques that make it simple to adjust the size of your garments. With these methods, you'll be able to alter garments to accommodate about a 20-pound weight change.

Assess Your Figure

Before you plan a wardrobe for weight change, it's important to assess your figure type. A full-length mirror, often a sewer's best friend, is less revealing than a photograph when it comes to analyzing your shape, so grab a digital camera and a trusted friend and take some pictures.

Determine where you carry most of your excess weight, and think about where you gain or lose inches when your weight changes. For some, those inches come and go from the tummy and waist; for others, from the hips and thighs. Knowing where your shape will change first and most dramatically will help you select appropriate pattern styles.

Plan for Easy Alterations

Any seam in a garment offers an opportunity to adjust fit, but vertical seams are the most helpful when it comes to increasing or decreasing circumference measurements. For this reason, princess-seamed styles, especially those with seams running from the shoulder (rather than the armscye) to the hem, are ideal for making fit changes. A princess-seamed dress or blouse, for example, offers six seams where alterations can be made: If you deepen each seam by just ¼ in., you'll tighten the dress by a total of 3 in. without affecting the hang or look of the garment. In fact, you can take even more than ¼ in. out of each seam, and altering seamlines unevenly (taking out more where you've slimmed down most, less in other areas) contours your garment beautifully to your figure.

For skirts and pants, a similar principle holds true. Look for skirts with gores and pants that include seams down the front and back of each leg. You can also add vertical seams to skirts and pants that don't have them: Start a seam at one of the waist darts and continue it to the hem, keeping it parallel to the grainline.

Select Flattering Fabrics

Each of the styles suggested here introduces vertical lines, some of which will run across the fullest part of your figure. Although up-and-down lines can create a slimming effect, you may prefer less obtrusive seams. If so, camouflage the style lines by using textured fabrics, such as tweed or pique. Allover prints, too, hide seams well, but avoid extremely bold prints and plaids; fragmented motifs and mismatched repeats can call attention to seams you want to conceal. Taking in and letting out seams puts stress on fabric, so it's important to select fabric that has some body (which is more appropriate for fitted garments than flimsy fabric), doesn't show needle holes when stitching is removed, and, when pressed, doesn't let seam allowances show through.

Change the Sewing Sequence

It's a bit tedious to alter most garments—opening all those intersecting seams certainly doesn't seem like a creative way to spend your sewing time. But by rethinking the way you construct your clothes, you can build alterability into them. On pp. 168–169, you'll find instructions for reconfiguring facing shapes and for changing the sewing sequence for pants and skirts and for dresses and tops so that all the vertical fitting seams are simple to take in or let out when needed.

To make quick work of alterations at vertical seamlines, create individual facing pieces for each garment section that flanks a seam where you expect to make adjustments, as shown below.

MAKE SEPARATE FACINGS

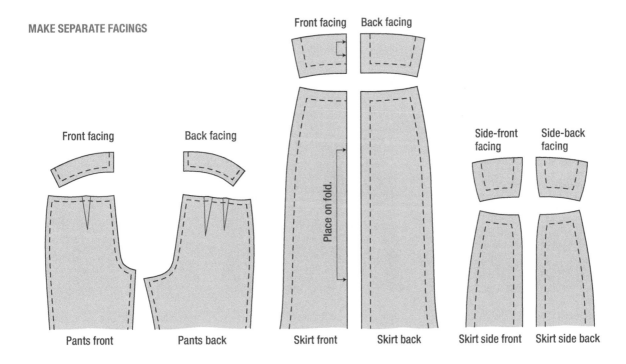

Front facing   Back facing

Front facing   Back facing

Side-front facing   Side-back facing

Place on fold.

Pants front   Pants back   Skirt front   Skirt back   Skirt side front   Skirt side back

By revising your sewing sequence from the traditional one, you can plan for seam intersections that facilitate, rather than interfere with, adjustments at vertical fitting seams. First, create any new facing pieces you might need, and finish the facing edges by serging, zigzagging, or pinking; avoid the turn-and-stitch method. Then, follow the construction sequences shown here.

PANTS AND SKIRTS

Sew all darts. Attach each facing section to its corresponding pattern piece, then press all the waistline seams open. For pants, sew the inseams. Insert a zipper in the center-back seam (see the left drawing below).

Join the gore seams for skirts and the center-leg seams on pants (if present), beginning at the facing edge and stitching toward the waist-seam intersection. Stop with the needle down at the waist seam, pivot the garment, and continue sewing to the hem. Sew the side seams in the same way (see the center drawing below).

For pants, insert one leg inside the other, with right sides together. Sew the crotch seam, starting at the bottom of the zipper and continuing to the front-waist seam. Stop with the needle down, pivot the garment, and continue sewing to the edge of the facing (see the right drawing below).

Press the facings to the inside of the garment, and anchor them to the seam allowances with a few hand stitches; don't understitch. Blind-hem the garment by hand or machine.

PRINCESS-SEAMED TOPS AND DRESSES

Insert a zipper in the center-back seam (omit this step if the garment has a center-front opening). Join the center front to the center back at shoulder seams, and the side fronts to the side backs at shoulder seams. Stitch the side panels to the center panels by sewing a continuous seam from the front hem to the back hem, passing through the shoulder seam (see the bottom left drawing on the facing page).

Leaving the side seams open, attach the sleeve or armscye facing to the armscyes. Press the seam open in the underarm area (see the bottom center drawing on the facing page).

Beginning at the facing edge or the sleeve hem, stitch toward the side seam. At the intersection with the sleeve seam, stop with the needle down, pivot the garment, and sew the side seam, ending at the hem. Press facings to the inside of the garment, but skip the understitching, which is time-consuming to remove for alterations. Hem sleeves by hand; tack facings to the side and shoulder seams. Finish the neckline as desired, and blind-hem the garment by hand or machine (see the bottom right drawing on the facing page).

CONSTRUCTION SEQUENCE FOR EASY ALTERATION OF PANTS AND SKIRTS

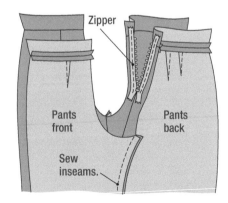

Attach each facing. For pants, sew inseams and zipper.

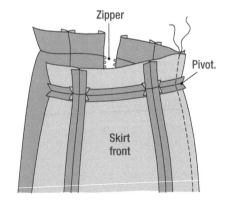

Join gore seam for skirts and center-leg seam on pants.

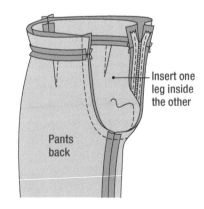

For pants, insert one leg inside the other and sew crotch seam.

Adjust at the Vertical Seams

After reengineering the garment with your new construction techniques, all you need to do to adjust the piece is loosen facings and hem edges, and adjust the seams (see the drawing at right).

First, undo the hem—entirely or just in the seam areas. Untack facings that were fastened to seam allowances.

Then, turn the garment inside out and put it on. To take it in, pin the vertical seams and facings to match any seam changes. (To increase the circumference, unstitch the needed seams and repin with narrower seam allowances.) Remove the garment, and—before removing the previous stitching—resew it and the facing seams as pinned. Remove the previous stitching, press the seam allowances open, and trim if you wish.

Next, try on the garment and adjust the hem. Resew the hem and tack the facings to the inside.

There's no easy way to adjust a fully lined garment, so it's more efficient to simply omit linings. In fact, don't sweat the finer details when you're sewing for weight changes, and focus instead on experimenting with fashion trends, using up stashed fabric, or playing with new fabrics that might not be in style next year. This approach to sewing isn't necessarily the way you might choose to make garments you anticipate wearing for many years to come, but it's perfect for temporary clothes that will see you through a season or so.

TIP For a quick hem when making minor adjustments, stitch a portion of the hem separately at each side of the seams, so you can undo just the seam area to take in or let out, and leave the rest in place.

CONSTRUCTION SEQUENCE FOR EASY ALTERATION OF PRINCESS-SEAMED TOPS AND DRESSES

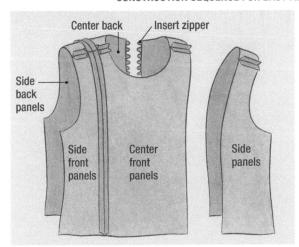

Join the center front to the center back and the side panels to center panels.

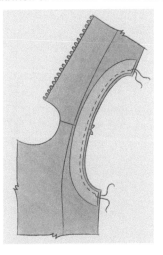

Leaving side seams open, attach the sleeve or armscye.

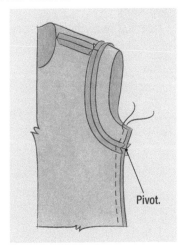

Finish the garment.

Sewing for a Mature Figure

Just when most of us have finally perfected the fit of our favorite patterns after years of altering them, our bodies start to play tricks on us. Regardless of what shape we're in, our shapes begin to change, and our clothing just doesn't fit the same way it once did. The most common of these changes are the following:

- **Rounding shoulders:** Shoulder seams slide toward the neck, jewel necklines feel too high and tight, and horizontal folds may appear above the bust.

- **Narrowing chests:** Even if the shoulders still fit, armscye seams may start to cut into the arm, and vertical wrinkles may appear at the arm crease.

- **Broadening backs:** Along with the two previous shifts, you'll usually feel pulling at the back of the sleeves and across the upper back. The intersection between side seam and armscye may feel strained.

- **Lowering bustline:** Bust darts and princess seams no longer feel well placed or properly shaped.

- **Protruding abdomen:** Skirts ride up in front, waistlines tilt up, and side seams start slanting and wrinkling diagonally.

- **Thickening waists:** Waistbands feel tight and side seams pull forward above the hipline.

- **Increasing high hip:** Skirts seem to ride up all around, and feel tight above the hipline.

- **Lowered, flattened seat:** Pants look droopy in back, and skirts look too wide.

The changes needed to fit the mature figure are shown in the drawings below and on the facing page. You may not need all of these adjustments.

Rounding Shoulders

For minor shoulder-seam shifts when the neckline is okay, simply remove a portion of the front shoulder seam, and add it to the back. Then shift the shoulder dot on the sleeve forward by the same amount (see the far left drawings below).

For a rounded upper back, or dowager's curve, add length at the center back with shoulder darts to take up the excess at the shoulder seam (see the center left drawing below). For more details on fitting rounded shoulders, see pp. 75–79.

For more severe rounding, add length in back and remove it in front through the middle of the armscye, raising the back neckline and lowering the front neckline at the same time (see the center right drawings below). Check the shoulder seam placement at the base of the neck and the shoulder tip by pin fitting, adjusting the seam angle as needed. Adjust the sleeves to match by shifting the sleeve cap forward by the amount of the change, thereby adding length to the back cap and removing it from the front cap (see the far right drawing below).

ALTERATIONS FOR ROUNDING SHOULDERS

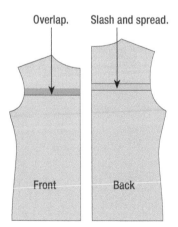
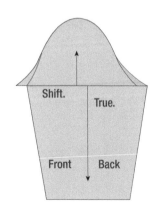

For a minor shoulder seam shift, remove length from front seam and add to back.

For slightly rounded shoulders, add length.

For severe rounding, add length in the back and remove it from the front. Adjust the sleeves.

Narrow Chest and Broad Back

Related to rounded shoulders, these changes usually go together. Decrease the pattern across the chest by reshaping the armscye. Increase the pattern across the back by adding at the armscye and side seam. Add to the sleeve underarm in back the same amount as you add to the side seam (see the far left drawings below).

Lowered Bustline

Redirect darts to point to the bust apex, or shift the entire side or underarm darts downward if they would point downward when redirected (see the center left drawing below). For more information on reshaping princess seams, see pp. 43–45.

Protruding Abdomen

Extra length and width are needed at the center front to go over the abdomen. Measure across the abdomen from side to side, then allow 1-in. ease for width.

Measure from the waist to the floor at the center and side to find the extra length needed at center front (see the center left drawing below).

Thickening Waist and High Hip

Add more width above the hips at the side seams, and make the darts shallower, or add soft pleats. Adjust the waistband to match.

Lower Seat

Remove excess width from the back of a skirt at the back side seams in the hip area. Pants need less length along the center-back seam, less width at the hip, and a shorter back crotch point, with a straighter center-back seam (see the far right drawing below).

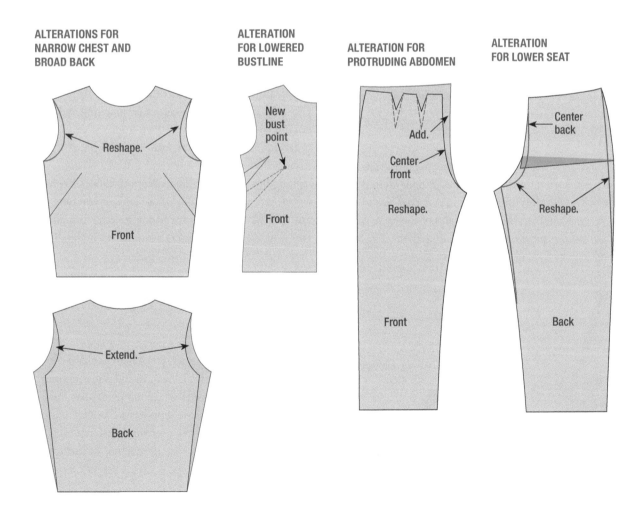

ALTERATIONS FOR NARROW CHEST AND BROAD BACK

Reshape.

Front

Extend.

Back

ALTERATION FOR LOWERED BUSTLINE

New bust point

Front

ALTERATION FOR PROTRUDING ABDOMEN

Add.

Center front

Reshape.

Front

ALTERATION FOR LOWER SEAT

Center back

Reshape.

Back

Fitting Bras

A well-fitting outfit starts with well-fitting foundation garments. For many women, finding a bra that fits properly is difficult, but you don't have to settle for a less-than-flattering silhouette. You can learn not only how to buy a bra with a great fit, but also how to copy it so you can always have the support and shaping you want.

Making your own custom-fitted bra can be a quick and rewarding project. If you're able to cut accurately and sew a precise ¼-in. seam, you can make a bra. For the first bra, plan to spend an evening or so. After this one is fitted and finished, you'll find that subsequent bras take two hours or less. Best of all, once you perfect the fit, you can keep the pattern forever, secure in the knowledge that you've solved one of a woman's trickiest wardrobe problems.

Anatomy of a Bra

The four elements of a basic bra include a bra band, cups, straps, and a closure. Variations in these key elements determine the bra style.

BAND
A full-band style, for example, offers the most support; it has a continuous band that extends around the body, with the cups set into it. A partial-band style has a band attached at the sides of the cups, with a center-front piece or hook separating them. The bra band may be a single layer or lined.

CUPS
Cups can be made of one, two, or three lined or unlined sections, with two being the most common. Cups may or may not include underwires for shaping. Lace cups are often lined with sheer tricot to add stability and reduce scratchiness. You can even add padding to the cups to make a push-up bra.

STRAPS
Straps can be made of strap elastic (less stretchy than regular elastic), nonstretchy strapping, or self-fabric, with or without an adjuster (the most common is a ring-and-slide adjustment). Nonstretchy straps usually have some elastic at the back for ease of movement.

CLOSURE
Bras close in either the front or back with hooks, and back closures usually have two or three size adjustments. Many sports bras pull on, with no closures at all.

For maximum shaping and support, an underwire bra is the best choice for most women. The underwire shapes and holds the cup to a fixed diameter, which can benefit even a small-busted woman. Complaints about underwires are due mainly to poorly fitting bras, which can cause pinching and poking wires. You'll see bras sewn from a wide variety of fabrics, including tricot, lace, stretch satin, cotton/Lycra®, and all-cotton knits and wovens. When making bras, you have the freedom to choose bright colors, jacquards, polka dots, or plaids, if you like. For your first attempt, start with a stretch fabric like two-way stretch nylon/Lycra satin, which makes fitting easier and forgives small errors.

Getting Started

Bra patterns (see Resources, p. 192) are available in a range of styles and sizes. Each includes instructions for sewing the bra, as well as recommendations for fabrics and notions. Some suppliers sell bra kits, as well, which include all the necessary materials to create a bra (the pattern may or may not be included in the kit).

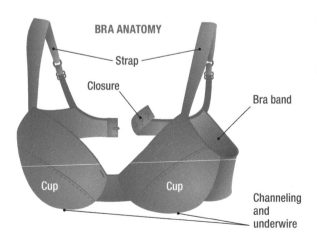

BRA ANATOMY
Strap
Closure
Bra band
Cup
Cup
Channeling and underwire

Calculating Your Bra Size

The first step in making a well-fitting bra is measuring your body so you know what size pattern to start with. You'll need to calculate your bra-band size and your cup size, wearing your best-fitting bra. (Large-busted women especially need support for accurate measurements.) For all the measurements, use a full-length mirror to make sure the tape is kept level around the body. For the measurement under your bust, be sure to keep the tape snug. Once you have your measurement, calculate your bra-band size as directed in "Measuring for a Bra," at right. When taking your full-bust measurement, again, keep the tape level but don't pull it snug. To determine the cup size, subtract the high-bust measurement from the full-bust measurement.

The difference, in inches, tells you the cup size (see "Bra Cup Size," below right). For example, if your bra band is 36 in. and your full bust is 38 in., your cup size is B; you'll make a size 36B. Remember that this is just a starting point. Your actual bra size may be slightly different.

Defining Good Fit

A well-fitting bra is comfortably snug around the body, with the breasts filling the cups completely—no excess fabric in the cups, and no breast tissue spilling out of the cup at the top, side, or bottom. The bra's center front touches, or very nearly touches, the breastbone. The bra band doesn't ride up in back, and the straps stay in place without slipping or digging into the shoulders. Ideally, the bust level is about halfway between elbow and shoulder, although this may not be practical for a heavy-busted woman.

BRA-MAKING NOTIONS

Measuring for a Bra

Most pattern companies design bodice patterns to fit a B cup. That's great if that's your correct size, but many women with bust-fitting issues don't know their correct bra size. It takes three measurements to determine your bra size.

- While wearing your best-fitting bra, measure the circumference under your bust. Keep the tape measure snug. To this measurement, add either 4 in. or 5 in. to get an even number. This total is your bra-band size **(A)**.

- Next, measure the circumference above your bust. This measurement is taken high under your arms. It is your chest—excluding your bust—and is called the "high bust" measurement **(B)**.

- Then, measure around your full bust. Make sure the tape measure is parallel to the floor all around the body and is positioned over the fullest part of your bust **(C)**.

Subtract the high-bust measurement from the full-bust measurement. The difference determines your cup size.

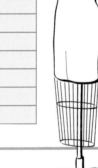

Bra Cup Size

The difference between your high-bust and full-bust measurements determines your cup size.

DIFFERENCE	BRA CUP SIZE
Less than 1 in.	AA
1 in.	A
2 in.	B
3 in.	C
4 in.	D
5 in.	DD or E
6 in.	DDD, EE, or F

When making a bra, check the fit with a sample: Make a sample cup with the pattern and fabric you plan to use, and hold it up to yourself. It should completely cover the breast from the center front to the side, and under the breast to the rib cage, with a little extra all around for seam allowances. Check that the breast fills the cup completely, without bulging at the sides or bottom. Can you pinch any excess fabric at the bust point? If so, make a note of how much and adjust the pattern pieces accordingly. (Two women may have the same rib-cage and full-bust measurements, yet still be different cup sizes.)

Now try the cup on the other breast. Many women aren't symmetrical, so it's important to check both sides. If your left side differs noticeably from your right, make separate pattern pieces for each side and label them. You can really customize the fit with the help of a family member or close friend (you'll need four hands). Hold the fitting cup up to yourself and have your helper hold the underwire against the cup in the correct position. Trace the entire bottom edge of the wire, using a pencil or fabric marker. Take it off and add ⅜ in. to the bottom for the channeling and seam allowance.

Common Fitting Problems

Most fitting problems are easy to remedy and often result from the mismatch of cup and band size.

- **Cup size needs adjusting:** Cups that are too small will need to be larger (and vice versa). If the cups fit correctly but the bra band is too tight or loose, changing the band size will also alter cup size. The C cup on a size 36 is about the same size as B cup on a 38. And if you go down a band size, you'll go up a cup size.

Pin out excess to shape the cup.

Upper cup (WS)

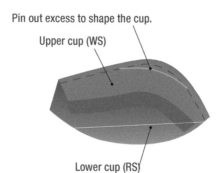

Lower cup (RS)

- **Cup needs reshaping:** If the cup is too small, you can go up to a larger cup size and reshape the tip, if needed. To remove excess fabric, pin out the excess on the test cup, tapering to zero. Make the same changes to the pattern, as shown below.
- **Bra band rides up in back:** If the band is too loose, the cups are too small, or both, try going up a cup size or down a band size. A larger bust needs a wider, closer-fitting band to support the weight of the bust.
- **Straps won't stay on the shoulders:** They may be too loose or set too far apart for narrow or sloping shoulders. Adjust the straps to give some lift to the bust. If you like, stitch the straps to stay in place. (A custom-fitted bra does not really need adjustable straps. Manufacturers use them to fit more women with fewer sizes.) You can move the straps closer together in back, or choose a different pattern.
- **Straps dig into the shoulders:** This also indicates a loose band or cups that are too small. A wider band and wider, padded straps help.

Making a sample bra (or two) will help you perfect the size of your pattern, and it's worth the time and effort. You can use the fabrics and notions recommended by the pattern, but don't hesitate to experiment with others as well. With experience, you'll learn what's most comfortable and supportive.

Cloning a Favorite Bra

If you've purchased a bra that fits just the way you want, you can use the method shown here to copy it.

Start by evaluating the fit of the bra you want to copy (see "Defining Good Fit," p. 173). The cup is the crucial area for fitting; you can adjust the band and the bridge (the short band of fabric that joins the cups at center front; this isn't present on all bras) once you have a pattern to work with. After developing a pattern from an existing bra, it's a good idea to refer to either a book on bra making or pattern instructions for a similarly styled bra, for help in constructing the garment. (See Resources, p. 192.)

Locate Stretch

Test each part of the bra that stretches for give, and draw an arrow on each piece with a water-soluble marker to indicate the direction of greatest stretch. The cups can be made of stretch or nonstretch fabric, depending on the style and support level of the original. If your cups are nonstretch, you'll still need to mark the direction of the greatest give on these pieces so that, no matter what fabrics you use, you can match the stretch on your bra to the original. You'll also need to mark the center front with a ruler, from top to bottom, at the bridge, if there is one. If your cups are seamless, also mark the bust apex on one cup with a dot. The bridge is always nonstretch; this area needs to be rigid for correct support.

Prepare the Copying Surface

The primary tool for cloning your bra is a firm, flat, pinnable surface you can attach the bra to and pin into as you trace its outlines with pin pricks. The best surface is foam-core board, available from most arts-and-crafts stores and office suppliers. The advantage of foam core is its stiffness; it holds pins firmly, and each pin leaves a clear, easy-to-see hole. Foam core that is ½ in. thick is ideal, but ¼-in. board will do in a pinch. One standard-sized 20-in. by 30-in. sheet will accommodate the largest bras.

You'll also need thin, see-through drafting paper, such as doctor's examination-table paper, available at medical-supply houses. Don't bother with freezer paper and brown kraft paper, which aren't see-through, or a synthetic paper like Do-Sew®, which won't show the pinholes. You'll also need glass- or plastic-headed pins, a sharp pencil, and a small, transparent ruler. When you're ready to start, cover the foam-core board with paper and pin it in place.

To prepare the bra, remove the underwire, if there is one, from one side of the bra. The wire is easiest to remove and return to its original state if you unpick a few stitches at the center-front end of the channel that holds the wire and slip it out; it will go neatly back in place with a couple of rows of machine stitches when you're done. Be sure to make a tracing or photocopy of the original wire, and send the drawing of it to your bra-supply source, where it can be matched for wires in the same size.

Cloning Basics

You'll copy your bra by systematically pulling each of its sections to its original flat-fabric size, stretching any attached elastic at the edges to allow the section to lie flat, unstretched, just as it would have been cut from yardage. You'll know you've stretched the attached elastic enough when all the wrinkles are gone from the fabric, but the fabric itself is not stretched. You'll pin the fabric down that way, at its edges along every seamline, and your pins will trace the outline of the piece with pinpricks through the paper underneath. Copy only one side of the bra; you can use either side, but be sure to stay with it throughout the cloning. Keep the top edge of the bra facing up when pinning and mark each piece as to its vertical orientation, because the pieces are easily turned upside down and confused during construction.

Don't get seamlines confused with topstitching, which is found on every bra, and be observant about possible seamline locations; for example, often there's a short seamline on the band under the cup area. Stick the pins fairly deep into the fabric and foam core, about ½ in. apart and as close together as ⅛ in. in really complex areas. When the pinning is complete, you'll remove the pins and connect the pinholes with a pencil to create a solid outline on the paper. These outlines, plus seam allowances, will be the pattern pieces for your new bra.

You only need to pin-trace one half of the bridge, even if there's no center-front seam, in which case you'll cut the pattern (but not the fabric) on the fold. Be accurate about the center front and draw the center-front line with a ruler, since this is an area where a little misjudgment can spell disaster.

PIN-TRACE THE BAND

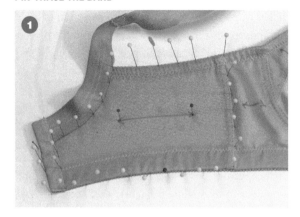

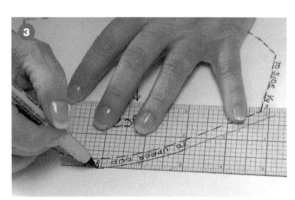

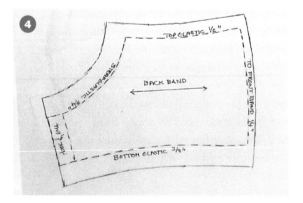

Pin-Trace the Band

1. Place pins at each end of the stretch-direction marks to transfer these, and pin-mark the shape of the hook-and-eye panel at the same time. Elastics are typically folded under along their seamlines, so the pins marking elasticized edges are placed along the perimeter, not at the inner edge of the elastic.

2. After removing the pins, connect the pinholes to outline the pattern shape. There are no jagged or wobbly edges on any bra pieces, so smooth the line around any misplaced or moved holes.

3. Add seam allowances using a clear ruler as a guide, and label them so you can be sure what gets attached to what. Note which edges are seams and which have elastic applied, and mark where seams intersect. For example, if a two-piece lower cup joins a one-piece upper cup, add a dot to mark where the junction should be positioned on the upper-cup seamline.

4. Differentiate seam allowances: ¼ in. for fabric-to-fabric seam allowances, and ⅜ in. for seams with underwire channeling sewn to it. Allowances for elastic equal the width of the elastic being used. You can change elastic widths later, but it's less confusing if you duplicate everything first.

Repeat the process for the cup and all the other flat parts of half of the original bra, being careful to pin exactly at the seamlines, and not at topstitching lines.

Pin-Trace the Cup

1. Copy the shape of the cup. The cup can't usually be pinned flat because it's attached to other pieces.

2. Pin as much as you can flat, then unpin the beginning to free the end of the fabric, leaving in the most recently set pins to keep the piece from shifting as you continue pinning the rest of the outline.

3. Move across the entire section this way, releasing the finished section as necessary until the piece is finished.

PIN-TRACE THE CUP

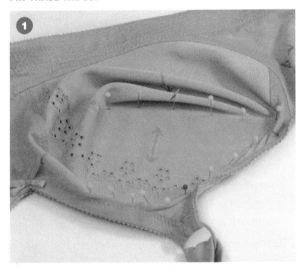
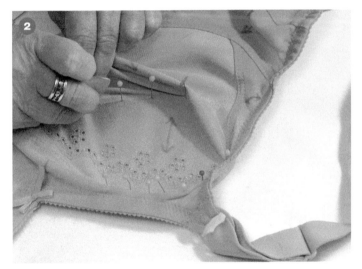
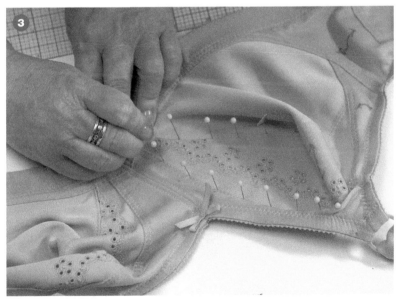

PIN-TRACING A SEAMLESS CUP

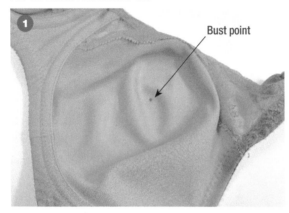

Bust point

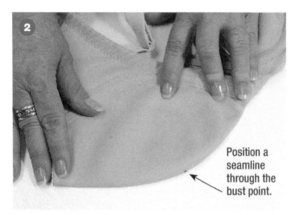

Position a seamline through the bust point.

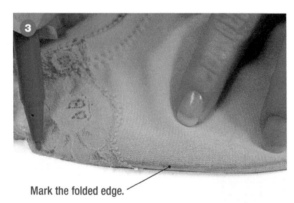

Mark the folded edge.

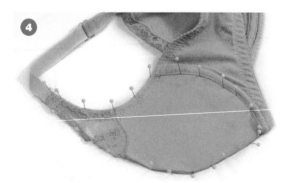

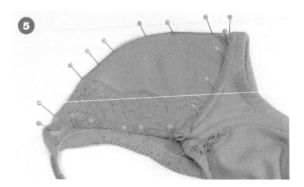

Cloning a Seamless Cup

Seamless cups are shaped in the factory by heat-setting the fabric over a hot, breast-shaped mold. You can duplicate these molded cup shapes simply by adding a seam, as shown in the drawings on the facing page.

First, put the bra on, adjust it to fit properly, and mark the bust point. Next, choose a seamline direction for your clone. Whatever direction you choose, the seam must pass through the bust point. This is true for any cup seams on any bra. Once you've decided on a direction, fold the bra where you want the seam to be, making sure it runs through the bust point. You'll know the fold is placed properly when the cup fabric lies as flat as possible. On an older, stretched-out bra, the fabric might not lie as flat as on a new one, but it will always lie flattest when the fold runs through the bust point.

1. Mark the bust point on the cup.

2. Fold the cup to position a seamline where you want it, making sure it passes through the marked point. If the fold doesn't pass through the bust point, you won't be able to smooth the cup flat.

3. Mark the folded edge with a water-soluble marker.

4. Pin one side of the cup with the other side folded under it, keeping the marker line right at the fold and pinning right through the layers underneath.

5. Unpin and trace the outline on paper. Then flip the cup over, position it elsewhere on the paper, and pin and trace the other side.

Construction and Fitting Tips

Once your pattern is made and cut out, with all seam allowances added, check it for accuracy by abutting the pattern pieces at the seamlines and "walking" one piece around the adjoining piece. This ensures that all joining seamlines are the same length, making adjustments if necessary.

Make the cloned bra from fabrics that are as similar as possible to the original. For example, if the original cups were Antron® tricot, there's no point in making the new cups from spandex, because they won't fit the same way. Likewise, if the band is made from power net, you'll want to look for a fabric that offers the same firm stretch characteristics. Your bra supplier should be able to help you with these choices.

Once you make a trial bra, you may wish to fine-tune some of the fitting areas. Common areas for fit adjustments include the strap position and the bridge

width. You can easily move the strap position closer to the center front if the straps are inclined to fall off the shoulder. The back strap position can be moved closer to the hook and eye, too.

A telltale sign of needed bridge alteration occurs when the bridge sits against the chest wall at the bottom, but projects at an angle away from the body at the top edge. This means the bridge needs to be made wider at the bottom. There may even be horizontal stress marks on the bridge. To widen the base of the bridge, simply slash the pattern piece from the bottom up to, but not through, the top edge and spread the necessary amount, then redraw the bottom edge.

It's usually the case that the wider the bottom band elastic, the greater the support and comfort level—no doubt because the band elastic provides most of the support in a bra. Most commercial bras use a standard ⅜-in. elastic for all parts of the band, top and bottom. More expensive, high-quality bras may use ½-in. elastic for the bottom band.

Seam Options for Bra Cups

As long as the seam passes through the bust point, bra cups can have seams oriented in any direction, whether diagonally, horizontally, or vertically.

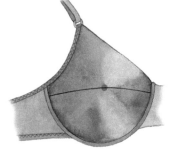

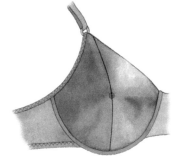

DIAGONAL
A diagonal seam runs from higher on the side to lower at the front, starting anywhere in the armhole curve. This is the most common and flattering placement, both to the shape of the bust and for the look of the bra itself.

HORIZONTAL
A horizontal seam runs side to side, starting anywhere in the wire line or band area below the armhole. A seam in this position allows the lower cup maximum curve, but is not considered the most flattering seam orientation.

VERTICAL
A vertical seam runs up and down, starting anywhere from the strap to the center front. A seam in this position flattens the cup below the point, creating a push-out effect to anything above it. The vertical seam offers the greatest support.

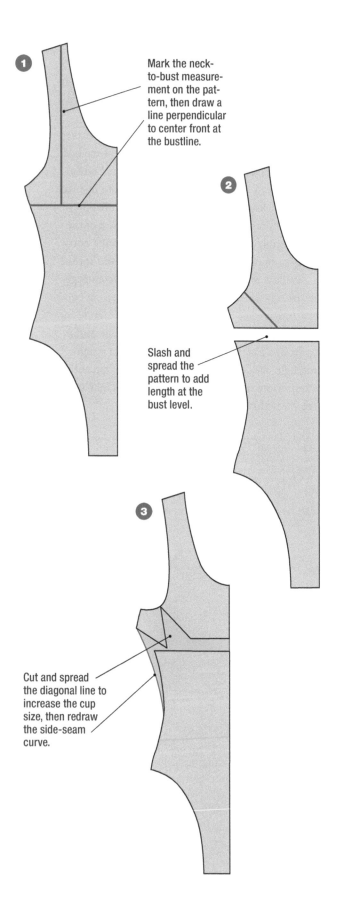

Mark the neck-to-bust measurement on the pattern, then draw a line perpendicular to center front at the bustline.

Slash and spread the pattern to add length at the bust level.

Cut and spread the diagonal line to increase the cup size, then redraw the side-seam curve.

Fitting Swimsuits

Most swimsuit patterns are designed to fit up to a C-cup bust. For larger bust sizes, altering the bustline to add extra fabric in the width and length will result in a much more comfortable and well-fitting suit.

The bustline is the horizontal line that marks the location of the widest measurement across the bust. To find out where to mark this line on a swimsuit pattern, you first need to locate your bustline. Next, measure the distance from your shoulder seam, just at the base of the neck, straight down to your bustline with the tape perpendicular to the bustline, not slanted. Transfer this measurement to the front pattern piece by measuring from the shoulder down, remembering to account for the pattern's seam allowance (1). Draw the bustline on the pattern at the measurement point, perpendicular to center front.

Next, draw a second line that runs from the armhole to about the middle of the front pattern piece, then slash the horizontal line and spread ½ in. for each cup size above C (add ½ in. for a D cup, 1 in. for DD, and so on) (2). After altering for a larger cup size, be sure to follow up by adjusting your overall torso length, if needed.

Cut a diagonal line just to the armhole and, without changing the armhole length, spread the "dart" ½ in. for each cup size above C. Redraw the curve of the side-seam line from the waist to the armhole (3). Gather the added amount at the front side seam in the bust area to match the back side seam.

This process works well, providing your pattern is a basic tank style. If your swimsuit has spaghetti straps, the best approach is to figure out where you want the neckline of the suit to sit on your body and mark the bustline from there, similar to the way you mark a tank style.

One great feature of sewing with Lycra-blend fabrics is that their stretch properties are very forgiving, so the fit doesn't have to be as perfect. If your adjustment point is slightly off, no one will notice.

Tools for Fitting and Alteration

Garment fitting involves working both with patterns and with garments—either test garments or fashion pieces you want to fine-tune on the body. Having the right tools and knowing how to use them is basic to the mastery of fitting. The tools shown here make accurate measuring and marking a sure thing for sewers of every skill level.

Measuring Tools

The prerequisite for any successful garment-sewing project is taking accurate measurements of the body. Measuring a body that's standing is a two-person job, and the right tape measure can make the activity more accurate and less embarrassing, whether you're the measurer or the one being measured. Over time,

tape measures, especially those made from treated cloth, can stretch, fray, or tear, Nowadays, most models are made from plastic or reinforced fiberglass. Check them occasionally against a hard (metal, wooden, or plastic) ruler for accuracy and replace when needed. Choose a tape with reinforced metal tips; the most convenient ones have numbers printed on both sides, with the numeral 1 on opposite ends. With these, no matter which end of the tape you grab, you can always start at zero.

"MODESTY" TAPE MEASURE

A rigid support backs one end of this tape. To measure someone else's inseam with minimal embarrassment or awkwardness, hold the bottom of the support as you position the tape end at the crotch.

TWO EASY TAPE™ AND INSEAM COMPANION

This pair of measuring tapes is configured to easily measure the crotch length and inseam from a secure reference point. One tape measures in both directions from a zero marking at its center, and a second tape is attached by a metal loop. To use it, pass the first tape through the crotch from center front to center back and secure it with a piece of elastic tied around the waist. Then adjust the tape so the zero and the metal loop are at the inseam. You can take very accurate crotch front, crotch back, and inseam measurements with this tool.

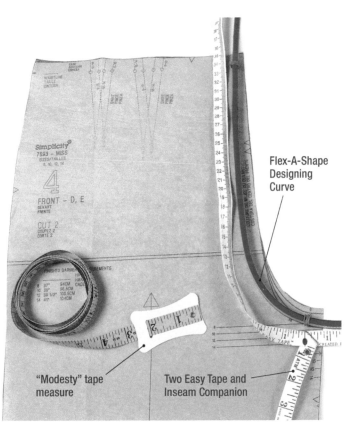

Flex-A-Shape
Designing
Curve

"Modesty" tape
measure

Two Easy Tape and
Inseam Companion

Tools for Adjusting and Drafting Patterns

Once armed with accurate measurements, you can adjust lines and curves on commercial patterns to personalize the fit, or draft original patterns. The following tools facilitate laying out and drawing smooth curves and straight lines, whether altering or designing.

C-THRU® RULER

Many sewers count this transparent ruler among their favorite tools. It's marked in an ⅛-in. grid and divided into inches counting both from end to end and out from the center. Use this ruler to check for symmetry, alter patterns, measure and mark seam and hem allowances, and establish perfectly parallel or perpendicular lines. Since you can see through the grid, it's easy to make parallel adjustments. You'll find this ruler in several sizes and colors at an office or art supply store.

TAILOR'S SQUARE

This L-square is unique because it makes it easy for you to mark a specific inch span into thirds (or halves, two-thirds, quarters, eighths, or sixteenths) at a glance, a function designed for use in pattern drafting but handy when you want to distribute repeating elements evenly in a given space. You can see the fractional divisions printed along one edge. The right angle allows you to establish lengthwise and crosswise grainlines on slopers or master patterns, and you can square it against a corner edge of fabric to confirm the grainline, or use it to check that your quilt corners are square. If you connect the inside and outside corners diagonally with a straightedge, you will establish a 45-degree angle, which you can use to draw a perfect bias line.

Tailor's square

FLEXIBLE RULER

When it comes to replicating and outlining any curved shape, you really can't beat the wonderful properties of a flexible ruler. This ruler with an inner lead core comes in a variety of sizes and can follow the contour of almost anything. A flexible ruler copies a shape, holds it in place, and enables you to transform it into a flat pattern.

Flexible rulers come in lengths from 16 in. to 40 in. and are bendable, pliable, and twistable. A flexible ruler has a measuring tape within the plastic coating on each side of it; one side gives measurements in inches and the other in centimeters. When you are outlining a shape, this multifaceted tool allows you to measure the shape's length and add seam allowances to it at the same time. These rulers are especially useful for copying very precise curves, shapes, and sizes. Just contour the inner edge of the ruler against the outer edge of the shape you want replicated, and trace.

The dimensions of the flexible ruler itself can also be an aid to your patternmaking. Since it measures ⅜ in. wide when lying flat or ¼ in. wide when on its side, it can easily help you alter your pattern by those dimensions. Just hold the flexible ruler on its side and trace along it to add a clean ¼-in. seam allowance as it outlines any shape it's replicating. By turning it over and laying it flat against the seamline, you can instantly add a ⅜-in. seam allowance to all of your pattern's seamlines.

When using the ruler against the body or any pattern seamlines, remember to lay the side facing the inch measurements next to the shape that you are following. Since the width of the ruler is ¼ in., you should record the measurement side that is closest to the body, otherwise you will increase the dimensions

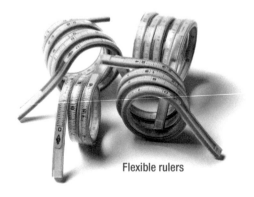

Flexible rulers

Designing with a Flexible Ruler

For both fitting and designing purposes, a flexible ruler comes in handy. It conforms to two- and three-dimensional shapes so you can transfer them to a pattern.

DESIGNING BEAUTIFUL NECKLINES

A. To make a plunging back V neck, wrap the ends of a 40-in. flexible ruler together with a rubber band. Then, position the ruler around the neckline with the ends in the back. Let the ruler gracefully shape where it naturally falls.

B. Trace the desired shape onto your muslin or tissue pattern.

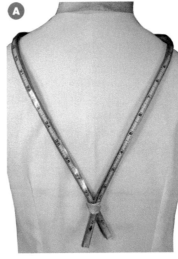

Position the ruler around the neckline.

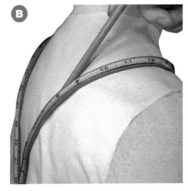

Trace the desired shape.

COPYING THE FIT OF YOUR FAVORITE PANTS

A. Turn the pants inside out. Place one pant leg inside the other to reveal the inside of the crotch curve. Pin to anchor at the waistline so that the curve doesn't shift. Then, lay the inches side of the flexible ruler along the seamline of the pants and record the front crotch measurement (the distance along the curve from front waist to inseam).

B. On your pattern, start the ruler at zero at the center-front waist and alter the front crotch/inseam tissue to meet the front length measurement. Pin the tissue pattern inseam together at the new crotch point.

C. Align your newly shaped flexible ruler onto your tissue pattern and draw in the rest of the crotch seam (use the inside of the ruler).

D. Mark the new seamline following the flexible curve, then add seam allowances to it.

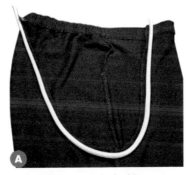

Lay the ruler along the inside seam.

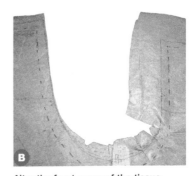

Alter the front curve of the tissue pattern to meet the front length measurement. Pin the tissue pattern inseam together.

Draw in the rest of the curve.

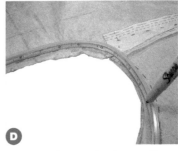

Mark seamlines on the tissue pattern.

you are measuring by ¼ in. If you prefer centimeters, then just flip it over to the other side and lay the metric portion against the shape to get that reading as well.

You will find it easy to outline around the ruler with a marker, as its plastic outer shell is waterproof. This is another convenient feature if you use water-soluble pens.

PATTERN NOTCHER

Designed for use by train conductors, this nickel-plated, cast-iron punch is heavy enough to make distinctive ⅟₁₆-in. by ¼-in. notches in patterns cut from oak tag or paper. Use it to mark strategic match points, dart placements, and pleats. To punch interior marks like dart tips, fold the paper and punch

through the fold. Use tailor's tacks, marking pens, or chalk through the punched notches to transfer their location to fabric.

SEAM GAUGE

This multitasking 6-in. metal ruler has a sliding indicator that you set to a specific measurement. This easily portable reference makes measuring, comparing, and establishing the size of hems, seam allowances, tucks, pleats, buttons, and buttonholes uncomplicated and memory-free because the slider holds the measurement until you reposition it.

A plus: The seam gauge and slider each contain a hole that you can use to create a compass. Put a pin through one hole to pivot on and a pencil through the other as shown.

You can also use a seam gauge as a compass.

Tools for Marking Information

To transfer measurements, shapes, or markings from a muslin to a pattern or from a pattern to fabric, use a tool designed for the task at hand.

MARKING WHEELS

The points of a **pinpoint tracing wheel** leave a punctured trail beneath any line they pass through, making this wheel ideal for transferring a pattern onto paper. If you're making a symmetrical pattern, draw half, fold the paper, and run the wheel over the lines to transfer the reversed image to the other half. You can make a pattern from finished clothing by spreading out a garment onto paper and running the pinpoint wheel along the edges and through the seamlines. But be cautious, because the points may mar the fabric—that's why this wheel shouldn't be used with dressmaker's tracing paper to mark most fashion fabrics.

Use **notched or smooth tracing wheels** with dressmaker's tracing paper to transfer marks from patterns to fabric prior to sewing. These days, specialized tracing papers wash or brush away easily, but it's a good idea to first test them on fabric scraps.

Roll-A-Pattern is a smooth-surfaced rubber wheel that produces a permanent ink line on leather, upholstery, and wood. The wheel picks up its color from a felt-tipped marker in the handle. Use it to trace around a pattern or template; it will glide along an edge without leaving ink residue on the template.

CHALKS

Tailor's chalk is widely used by professionals to mark clothes for alteration or record seamlines and match points on muslins that have been pin-fit. It is inexpensive, is long-lasting, and won't evaporate or dissolve in water.

Wax chalk leaves marks that disappear when touched with a hot iron and is most often used on thick fabrics that readily absorb the mark as it melts. **Clay chalk** is usually used on thinner or delicate fabrics because you can brush it away. You can purchase a plastic holder and sharpener that make the chalk more efficient to use.

To draw precise but temporary lines on fabric, run a **powdered chalk marker** along a ruler or use it freehand. These markers dispense a thin line of powdered clay chalk via a tiny perforated wheel, which is set into a handle that doubles as the chalk container. They come in a variety of handle shapes and colors, can be refilled, and never require sharpening.

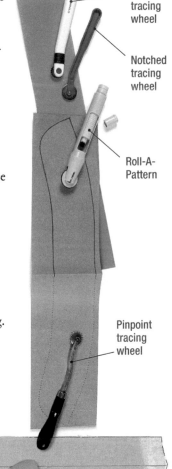

Smooth tracing wheel

Notched tracing wheel

Roll-A-Pattern

Pinpoint tracing wheel

Wax chalk

Clay chalk

Powdered chalk markers

The Designer's Curve

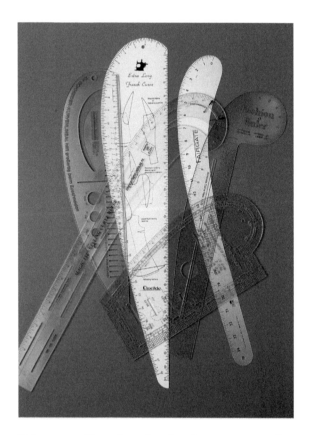

Pick a curve with numbers along the edge so you can easily identify the section you need. Each of these curves will help you do the job.

Designer's curves (including the more gently curved hip curve, which is marked for measuring) are a basic part of the professional patternmaker's tool kit. Every curved line on a pattern comes right out of some section of the designer's curve, or a combination of sections. Knowing how to use the curve yourself can make altering patterns easier and more accurate. You can redraw a curve when you've cut across it during fitting, or you can use the curve as a guide when making the alteration in the first place.

When a pattern for a ready-to-wear garment is made, the curves within it are derived from some ideal or average body shape the designer has chosen. The pattern will not fit everyone, nor is it meant to. If the pattern is for sewers, those curves are also guesses at what will work best, but it's assumed that they'll have to be customized. To do so, it is best to use the tool the curves were originally drawn with, the designer's curve, or something very similar. For example, there are two positions of the designer's curve commonly used to create the waist-to-hip curve on a skirt or pants pattern. Many women are built so the more shaped end of the curve fits them best from waist to hip. Women with straighter figures will get better results when the straighter end of the curve is used to draw their patterns from waist to hip. Designers and patternmakers must make similar choices: Some ready-to-wear lines are designed for curvy figures, others for straighter shapes.

USING THE CURVE

There are many designer's curves for sewers as well as similar curves. Hip curves have a gradually tightening curve that starts quite straight and takes about 15 in. to 20 in. to reach maximum curve. One that's preferred by many sewers is the transparent Fashion Ruler, which you can see pattern lines through. The curve should also have printed numbers along its curved edge. These features make it easy to record the portions of the curve you've used, so you can repeat the shape, either from pattern to pattern or symmetrically within the same pattern.

For example, once you have a skirt pattern that fits your hips perfectly, you can shift the designer's curve along the skirt side seam until the curves match as closely as possible from waist to hip. And because the curve has numbers on it, you can record the shape of the hip by simply noting the numbers at the points where the curve starts and ends. Then you can use that same set of numbers to reshape the waist-to-hip section on all patterns

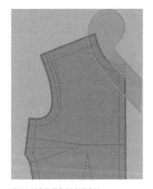

CHANGE TO V NECK

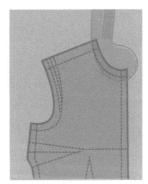

LOWER NECKLINE

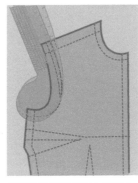

SHORTEN SHOULDER SEAM

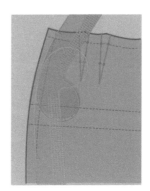

CHANGE SIDE-SEAM SHAPE

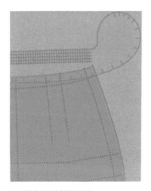

RAISE WAISTLINE

LOWER WAISTLINE

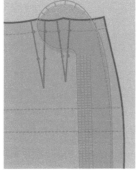

HIGH-HIP ADJUSTMENT

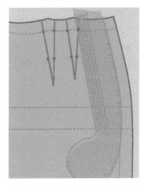

STRAIGHT-HIP ADJUSTMENT

that extend below your waist and need to follow your hips. The same principle works with all typical pattern curves; above you'll find eight examples of ways you can use a curve to correct a pattern. Once you know your numbers, you know that all pattern curves need to be at least as big as, or shaped similarly to, those sections of the designer's curve.

TRUING REDRAFTED CURVES

After you've corrected or transferred a curve to your pattern, you still have to smooth and refine it, a process called truing. You need to make sure that joining seams are the same length if they aren't meant to be eased together. Also, curves that join across

seams, such as front and back armholes, or across closures, such as left and right necklines, need to meet as straight lines without creating a peak or a dip. And most basic: Wherever curves blend into straight lines, the transition must be perfectly smooth, without angles or abrupt changes. In each case, the curve is usually the best tool for truing these small sections at the start or end of pattern lines taken from the curve. To wield the curve like a professional, just practice sliding it up and down along existing lines to find the most appropriate portion to use.

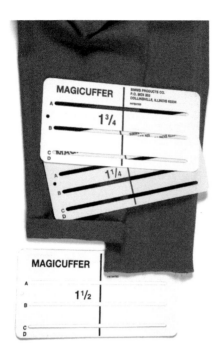

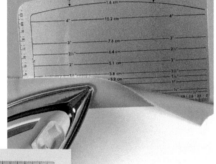

The Ezy-Hem Gauge lets you turn up and press an even hem allowance, whether straight (right) or curved (below).

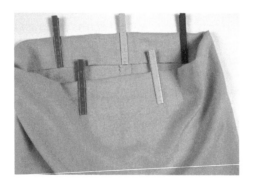

With Hemming Bird clamps, you can simultaneously measure and secure a hem allowance.

Tools for Finishing Details

These tools facilitate getting your buttons evenly spaced, your hems straight, and your cuffs even.

MAGICUFFER

Making cuffs is confusing for many sewers. With this tool, you can mark pants hems and calculate cuff measurements as fast as you can draw lines. Simply match up the Magicuffer to the inseam and align slot A with the desired length. Draw chalklines in slots A, B, C, and along the edge of D; cut off the excess fabric at D. Fold to the inside on line B and sew the hem along the cut edge. Turn the cuff to the outside along line A and press; then tack in place at the seams. **Caution:** The clearly marked templates are made of heavy-duty plastic, but will melt when touched with an iron.

EZY-HEM® GAUGE

Use this tool to turn up and press an even hem allowance, whether or not the hemline itself is marked on the right side of your garment. The gauge is marked for straight hems from ¾ in. to 4 in. deep and for curved hems from ¼ in. to 2½ in. deep. With the wrong side of the garment up, place the appropriate gauge edge (curved or straight) on the hemline, fold up the hem allowance so the edge aligns with the correct depth mark, and press it in place right over the gauge. For deep curved hems, sew a basting stitch along the allowance edge so you can tighten it evenly against the gauge.

HEMMING BIRD®

At 3 in. long, these handy metal clothespin-like clamps double as a depth gauge while securing a folded hem allowance. Because they hold the fabric flat, you can try on the garment and get a realistic idea of how it will look when finished. They are sold three to a package, and are especially good for establishing pants hems.

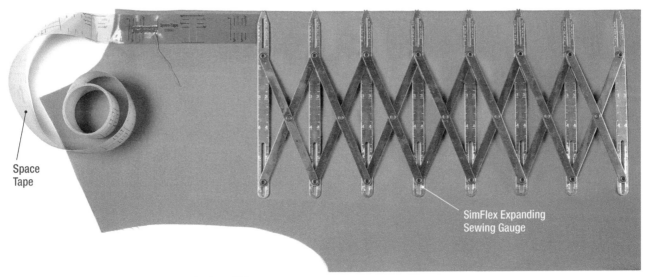

Space
Tape

SimFlex Expanding
Sewing Gauge

SIMFLEX™ EXPANDING SEWING GAUGE

Expand or retract this metal gauge to establish evenly
spaced button and buttonhole placements within a
given span. To get the best results, always expand the
gauge fully and then reduce it so the desired number
of points fits within the span.

SPACE TAPE™

Spacing buttonholes is usually easier than marking
them for stitching. Adhesive-backed Space Tape is
marked with a variety of buttonhole sizes, in both
vertical and horizontal orientation. Use the tape to
establish your buttonhole placements, and then stitch
the buttonholes directly through it using the printed
measurements; tear away the excess tape when you're
done. Any Space Tape that remains under the stitching acts as a stabilizer.

CHALK HEM MARKER

This tool is handy for marking hems on yourself and
others. To use, first decide how far off the floor the
hemline should be and set the top of the slider at that
level. Then put on the garment and stand close to
the marker so that the powder-dispensing slider just
touches the fabric. Squeeze the rubber bulb to dispense a neat chalk line. Rotate, and squeeze continu-
ously until you've marked a line perfectly parallel to
the floor around the entire skirt hem. If you want a
floor-length hem, and the marker doesn't go that low,
mark a line and measure down from it.

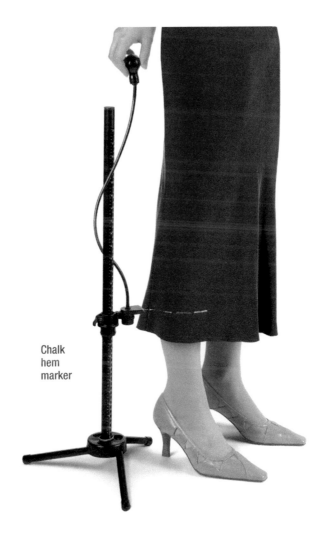

Chalk
hem
marker

Measurement Notes

Measurement Chart

THE CHART BELOW ALLOWS SPACE TO RECORD DIMENSIONS FOR BOTH THE LEFT AND RIGHT SIDES OF THE BODY, WHICH MAY BE HELPFUL WHEN FITTING AN ASYMMETRICAL FIGURE.

SHOULDERS

Shoulder length/left:　　　　right:

Shoulder to shoulder/front:

Shoulder to shoulder/back:

Back width:

Front shoulder slope/left:　　　right:

Back shoulder slope/left:　　　right:

Neck to waist/front:

Neck to waist/back:

ARMS

Arm length (over arm)/left:　　　right:

Biceps/upper arm circumference/left:　　right:

Armhole depth/left:　　　right:

BUST

Bust circumference:

Upper bust circumference:

Under bust circumference:

Chest width:

NECK

Natural neckline:

Neck edge to bust point (bust depth)/left:　　right:

Neck edge to waist/left:　　　right:

LEGS

Outer seam/left:　　　right:

Inseam:

Waist to floor/front:

Waist to floor/back:

CROTCH

Crotch length/total:

Crotch length/front:

Crotch length/back:

Crotch depth:

WAIST AND HIPS

Waist circumference:

Abdomen:

Abdomen depth:

Hip circumference:

Hip depth:

Fullest part of hip:

Fullest hip depth:

Ease Measurements from Your Favorite Clothes

FOR INSTRUCTIONS ON ASSESSING THE AMOUNT OF EASE YOU LIKE IN A GARMENT, SEE "DETERMINING A GARMENT'S EASE" ON p. 13

EASE	
Preferred ease for fitted clothes	
BUST ____ in. pinch X 4 = _____ total	HIP ___ in. pinch X 4 = = _____ total
Preferred ease for semifitted clothes	
BUST ____ in. pinch X 4 = _____ total	HIP ___ in. pinch X 4 = = _____ total
Preferred ease for loosely fit clothes	
BUST ____ in. pinch X 4 = _____ total	HIP ___ in. pinch X 4 = _____ total
Preferred ease for nonfitted clothes	
BUST ____ in. pinch X 4 = _____ total	HIP ___ in. pinch X 4 = _____ total
Preferred ease for _____ clothes	
BUST ____ in. pinch X 4 = _____ total	HIP ___ in. pinch X 4 = _____ total
Preferred ease for fitted sleeves	
_____ in. pinch X 2 = _____ total	
Preferred ease for nonfitted sleeves	
_____ in. pinch X 2 = = _____ total	

BODY DIMENSIONS

Head circumference* _____

Chest circumference _____

Waist circumference _____

Hip circumference _____

Biceps _____

Wrist _____

Other _____

*For judging neck openings on pullover garments

RESOURCES

NOTIONS

BANASCH'S
www.banaschs.com

CLASSACT DESIGNS
www.dressformdesigning.com
www.drapingforbeginners.com

CLOTILDE
www.clotilde.com

JOANN'S FABRIC AND CRAFT STORES
www.joann.com

NANCY'S NOTIONS
www.nancysnotions.com

STEINLAUF & STOLLER, INC.
www.steinlaufandstoller.com

WAWAK
www.wawak.com

DRESS FORMS

Professional Dress Forms

RONIS BROS.
www.ronis.com

SUPERIOR MODEL FORM CO.
www.superiormodel.com

WOLF FORM COMPANY, INC.
www.wolfform.com

Customizable Dress Forms

FABULOUS FIT
www.fabulousfit.com

MY TWIN DRESSFORMS & PANTSFORMS
www.mytwindressforms.com

Dial-Adjust Dress Forms

PRYM CONSUMER USA INC./DRITZ
www.dritz.com

PERSONALIZED DRESS FORM SERVICES AND WORKSHOPS

CLASSACT DESIGNS
www.dressformdesigning.com

LINGERIE SECRETS
www.sewinglingerie.com

MY TWIN DRESSFORMS & PANTSFORMS
www.mytwindressforms.com

BRA-MAKING PATTERNS, BOOKS, AND SUPPLIES

BRA-MAKERS SUPPLY
www.bramakerssupply.com

CORSET MAKING SUPPLIES
www.corsetmaking.com

ELINGERIA
www.elingeria.de

ETSY.COM
www.etsy.com

FABRIC.COM
www.fabric.com

FABRIC DEPOT
www.fabricdepotco.com

LOGANKITS AND JEWELRY
www.logankits.com

MAKING BEAUTIFUL BRAS
www.beautifulbras.com.au

SEW SASSY FABRICS
www.sewsassy.com

THE BRA-MAKERS MANUAL
www.bramakersmanual.com

PHOTO CREDITS

p. i: Sloan Howard

pp. iv (far left), v (far left): Joseph Kugielsky

pp. iv (two center), v (two on the right): Scott Phillips © The Taunton Press, Inc.

p. v (second from left): Sloan Howard

p. vi [133 MC_062.tif]: Jack Deutsch

Illustrations:

p. iv: Christine Erikson

p. iv (far right): Deb Bussino

CHAPTER 1

pp. 6 - 10: Joseph Kugielsky

p. 15, 17: Scott Phillips © The Taunton Press, Inc.

p. 23: David Page Coffin

Illustrations:

pp. 11, 13: Carol Ruzicka

pp. 18 - 21: Christine Erikson

CHAPTER 2

pp. 27, 30-31: Sloan Howard

pp. 32- 35: Scott Phillips © The Taunton Press, Inc.

Illustrations:

pp. 28, 29: Carol Ruzicka

p. 30 (bottom right): Rosann Berry © The Taunton Press, Inc.

CHAPTER 3

pp. 51, 97: Scott Phillips © The Taunton Press, Inc.

pp. 82, 83: Susan P. Nelson

pp. 84 - 89: Sloan Howard

pp. 90 - 95: Kenneth D. King

Illustrations:

pp. 37- 39, 42, 43, 48, 49, 54, 55, 63, 65, 66: Carol Ruzicka

pp. 40, 41: Gloria Melfi © The Taunton Press, Inc.

pp. 44 - 47: Karen Meyer

pp. 50, 52, 53, 71: Christine Erikson

pp. 56, 62 (left and right), 75: Robin Mazzola

pp. 57 - 62 (center): Deb Bussino

pp. 67, 68, 69, 78 - 81: Linda Boston

pp. 72, 73, 74: Rosann Berry © The Taunton Press, Inc.

pp. 76, 77: Karen Meyer

p. 98 - 101: Connie Crawford, Rosann Berry © The Taunton Press, Inc.

CHAPTER 4

pp. 103, 105, 106, 107, 108: David Page Coffin

p. 109 Scott Philips © The Taunton Press, Inc.

p. 123: David Page Coffin

pp. 124 -125: Joseph Kugielsky

pp. 128 – 131, 135: Sloan Howard

Illustrations:

pp. 112, 113: Christine Erikson

pp. 118, 119: Karen Meyer

pp. 120, 121, 122 (top): Carol Ruzicka

pp. 114, 122 (bottom), 126, 127: Rosann Berry © The Taunton Press, Inc.

pp. 132 - 135: Rosann Berry © The Taunton Press, Inc. and David Rohm

CHAPTER 5

pp. 138 -141, 143- 149, 151, 152, 155 - 160, 173: Scott Phillips © The Taunton Press, Inc.

pp. 161 - 165: Sloan Howard

pp. 176, 177, 178: David Page Coffin

Illustrations:

p. 138: Rosann Berry © The Taunton Press, Inc.

pp. 142, 143: Lisa Summerell

pp. 167, 168, 169, 170, 171, 179: Christine Erikson

pp. 172, 173 (right), 174: Carol Ruzicka

p. 180: Linda Boston

APPENDICES

pp. 181, 182 (left), 184, 185, 188, 189: Sloan Howard

p. 182 (right), 186: Scott Phillips © The Taunton Press, Inc.

p. 183: Jean Haas

Illustrations:

p. 187: Julia Talcott

If you like this book, you'll love everything about *Threads*.